Spirituality For Everyone

by Sharon "Kumuda" Janis

Based on the 2nd edition of
Spirituality For Dummies

Night Lotus Books

Spirituality For Everyone

Table of Contents

Part Two: Spiritual Practice Makes Perfect

Part Five: Ten Things...

When You're Under Ongoing Pressures
When You Don't Like Your Job
When You've Experienced a Difficult Childhood
When You Feel Spiritually Lost
When Something Awful Happens
When Good Fortune Comes Your Way

Do Unto Others As You Would Have Them Do Unto You
Think Good Thoughts
Look Beyond Matter to Spirit
Keep Good Company
Turn Within for Guidance
Be Moderate and Balanced
Remember Death
Express Yourself Freely
Keep Your Word
Have a Good Sense of Humor
Never Let Your Creative Spirit be Limited by Numbers

Initial Quick Tips

What Spirituality Can Do for You

- Spirituality gives you greater appreciation for everything in your life.

- Spirituality gives you more awareness of the bigger picture.

- Spirituality gives your actions more power, along with guidance on how to use that power.

- Spirituality brings you to a place of independent contentment.

- Spirituality is the key to overcoming sorrow.

- Spirituality encourages honesty and self-acceptance.

- Spirituality reveals that what you seek is inside yourself.

- Spirituality dissolves your limited ideas of who you are and guides you into greater self-respect.

- Spirituality helps you remember that everything is divine, even when it doesn't feel divine!

Dispelling Several Myths about Spirituality

- Spirituality is not the same as religion. Religion is the shell, while spirituality is the kernel within that shell. Religion is the map; spirituality is the territory.

- Being spiritual doesn't mean becoming something you weren't before. Although the light of spirituality may soften some of your personality's rough edges, your individuality is an important part of how spirit expresses in this world through and as you.

- Spirituality isn't just for a chosen few. The universe doesn't run with a class curve. Everyone can get an A in this class! In fact, everyone who gets an A helps more people get an A. One spiritually aware person can awaken many others, without even trying — through their positive efforts and expressions, and through the vibration of higher consciousness they contribute to the world.

- Spirituality is not about using metaphysical techniques to bend the universe to fulfill your material desires. Spirituality is about bringing yourself in harmony with the greater good of this universe so that blessings can unfold around you naturally without your having to grab them.

- Spirituality is not beholden to one or the other doctrine. Nor is it possible to fully express spirituality in any doctrine. Spirituality is alive in and personal to each soul.

- Spirituality is not about being outwardly smart or well-versed in theological debates. In fact, spirituality is one place where being simple, humble, and open is the first step! Spirituality is a shift to the wisdom of the heart.

- You don't have to do anything in particular to be spiritual. Spirituality doesn't require a list of specific actions. In fact, anything can be a spiritual practice, depending on your attitude. Spirituality inspires you to act with skill, freedom, gratitude, and a sense of service.

- You don't have to go anywhere to be spiritual. Of course, certain spiritual places can bring positive energy and inspiration to you — which is one reason spiritual seekers often take pilgrimages to holy places. Nevertheless, the ultimate goal of spirituality is to become a beacon of positive energy and inspiration unto yourself and the world. True spirituality comes with you wherever you go.

- You don't have to wait to be spiritual. Spirituality is a shift of awareness that can happen in a moment. Although external efforts can help trigger the inner shift, you can become spiritually aware right where you are — right here and right now, while reading this yellow Cheat Sheet!

Ten Places to Meditate Before You're Spiritually Enlightened

- In a quiet room
- Outside, in nature
- In a church
- In a meditation center
- In a temple
- In a monastery
- In a yoga studio
- By the ocean
- At the foot of a tree
- In the company of spiritually awakened beings

Ten Places to Meditate After You're Spiritually Enlightened

- Anywhere
- Anywhere
- Anywhere
- Anywhere
- Anywhere
- Anywhere
- Anywhere
- Anywhere
- Anywhere
- Anywhere

Dedication

This book is dedicated to my beloved gurus, Baba Muktananda and Gurumayi Chidvilasananda.

To the great beings and masters of all traditions.

To my dear reader: I know that the same Divine Consciousness who has composed these words also reads them through your eyes. I bow to the great spirit that exists in you and as you.

Introduction

After the first edition of *Spirituality For Dummies* was published, I was surprised to find that some spiritual folks were embarrassed to buy the book. The very first email I received was from a fellow who said that he'd hid it between the Bible and Koran on his way to the bookstore's cash register. A college professor told me he was afraid that one of his students might see him purchasing the book (I suggested that he could order a copy online and receive it in a plain brown box), and a woman told me that she loved reading the book but had covered the title with pretty wrapping paper.

Of course, spiritual people like to use positive thoughts and words to describe themselves, as well they should. Yet, at the same time, humility and honesty (not to mention a good sense of humor) are also important aspects of spirituality. During the seven years since the first edition was published, I've also met many top quality spiritual priests, ministers, swamis, and monks who responded to hearing the title *Spirituality For Dummies* by saying: "That's the book for me!" These accomplished spiritual folks were not calling themselves spiritual dummies to put themselves down at all. Rather, they realize the vast and profound nature of spirituality and acknowledge the inevitable truth that much more can always be known. Nevertheless, with *Spirituality For Dummies* now out of print after seventeen years, I bring to you, *Spirituality For Everyone*.

About This Book

Spirituality For Everyone presents basic spiritual concepts from various traditions, combined with relevant psychological and scientific studies and my own personal understandings, insights, experiences, and occasionally, opinions.

In college, I considered taking a physics class because I was interested in learning more about a cool new theory called holography. But then I discovered that students had to first take two semesters of courses about the most boring and basic aspects of physics before they could begin to learn about the more interesting new research. The same thing happened if you enrolled in the university's art school. First you had to take a semester-long class on how to draw straight lines, and if that didn't kill your creative spirit, you'd get to move on to some actual art courses. But that's not what you're going to get here.

My intention is to give you the goods and introduce you to the most beneficial words, concepts, analogies, and insights that I've come across on my journey. I don't put in politically correct disclaimers or try to fit within every belief system out there. I won't apologize for extending my insights out to where they lead and sharing that place with you. I don't intentionally propagate any particular point of view outside of my own appreciation for that view as a useful ladder to higher spiritual understanding.

You don't have to join anything, you don't have to believe anything, and you don't have to sign anything. This book is an offering of love and service to the God who dwells in you from the same God who dwells in you, in me, and in everyone and everything (See Chapter 2 for a discussion of the word "God).

A Variety of Sources

My goal is for this book to be accessible to seekers from all walks of life and all faiths — including those with no specific religious orientation at all. This book focuses on nondenominational spirituality and is intended to resonate with many doctrines and paths.

Knowing that this book is intended to be nondenominational, you may start reading about topics like *karma* (Chapter 15) and *dharma* (Chapter 13), and wonder, "Hey, there are a lot of eastern references here!" And you would be right.

Many of the ideas in this book are presented in the context of Christian and Indian philosophies, although in most cases, the same basic concepts also appear in other religious traditions.

I focus a bit more on eastern philosophy due to my experiences with Indian-based philosophies and practices. I spent ten years living in an Indian-based ashram with two Indian gurus. During these years, I chanted in Sanskrit and studied primarily eastern scriptures. Therefore, using these terms and concepts allows me to share certain ideas more clearly than if I were to run around trying to research parallel examples from other religions that I'm not as familiar with.

Still, even though eastern teachings are not so common or well-publicized in western countries, some of the most beloved and inspired western artists, writers, and thinkers spent time studying eastern philosophies — including Albert Einstein, Albert Schweitzer, Aldous Huxley, Henry David Thoreau, Herman Hesse, Ralph Waldo Emerson, and many others.

All this said, I do make an effort to present ideas in a way that is not bound to any one tradition or religion. One way I bring greater balance to the book is by including an abundance of quotes from spiritual figures, artists, and thinkers from many cultures and traditions. I personally like to hear about spiritual matters in different styles, so these quotes allow me to give you a rich buffet of spiritual wisdom and ideas.

I've attributed these quotes using only the names of those being quoted, rather than trying to limit their accomplished lives to a three-word description. Today's information explosion makes it very easy for you to look up the sources of any quotes you like so that you can find out more about their history and other works.

One mistaken assumption would be for you to think that I expect you to agree with all my ideas and contemplations. After many years of ongoing personal and spiritual exploration, I am taking the opportunity to share some of the more interesting and useful concepts and understandings I have encountered and unfolded along the way.

If I prefaced every sentence with the obvious, "This is my opinion…," you'd probably get bored very soon, and my editor would get mad at me. So please, right now, just place one big IMHO ("in my humble opinion") over this entire book, and I'll do my best to present the information and ideas clearly for you.

I'd like to address another mistaken assumption with a prayer that was written many centuries ago by a prolific Indian poet named Pushpadanta to express how futile it is to think that the grand, glorious, creative, spiritual expansiveness can ever be fully expressed in words:

Spiritual Wisdom

Oh Lord! If the Goddess of wisdom were to write for all eternity with a pen made from a branch of the best of all celestial trees, using the whole earth as Her writing pad; and if the mass of ink used equaled the blue mountains, and the ocean were Her ink-pot — still, it would be impossible to express the true fullness of Your attributes.

—Pushpadantacharya

As for my assumptions about you, I assume that you're a human soul, made in the divine image and likeness, and of the substance of pure spirit. I assume that you're open to considering ideas while using your own discrimination to choose which ones work for you. Perhaps you've been deeply involved with a spiritual path, or maybe this book is your first exploration.

Regardless, I assume and hope that you read these words with an open mind and heart and allow them to trigger your own inner understanding, along with a greater appreciation, awe, and reverence for your own divine spirit, wise soul, and amazing journey.

Main Sections

This book is organized into five parts that guide you through spiritual theories and practices.

Part One: Getting Acquainted with Spirituality

This part introduces the whole idea of spirituality and explores what it means for you in your life. What's the difference between religion and spirituality? Who are you really? Why are you here and where will you go next? This part addresses many of the questions you may have about spirituality and includes analogies and stories to help you understand that you already are spiritual!

Part Two: Spiritual Practice Makes Perfect

This part introduces you to spiritual practices that can energize your body, empower your mind, and nourish your spirit — including exercises, contemplations, meditations, spiritual studies, prayers, and devotional singing. If you're looking for something spiritual to do right now, flip to this part.

Part Three: Living a Spiritual Life

This part gives a philosophical exploration of spiritual virtues such as honesty, compassion, and humility, and shows you how to uplift every aspect of your life: from greed to abundance, from attachments to freedom, from pleasure to bliss, from trials to transcendence, and from relationships to divine love.

Part Four: Connecting with this Conscious Universe

This part gives you a solid philosophical foundation for understanding the spiritual nature of this universe and explains how karmic laws work in your life.

Part Five: Ten Things

This part gives you several quick spiritual picker-uppers, with ten simple things you can do to bring more spirit into your life, ten spiritual-sounding lines and what they may really mean, ten more "commandments," and ten examples of seeing your life with spiritual eyes.

Ways to read this book

This book is designed for skimming, cover-to-cover reading, or exploration of specific topics, depending on your preference.

- **Skimming:** My goal is to have each page, part, and section stand on its own. That's because my favorite way to approach a book is to hold it in my hands, close my eyes, ask God and the Spirit to reveal to me what I need to know right now, and then randomly open the pages. It works!

- **Cover-to-cover reading:** If you're interested in all facets of spirituality, I recommend starting at the beginning of this book and reading through to the end. I intentionally wrote this book in an order that builds on itself, in case you choose to start with the first and end at the last page.

- **Exploring specific topics:** This book touches on a diverse array of spiritual topics that are listed in both the Table of Contents and the Index. If you're interested in starting a daily practice, head on over to Part II. If you've always wondered why you're here and where your soul will go next, you'll find some interesting ideas about this in Part I. If you're wondering how to uplift your life, the chapters in Parts III and IV can give some theoretical and practical guidance.

My recommendation is to read this book in any or all three of the preceding ways, as you are guided. Open it at random, look up specific topics, and also read the whole book from cover to cover. However you read this book, I hope and pray that it is a beneficial blessing for your journey.

Part One:

Getting Acquainted with Spirituality

Chapter 1

Finding Authentic Spirituality

Topics in this Chapter:

* *   Understanding the importance of spirituality in today's world
* *   Finding your way around this book
* *   Tasting what lies ahead

Today's topsy-turvy world brings a unique array of spiritual challenges. Religions east and west stand accused of indiscretions and violations, while spiritual teachers who should be lifting seekers into higher wisdom are often concerned with uplifting their own bottom line. Some modern prophets cater to desire-obsessed audiences by teaching a kind of "Santa Claus" theology that is guaranteed to get you that new car you want, or if nothing else, that will get these "profit prophets" the new cars *they've* always wanted. What is a spiritual seeker to do?

Newsflashes warn about small and large apocalypses that have or could happen at any moment in-between investigations about which star has revealed which bad quality to the paparazzi and which politicians are supposedly colluding with whom. Countrymen don't trust their leaders; family structures are crumbling; autism rates are climbing, citizens of all ages are being overmedicated with pharmaceutical industry fare, and most people feel cut off from or unable to experience and understand their divine spiritual heritage.

An important key to turning these and other troubling things around and bringing greater light and healing into our world in all sectors and realms is authentic spiritual knowledge, awareness, and blessings.

What our world needs now is the kind of spiritual love, wisdom, and practices that provide an anchor into the peaceful, sublime happiness of the eternal universal soul. We need authentic, intelligent explanations of higher-consciousness spiritual principles that honor, support, and guide them right in the midst of our lives. The goal of *Spirituality For Everyone* is to be a helpful guide for your journey — a friend on your path that opens new doors of awareness, understanding, and experience.

In this chapter, I share with you some spiritual basics and tell you where to go in this book to explore its ideas more fully.

Spirituality and Self-Knowledge

In a nutshell, spirituality relates to your own personal experience and relationship with the divine. People tend to confuse spirituality with religion, because the two often come together. Religions are sets of practices and beliefs that have been created based on the epiphanies and teachings of prophets, saints, or sages. Most religions are intended to lead you into the light of spirituality, either by focusing on an outer form of divinity, or on the spiritual presence within yourself, or both. (See Chapter 2.)

Self-knowledge is one of the main keys to spirituality. First you explore who you think you are, and from there, you can move into a deeper spiritual view of who you *really* are. When you have a strong foundation of spiritual self-respect, you aren't as easily brought down by the judgments and errors of yourself and others. With spiritual self-respect, you become your own best friend. You find ways to increase your spiritual understanding and uplift every aspect of your life. Through your upliftment, you also naturally help to uplift the world around you. The divine flame shines in your very own soul – shouldn't you at least know it is there? (See Chapter 3)

Self knowledge also helps you to ask big-picture questions, such as: "Why am I here on this earth and in my body?" and "What am I supposed to do while I'm here?"

According to many spiritual sages, the most important thing to do while you're here is to expand into a spiritual awareness that guides your actions and thoughts to be powerful and positive. But how does one learn to do this? Where can you go to find out about spiritual principles and practices? Where can you meet others who will support and share your spiritual journeys together?

Since the original *Spirituality For Dummies* was published, many people have asked me to recommend a spiritual path or group for them to follow. However, in spiritual journeys, there is no "one size fits all" group or path to recommend to everyone. In Chapter 5, I give you suggestions and warnings about what to look for in outer spiritual guidance such as groups, teachers, and writings.

 **Consider**

Ultimately, you have to do some research to find and recognize what works for you, because each person's spiritual path is unique and personal. You can take many roads to the divine, and you can certainly get there from wherever you are right now (although you may have to make a few u-turns!).

Spiritual Practices

Even if you're not quite ready to leap into higher visions of universal creation, you can certainly follow simple practices such as sitting for meditation or improving the spiritual atmosphere of your environment with sacred images and sounds. Chapter 6 explains the importance of bringing spirituality into form through practices for body, mind, and spirit, and guides you in choosing which practices are right for your individual nature.

- **Practices for your body:** When you approach life with a spiritual perspective, it can be easier to treat your body with love and respect, as a temple of the divine and a gift from the universe that has brought you to live in this world. Physical practices, including hatha yoga, martial arts, religious dance, and breathing exercises, can help you anchor your awareness of the divine in your body and give you the stamina to have a long and vibrant spiritual journey (see Chapter 7).

- **Practices for your mind:** It is in your mind that everything you know and experience takes place. Therefore, many spiritual sages have given supreme importance to the clarity and power of the mind. Spiritual practices for your mind include meditation, study, and contemplation. These practices help you clear up the mental and emotional clutter that keeps you from experiencing spiritual freedom. Spiritual practices for your mind can open your ability to understand and experience the universe in a personal and joyful way (see Chapter 8).

- **Practices for your spirit:** Devotional practices unlock the hardened areas of your spiritual heart so that the river of grace and love can flow more freely through your life. You can nourish your spirit through practices such as prayer, charity, devotional singing, service and worship, and by turning your everyday environment into a sacred space (see Chapter 9).

Spiritual Living

As you integrate spiritual principles into your life, every aspect of your experience becomes uplifted and transformed into a spiritual field of experience. Virtues such as honesty, humility, and compassion are not just a set of uncomfortable rules that you must push yourself to follow, but with spiritual awareness, these virtuous qualities become natural ways of living that improve your life in countless ways.

You can apply spiritual principles to different areas of your daily life: work can become grace-filled service; limitations can open up into spiritual freedom; anger can melt into forgiveness and then into the great healing gift of gratitude.

Greed for material acquisitions can mature into a state of abundance and lasting fulfill-ment, and relationships can transform into blessings of good company and divine love.

Regardless of who you are and how spiritual you become, trials and tribulations are al-ways a part of life. In fact, without any struggles and challenges, you wouldn't be able to grow as well and beautifully as you do when you strengthen your spirit by going through troubles with a commitment to turning them into triumphs. (See Chapter 12 to find out how to approach challenges with a positive mindset and strength of spirit that allows you to not only survive, but also thrive through the inevitable storms of life.)

Part of spiritual living is to make good choices in all the small and large decisions of your life. To make decisions that are focused on your highest goals, you need to discover and honor the deeper calling of your soul and tap into divine inner guidance. Honoring your individual nature and style also opens the doors to experiencing and expressing your creative spirit, so you can give something great to this world through whatever you do. (Chapter 13)

Spiritual Wisdom

The way you look at the world decides how the world manifests for you. Therefore, studying spiritual concepts and theories can vastly expand and improve your understanding and experience of life.

Certain eastern philosophies declare that this universe is divine, perfect, and one, even in the midst of its appearance of multiplicity, disarray, and imperfection. Imagine how such a viewpoint of divine universal oneness and perfection can change your approach to life! (See Chapter 14.) With a higher spiritual awareness, you can take your rightful place as a con-scious co-creator of your world, and discover how to use your words and thoughts to create a happy, healthy, and spiritually enlightened life.

Some popular spiritual fads today give metaphysical principles that can help you create and manifest more of what you want in this world. These powers to create on a spiritual level tend to come naturally with spiritual maturity. However, many are using such techniques to tap into these powers of creation before they may be fully prepared to use them properly. This book is intended to give you a strong spiritual foundation that is lacking in many of these current spiritual fads.

One ultimate goal of spirituality is to attain the state of spiritual freedom and liberation that is sometimes referred to as enlightenment, nirvana, or self-realization. Becoming aware of your true nature changes everything. With self-realization, even if you're living the exact same outer life as you always have, your inner experience expands far beyond the mundane surface living that you may have settled for in the past. (Find more about spiritual liberation in Chapter 17.)

Two important instructions that will help you find and express authentic spirituality in your life are "Trust yourself" and "Serve joyfully." In a sense, everything in this book is intended to guide you in these two areas.

Trust yourself

To experience a powerful and positive spiritual journey, you have to trust yourself. You are the one who decides what you believe. You are the one who chooses what to do with your time and circumstances here on earth. Will your focus be on material pursuits, spiritual aspirations, or both together? You are the King of the kingdom that is your own amazing life — it is your thoughts and actions that mold your journey.

Choose your thoughts and actions wisely, and come to trust yourself so much that you are well-guided in every moment and every circumstance.

Even if you have a very good spiritual teacher who explains certain theories very nicely and whose presence brings uplifting inspiration to your spirit, still you have to trust yourself to understand the information correctly, to receive the blessings in a powerful and positive way, and to nurture and properly use what you've received. It is your calling to combine the best of what you've understood and experienced, and to bring that together in your own individual view of the world. Don't just jump into someone else's belief system; rather, discover, craft, and enhance your own.

When you read books, it is you who must discern what you do or don't believe, or what you want to focus on now versus later. For example, as you read this book, please drink in whatever speaks to you, shelve what doesn't for possible revisiting in the future, come up with converse examples to my assertions, and expand what I share through your own experiences, opinions, and wisdom. I'm just giving you some good materials — you have to use them to build your own spiritual house.

Trusting yourself is a big responsibility, but a necessary one. You are the conductor of the orchestra of your thoughts. Bring in whatever melodies resonate with you and combine them with your own inner music to create a beautiful symphony that is your journey of life.

Be trustworthy

Trusting yourself doesn't mean to trust your ignorance, but to strive, heart and soul, to be trustworthy. All the spiritual practices and virtues come together to make you trustworthy to yourself, to others, to God, and to this world. (Find more on spiritual practices in Part II and more on spiritual virtues in Chapter 10.)

Being trustworthy means being honest and keeping your word to yourself and others. Being trustworthy means that you've pushed aside lower emotions, such as greed, hatred, and jealousy, so that your thoughts and actions are coming from higher emotions, such as love, generosity, and joy.

It is not enough to lazily say that you trust yourself when you may only be trusting your most surface opinions, many of which have been planted in you by the very commercialized society we are living in today. You have to go deeper, through meditation, prayer, contemplation, and spiritual study, to find and express the part of yourself that is wise, divine, and trustworthy.

That trustworthy part of yourself will lead you through the jungles and mazes of life. It will guide you on what to do, who to spend time with, what to read, what goals to pursue, and where to go when. This trustworthy part of yourself is also your intuition, which knows a lot more about the world manifesting around you than you consciously do.

For example, your intuition knows if you're dealing with someone who is being dishonest with you. If you're in tune with your intuition, then you may be gently guided to avoid a situation that might otherwise cause a messy confrontation with the person who is being dishonest (unless a messy confrontation is something both of your souls need to experience). Your trustworthy guidance takes you through the most beneficial roads of life and protects you from pitfalls along the way.

Trusting "God"

Here, I use the word God to represent whatever you conceive the universal conscious divine presence to be. (Chapter 2 discusses the word God and various representations of divinity.)

By trusting God, you are trusting the beneficence of the universe; you are trusting the divine presence that presides over everything. When you trust God, you stop worrying so much about the twists and turns of life. Even if you do feel upset or concerned about some turns of events, you still can access a place inside yourself that trusts that whatever is happening has a higher purpose. Even awful experiences can have a higher purpose if they guide you to expand your awareness into greater realms of spiritual freedom.

Trusting God is an essential part of trusting yourself. Ultimately, the most trustworthy part of yourself is also a seed of God that came with your birth into this world. Trusting yourself and trusting God are ultimately two faces of the same coin.

In each moment, trusting God allows you to move happily and spontaneously through life. You courageously try things that you don't necessarily know how to do. You sign up for that class, write that book, offer to help, give that speech, or make that commitment.

Serve joyfully

Part of trusting yourself is to have clear intentions and motivations in everything you think, say, and do. Greedy desires and ulterior motives cover the light of spiritual intuition that is necessary for receiving inner guidance.

To have a vibrant journey, you have to shift from the usual perspective most people have of looking at each situation in terms of what they can get from it. Instead, you walk into each moment of your life with an openness and readiness to serve, connect, help, and bless.

Instead of grabbing at life, you walk with your hands open and ready to give and receive. When you cease grabbing for lesser things, the universe has the opportunity to give greater things that you may not have even thought to want.

Eventually, "How can I be of service?" becomes etched in your psyche so that it becomes a natural presence in your being. Then, you don't have to actively seek out ways to help — you are in harmony with this loving universe, and that harmony brings you exactly where you should be to naturally offer what is helpful, just by being who you are.

 **Consider**

Being of service to the universe is a great and personal way to relate to life.

Chapter 2

Defining Spirituality

Topics in this Chapter:

  *   Exploring the meaning of spirituality
  *   Understanding how spirituality relates to religion
  *   Contemplating that amazing, remarkable, wondrous God
  *   Preparing yourself for the great benefits of spirituality

Spirituality goes deep into the heart of every matter and extends far beyond the physical world of matter. Spirituality connects you with a profoundly powerful and divine force that's present in this universe and in yourself. Whether you're looking for happiness, inner peace, or supreme enlightenment, spiritual knowledge can propel you to achieve your personal goals and provide an effective a plan for living.

- No financial or societal stature helps you find as much fulfillment in life as spiritual wisdom.

- No amount of outer effort bears as much fruit as understanding and flowing with the spiritual laws of this universe.

- None of the powerful people you know can "connect" you like the power of knowing your own self.

- No friend can love and guide you as much as that truly best friend who exists behind all friends, behind all enemies, and in your very own soul.

In this chapter, I provide background information about spirituality and introduce spiritual ideas and theories that have the potential to immediately begin transforming your life for the better.

Spirituality: The Basic Idea

Spirituality is the one accomplishment that blesses every aspect of your life and remains with you even after your time on earth is done.

Spirituality brings you in touch with the great eternal nature of life. It invigorates and inspires your soul to reach for the highest and to do what is right instead of what may be easy or comfortable. Spirituality is like a stream of wisdom that flows through your very own being and guides you on your path.

The lion cub who thought he was a goat

While walking through the forest one day, a young lion cub became separated from his mother. Lost and hungry, the cub came upon a family of goats who took him in and brought the lion cub up as one of their own. Within a few months, the little cub even began to bleat like the other goats, though he never did get it quite right.

One day, the goats were dining in a grassy field, when a lion happened by. All the young goats went to hide behind the trees, in case the lion was looking for lunchmeat. The big lion had already eaten his meal, but was surprised to see a young lion cub running off to hide with the goats. He went over to the cub and asked, "What are you doing here with these goats?"

The cub eyed the lion nervously and replied, "These are my goat brothers and sisters, sir, and I am also a goat."

The older lion realized there was a problem here. "What on earth makes you think you're a goat?"

This question confused the cub. Couldn't this lion see he was a goat? Nobody had ever questioned his goatness before. The cub became suspicious. Maybe this lion was planning to get him involved in some dubious scheme. "Please, just let us be," implored the cub. "Everything is just fine here with us goats."

However, the elder lion couldn't bear to let this poor cub live on in such delusion. After all, this cub was king of the forest, not a lowly goat. "Come with me," the lion said, leading the cub to a nearby stream. "Look into the waters and see your true nature."

The cub walked up to the water's edge. He had drunk from these waters many times, but had never paused to look at his reflection before breaking the water's surface. As he peered into the waters, the cub saw his own majestic face and began to roar with amazement and joy.

This analogy illustrates the predicament most people are in. Not realizing their true identity, many base their self-image on the opinions of others. In Parts II and III of this book, I show you powerful spiritual practices and principles that can help you still the waters of worldly life and see your own majestic face, perhaps for the first time.

Some ways spirituality can manifest include

- Being conscious of the subtle power of grace that pulsates behind the physical appearance of your life
- Experiencing a higher universal love and respect for all, instead of only feeling connected with certain people
- Remembering that there is infinitely more to you and everything else than can be known by your mind and senses
- Surfing the waves of life with a lighthearted view that nurtures a positive sense of humor
- Not wanting to spend too much time watching and listening to manipulated and commercial media blasts that bring stress and worries about things over which you have no control.
- Staying aware of the divine nature of life as you move through events and experiences with faith, optimism, and an unfettered heart.
- Coming into your true inheritance and divine birthright as a human being
- Developing a mature approach that allows you to appreciate simplicity and peacefulness
- Achieving an ability to see the spiritual even in the ordinary
- Making your relationship with the divine more important than your relationships with this world
- Coming into your true inheritance and divine birthright as a valuable human being

Spirituality is a unique topic to explore, because it reaches beyond the boundaries of the physical world. Due to its ineffable nature, the nature of spirituality can't be perfectly captured or described in ordinary, everyday terms.

Yet, because the spiritual essence already exists inside of you, hearing the right words can trigger your own awakening into a higher perception.

I start this exploration of spirituality by contrasting it with the more common materialistic approach to life.

■ **The materialistic approach:** The materialistic approach relies primarily on the five senses — what can be seen, heard, tasted, touched, or smelled. Someone following a materialistic approach depends on outer appearances of things to determine what to think and feel about them, and seeks to fix whatever is wrong or out of place solely by moving things around and making outer changes.

■ **The spiritual approach:** In contrast, the spiritual way is to see beyond outer appearances and the five senses into an intuitive perception of the deeper causes behind outer conditions. Someone following a spiritual approach:

- Seeks to change and uplift the world by first transforming and improving his own vision

- Relies on inner guidance to show the best way to move forward with her efforts.

- Trusts, even while striving to solve a problem, that the problem is part of a good and kind universe that may be using this situation to teach ultimately beneficial lessons to everyone involved.

- Understands that both the worldly and spiritual levels are occurring simultaneously in his life and seeks to find a balance between his outer actions and inner vision.

- Appreciates that even the outer events in her life have their essence and source in the spiritual plane, with the effects of those seeds becoming visible as the outer events.

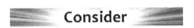 **Consider**

Including a spiritual approach benefits all your efforts because the spiritual laws of this universe connect your personal vision with the world around you in ways you may never have even imagined. (For more on this topic, see Chapter 15.)

Are you a beginner?

When it comes to spirituality, everyone is a beginner, and nobody is a beginner.

Whether you're a "young soul" or an "old soul," religious or atheist, good or bad, you're inherently spiritual just by being alive. Even thugs can become saints once they realize and remember their spiritual soul.

As with many other fields, the awakening to spirituality can sometimes be especially accessible to those with "beginner's mind" or "beginner's luck," although continual effort and practice will help keep your experience of spirituality strong and steady.

One of the great gifts of spirituality is to realign your sense of self with something you may not have ever imagined was within you. Spirituality says that even if you think you're limited and small, it simply isn't so. You're greater and more powerful than you have ever imagined. A great and divine light exists inside of you. This same light is also in everyone you know and in everyone you will ever know in the future. You may think that you're limited to just your physical body and state of affairs — including your gender, race, family, job, and status in life — but spirituality comes in and says, "There is more to you than all these qualities and labels."

Notice that *spirit* sounds similar to words like *inspire* and *expire*. This similarity is appropriate because when you're filled with spiritual energy, you feel great inspiration, and when the spiritual life force leaves your body, your time on this earth expires. Remembrance of your inspiration and eventual expiration are two main themes of the spiritual journey:

- **Remembering to be filled with inspiration**, which also translates into experiencing and expressing love, joy, wisdom, peacefulness, and service

- **Remembering the inevitable expiration** that waits to take you away at any moment from the physical circumstances you may think are so important right now

Making a best guess

Okay, I'll admit right off the bat that no one really knows completely and accurately why we're here on earth or what this game of life is all about. The ultimate truth simply doesn't fit into neat packages; therefore, all anybody can do is to make a best guess.

Will you choose to spend all your time and energy on acquiring more money, power, beauty, love, admiration, success, a nice house, good family, and devoted friends? These ambitions are all fine, but I propose that adding spiritual efforts and goals to the mix is also an especially good guess.

Spirituality has an importance beyond all these worldly achievements. It reaches into the depths of creation, into a part of your soul that's much greater than just your body or temporary circumstances.

Don't Forget

One of the main teachings of spirituality is to look within and find what you seek within yourself. The external world is temporary and ever changing; your body will die one day, sweeping all your worldly possessions away like a mere pile of dust. Your inner Self, on the other hand, is timeless, eternal, and deeply profound.

Spirituality: The true wealth

People say that "Health is the greatest wealth," or "A good mind is paramount," or "Having loving relationships is what's really important." One prayer from India entreats *Lakshmi*, the goddess of wealth, to shower blessings in the form of intelligence, enjoyments, success, worldly positions, prosperity — and most importantly according to this prayer, the wealth of becoming free from ego, the limited self-identification that keeps us from remembering the true greatness that exists beyond all these external accoutrements. (See Chapter 3 for more about ego.)

Wealth and riches come in many forms; however, there is a prosperity that only a small percentage of people attain. This precious treasure is the experience of expanded consciousness, inner peace, and serenity that comes from the light of spiritual awareness.

Consider

Got a good family? Great. Lots of money? Fine. Exciting career? Fabulous. Spiritual awareness? Priceless!

Spiritual wisdom reveals the hand of grace that uplifts all the ever-changing circumstances of your life into the eternal light of divine spirit.

With spiritual understanding, you may outwardly look nearly the same as you did before, but inside you'll have gained a great wealth of spiritual vision, peacefulness, faith, and love.

What does "spirituality" mean?

Although people sometimes confuse the word spirituality with a religious movement called *spiritualism*, the words *spirit, spiritual,* and *spirituality* originally referred to breath and wind and first appeared in the 13th, 14th, and 15th centuries, respectively. These terms weren't even around during the indeterminable antiquity when many world religions were formed, although other words have been available in world cultures and traditions throughout the ages to refer to aspects of what is now called spiritual energy. These words include Holy Ghost, Chi, Tao, Sefirah, Prana, Ki, Ruach, and for at least one bushman tribe in Africa, a clicking sound made with your tongue.

- Spirituality is a personal approach to connecting with the divine and experiencing the realms that exist beyond the sensory world.
- Spiritualism is a religious movement that was developed in the 18th and 19th centuries and focuses on communicating with the aspect of spirit that survives bodily death.

Spirituality is about following your heart

Spiritual Wisdom

Your vision will become clear only when you look into your heart. Who looks outside, dreams. Who looks inside, awakens.

—Carl Jung

The spiritual journey can be summed up in two phrases:

* Purify your heart.

* Follow your heart.

Spiritual practices and exercises such as prayer, meditation, yoga, contemplation, scriptural study, and devotional rituals (covered in Part II of this book), as well as spiritual qualities such as compassion, honesty, steadiness, and unconditional love (covered in Part III) contribute to this process of purifying your heart and following the guidance of your pure heart.

With a purified heart, you're better able to hear, trust, and follow the still, small whisper of universal guidance that speaks softly in every moment if you have the ears to hear.

 **Be Careful**

If you follow your heart before first purifying your heart, some of your inner promptings may in fact be regular old thoughts and desires disguised as inner inspirations and divine guidance!

Be sure your intentions are pure and not sullied by the muddy waters of greed, jealousy, anger, lust, and fear. Keeping your intentions pure will ensure that even if your inner guidance isn't always on target, you'll still be moving forward in a positive, spiritual way.

Discovering your smiling soul

When you shift into spiritual awareness, you may appear to be living the same life as before, with the same ambitions, joys, and sorrows as before. However, inside, you have a radiant smile that may or may not be visible to the world. Your spiritual soul smiles through the good times and the bad. In fact, as your smiling soul shines more and more into the world around you, the world also begins to reflect your smile back at you.

Do you ever find yourself smiling even when no one else is around? If not, try it! Smile to yourself. Smile at being alive. Smile to God, who is always present where you are — closer than your own breath.

Spirituality in Action

Experiencing self-awareness — right here and right now

One important element of spiritual growth is to become more self-aware. This is something you can practice anytime and anywhere. Try it now:

1. Observe yourself in this present moment.

How are you feeling? Are you taking nice, relaxed breaths? Is your posture gentle yet supportive of your body? Are you able to focus on the words you're reading, or is your mind flitting around to outer distractions, inner concerns, and random thoughts?

2. Look upon yourself with a kind and friendly eye.

If you aren't as peaceful or focused as you'd like to be, don't fret — because fretting definitely won't help you feel more harmonious and calm. Just be aware of your inner state without judging it as good or bad.

3. Gently align yourself, adjust your posture if necessary, and put a little more effort into focusing on the ideas you're reading.

Sometimes not-so-spiritual thoughts come up while you're contemplating spiritual teachings. If these unwelcome thoughts come up, your mind may just be doing a bit of housekeeping, such as sweeping up some old mental clutter that needs to be cleared. Be receptive to also receiving your own inner wisdom as it's churned up by all these spiritual words and contemplations.

4. Take a deep breath, allowing oxygen and energy to fill your entire body.

Breathing is how you live in continual union with the universe around you. The life force pours into your body, mind, and soul with each inhalation and then rides back out on the wave of exhalation, merging into the outer air. You may want to take a peaceful break right now by closing your eyes for a few moments and enjoying a few deep, slow breaths.

Getting to know your spiritual heart

Spirituality is a shift into the knowing of your heart — not your physical heart, but the inner, spiritual heart that represents all the ways of knowing that take place beyond the rational mind. The spiritual heart can transform this ordinary world into a heavenly realm.

Your spiritual heart is a nonphysical space of communion with spirit that is also your:

- **Seat of intuition:** This intuition comes from a deeper way of knowing than has been captured by scientists and psychologists. Through intuition, your spiritual heart guides you to move in harmony with the universe.

- **Realm of unconditional love:** To the spiritual heart, every person is a brother, sister, mother, and father. But unlike many worldly relationships, this flow of love can't be squashed even if someone acts against you. When you have true unconditional love, your vibration of love and the universal vibration of love become one — because universal love is inherently unconditional.

- **Abode of inner peace:** When peace begins to make its home in you, it is like a still lake after a thunderstorm — the air is gentle, yet vibrant and fresh. When you're in touch with your spiritual heart, even when you become frazzled from the storms and challenges of life, you can find your way back to the lake of your own inner peace. You can take a dip in the refreshing waters that flow within your spiritual heart.

- **Ocean of contentment:** The spiritual heart knows that true happiness doesn't come from outer objects, people, or events. Things and people can bring little blips of happy feelings, but the contentment of your spiritual heart is much better. Inner contentment may not always be as exciting or dramatic as having outer desires and passions fulfilled, but spiritual contentment becomes your soothing companion during easy times and hard times, and on both stormy and sunny days.

Oh, the contradictions!

There are two kinds of truth, small truth and great truth. You can recognize a small truth because its opposite is falsehood. The opposite of a great truth is another great truth.

—Niels Bohr

Spirituality encourages you to approach life with more responsibly and respect for the deeper meanings behind even the smallest details of life. At the same time, spirituality also gives you an awareness that everything is running quite well without your having to feel anxious or responsible for it all.

The spiritual journey is filled with these sorts of seemingly opposite viewpoints. Here are a few more:

- **Effort is of utmost importance, but you have to stop trying.** If you don't put effort into attaining the great benefits of spiritual life, these attainments will probably not fall right into your lap. However, there comes a time when your trying must lose its sense of effort, wanting, and striving for something that you don't have. You make the efforts, yet the attainments come as a gift, like when someone who has worked hard to become famous for years or decades is called an "overnight success."

- **You're a work in progress that's already done.** You may have a whole list of improvements you'd like to make in your self. Maybe you're unhappy with how you act at times, or with certain self-defeating habits or thought patterns you may have gathered along the way. In this way, you're still a work in progress, with great room and potential for change, growth, and improvement. On the other hand — and this is a big spiritual hand I'm talking about — after you glimpse the amazing beauty and perfection of this eternal universe, you also recognize that your deepest spiritual essence is ultimately eternal and perfectly complete.

- **Love thy neighbor, but not too much!** A love for humanity is paramount for spiritual growth, but this love doesn't mean you have to spend a lot of time with all kinds of people all the time. The company you keep affects your thoughts and life in ways you may not even imagine (see Chapter 11). Some spiritual seekers find that a certain amount of solitude allows them to explore the inner realms and become clearer about what they really feel and believe. Even while opening your heart to fellow human beings, tap into the invaluable spiritual freedom and growth that comes when you don't feel obliged to fit your expanding beliefs into the concepts of too many other people's belief systems.

- **You have to take care of your body, even though you're not really the body.** You know how all these spiritual teachers say that you aren't really the body, you are pure spirit and all that? Still, you can bet that most of them eat when they're hungry and sleep when they're tired and probably moan and groan like everyone else when their own bodies go through a painful experience. This discrepancy doesn't mean they were lying about this "not the body, but pure spirit" thing. Rather, it's one more dichotomy on the spiritual path: You are in the body, but not of it.

- **You are supreme consciousness, but you still have to wash the dishes.** In the depths of spiritual practices such as meditation, you begin to experience greater realms of thought. You may feel completely free, expansive, and powerful — even one with the whole universe. Then, you come out of meditation, and that pile of bills is still sitting there waiting to be paid, the house needs cleaning, or the phone is ringing and your boss, a creditor, or a relative wants to have an aggressive chat with you. Where did all that freedom and expansion go?

The Difference between Spirituality and Religion

Although the words *religion* and *spirituality* are sometimes used interchangeably, they really indicate two different aspects of the human experience.

- *Spirituality* is the wellspring of divinity that pulsates, dances, and flows as the source and essence of every soul. Spirituality relates mainly to your personal search and connection with the divine, as you look beyond outer appearances to find deeper significance and meaning.

- *Religion* is most often used to describe an organized group or culture that has been sparked by the fire of a spiritual or divine soul. Religions often act with a mission and intention of presenting specific teachings and doctrines while nurturing and propagating a particular way of life.

There is only one religion, though there are a hundred versions of it.

—George Bernard Shaw

Different religions can look quite unlike one another. Some participants bow to colorful statues of deities, some listen to inspired sermons while dressed in their Sunday finery, and others set out their prayer rugs five times a day to bow their heads to the ground. Regardless of these different outer forms of worship, the kernel of religion is spirituality – the relationship between the individual soul and divine universal spirit.

Here are some more ways to distinguish spirituality from religion:

- Spirituality is the mystical face of religion.

- Spirituality is being guided from within, while religion is being guided outwardly.

- Spirituality is the pearl within the shell of religion.

- Spirituality is the banana, while religion is the banana skin. Respect the banana skin, but eat the banana!.

Religion and spirituality can blend together beautifully.

Thou shalt nots

One way to describe the difference between religion and spirituality is to say that religion is about being outwardly guided, while spirituality is being inwardly guided. Here's a small sampling of the many prohibitions dictated by various religious traditions as part of their outer guidance:

- Thou shalt not kill any living thing (Buddhism)

- Thou shalt not eat pork (Judaism, Islam)

- Thou shalt not cut your hair (Sikhism)

- Thou shalt not disturb birds and other animals (Taoism)

- Thou shalt not commit adultery (Christianity, Buddhism, Judaism, Islam, Hinduism, and pretty much every religion)

- Thou shalt not wear head coverings in a house of worship if you are a male (Christianity)

- Thou shalt not go bareheaded into a house of worship if you are a male (Judaism, Sikhism)

- Thou shalt not point the bottoms of your feet toward an altar (Buddhism, Jainism, Hinduism, Sikhism)

Spirituality is:

- Beyond religion, yet contains all religions
- Beyond science, yet contains all science
- Beyond philosophy, yet contains all philosophy

GOD: Generous Omniscient Divinity

When you talk about spirituality, you have to also talk about God. Who is God? What is God? Is God?

These questions have been asked and answered in countless ways throughout human history. Some ancient ancestors sacrificed animals at the altars of stone representations of God, while others worshipped a multitude of colorful gods with strikingly human traits and desires. Some believe God is a conceptual repository for all the questions that have not yet received acceptable answers, while others speak to God as a child might address his or her mother or father.

What is God to you? Were you made in His image? Is God alive in your life? Did He die for your sins? Is She showering you with blessings or sending arrows into your heart? Is He keeping track of whether you've been bad or good (so, be good, for goodness sake!)?

In the beginning, there was nothing. God said, "Let there be light!" And there was light. There was still nothing, but you could see it a whole lot better.

—Ellen DeGeneres

Many people are fair weather friends with God. They ignore God when things are going well, and as soon as disaster hits, they'll be saying, "Um, God, remember me?"

Be Careful

Don't wait for a disaster to think of God or talk to God, or God may find that disaster is the best way to ring your phone!

In fact, you can make God an integral part of your daily life in a real way, where an open line of communication is gently present in even your smallest actions and thoughts.

Playing "My God is better than your God"

Spiritual Wisdom

It is more important to create a safer, kinder world than to recruit more people to the religion that happens to satisfy us.

—Dalai Lama

What wise ones say about God

"Looking for God is like seeking a path in a field of snow, if there is no path and you are looking for one, walk across it and there is your path."

   —Thomas Merton

"Once you have seen the face of God, you see the same face on everyone you meet."

   —Deng Ming-Da

"The eye with which I see God is the same eye by which God sees me."

   —Meister Eckhart

"God is simple, everything else is complex."

   —Paramahansa Yogananda

"God to me, it seems, is a verb and not a noun, proper or improper."

   —Buckminster Fuller

"The simplest person who in his integrity worships God, becomes God."

   —Ralph Waldo Emerson

"The mind that wishes to behold God must itself become God."

   —Plotinus

"If God made us in His image, we have certainly returned the compliment."

   —Voltaire

Many wars have been fought based on what amounts to fairly slight variations in religious theory and language. However, in the light of spirituality, no one needs to fight with anyone else over whose religion is better. No one needs to quarrel over every rule and detail of all the different doctrines. Rather, a spiritually aware person is open to learning and growing from everything in life. An ancient Indian scripture explains, "Truth is one, although sages call it differently." The Sufi poet Jelalud'Din Rumi expressed, "There are a hundred thousand ways to kneel and kiss the ground."

Your experience of God doesn't have to be the same as the experience of everybody or anybody else. One sign of spiritual awakening is an increased respect for all people, all religions, and all forms of God. This kinder, gentler approach replaces outdated tendencies toward intolerance and prejudice. As one becomes more spiritual, the animalistic aggressions of fighting and trying to control the beliefs of other people can be cast off like an old set of clothes that no longer fits.

In fact, many spiritual seekers begin to feel that every image of divinity, regardless of its religious context, is just one more face of the same, eternally present God.

Loving and respecting all religions and images of God doesn't mean that you have to agree with all their doctrines. In fact, you don't even have to believe and agree with every element and doctrine of your own religion! This suggestion goes for any teachings you may encounter along your path. For example, as you read this book, enjoy whatever words work for you and just skim over what doesn't. My goal is to share spiritual ideas that have been helpful on my journey, not to make you agree with them.

What Spirituality Can Do for You

Knowledge of your true spiritual nature can transform your entire world because the world you know is inherently limited by your ability to know it. The journey of spirituality gives you new eyes through which to see. My spiritual teacher used to call it "changing the prescription of your glasses." You still see the same world as before, but it is nothing like before:

- Within every joy and behind every sorrow, you begin to perceive the same underlying exhilaration of being alive.

- Your uncomfortable feeling of being separate from the world begins to dissolve into a subtle sense of oneness with all things.

- You take greater responsibility for the circumstances of your life as you realize that everything around you is a reflection of your inner being.

- Even when you're totally alone, you know that you're never really alone.

- When you're aggravated by an outer circumstance, you can sense that it is only a reflection of some deep lesson your soul is struggling to learn.

- As the ups and downs of life come like waves to your shore, you ride them with acceptance and detachment, knowing that your true home is in the ocean's great depths — in the peaceful calm beneath the ever-changing waves of worldly life.

You won't find this many benefits being promised on even the most enthusiastic info-mercial for any product! With spiritual awareness, you'll have:

- A greater sense of power in co-creating your life with the universal Spirit

- An enhanced appreciation for every moment of life, whether pleasurable or challenging

- A steadiness that carries you into the precious confidence that everything is all right, all the time

- Faith in a living God or Divine Nature that is present in even the smallest detail of your life

- Days filled with joyful service and inspirational inner growth

- A natural state of peacefulness and contentment

- Honesty and self-acceptance, without needing to hide who you really are

- The transformation of your limited self-identification into a greatness and magnificence you may never have imagined exists in you, *as* you

Great things about being spiritual today

The quest for spiritual realization is as valid and important now as ever, and today's technologies and advances offer an abundance of benefits to bless your vibrant spiritual journey. Here are some of the great advantages for spiritual seekers today:

- Recent advances in science and technology mean that more information about this world and your mind and body is available to contemplate and consider.

- Relatively widespread freedoms of religion around the world allow you to craft your spiritual beliefs in a personal way.

- Today's longer life spans give you more time to learn and grow.

- Running hot water — because hot showers must automatically be included on all lists about what is good about today!

- Magnificent telescopic photos of the universe are available to remind you of how big it all is.

- Wisdom from cultures past and present is readily accessible in libraries, bookstores, and at the click of a mouse.

- More time is potentially available than when people had to carry water from a well, cook meals over open fires, and milk the cows before dawn.

- Convenient opportunities for transportation give seekers the ability to go on spiritual pilgrimages and experience other cultures.

- More movies, television programming, news stories, and documentaries can give opportunities to contemplate and grow from a massive array of life lessons without having to travel to each place or go through each experience and event yourself.

Not so great things about being spiritual today

Obviously, I want to convince you that today is a great time to be spiritual, and indeed, it is. However, it wouldn't be fair if I didn't also point out some of the unique challenges facing a spiritual seeker today:

- Ever-present media machines blasting negative, violent, and manipulative energies into today's society, exposing even young children to a lot of unspiritual images.

- A pervasion of toxins, pesticides, junk foods, pollutants, and invisible radio, television, and telephone signals that can compromise your physical health and clarity of thought.

- A more scattered society, with less sense of family, community, and commitment to one another. (On the other hand, this trend toward social separation can also give more opportunity to spend time with yourself, which can be *helpful* to spiritual growth.)

- Cement cities that take people away from the colors, shapes, textures, and smells of nature that are so essential for nurturing the soul.

- The infiltration of commercialism and corporate greed into every aspect of worldly life, with companies spending millions of dollars to convince you that you won't be happy unless you acquire their product.

Chapter 3

Discovering Your Own Spirit

Topics in this Chapter:

* Discovering the spirituality in your life

* Understanding your higher self

* Seeing beyond your masks

* Exploring what keeps you from experiencing your greatness

This chapter is dedicated to helping you understand that you are a unique expression of pure spirit. One way to achieve this awareness is by contemplating the big questions of life, such as, "Who are you?" and more importantly, "Who are you *really*?"

Even if you think you can't be spiritual because you may have some faults, or even a lot of faults, you can still discover how to see those faults within a bigger picture of yourself as an individual expression of the great universal spirit.

The First Step: Knowing That You Don't Know

There are more things in heaven and earth, Horatio, than are dreamt of in your philosophy.
—William Shakespeare

One of my favorite spiritual texts says, "He who thinks he knows, knows not; while he who thinks he knows not, truly knows." This statement implies that the person who thinks he knows is the most ignorant. Why is this?

The truth is that humans don't and can't know everything. Countless layers of reality can be unraveled in every direction you look, from a seemingly infinite sea of galaxies to the invisible atoms on this page.

As a human being, you live and walk upon this floating pebble of water, rock, and moss that is called earth. You've come equipped with a body and approximately three pounds of electrochemical jelly, called your brain.

With these inherent limitations, you'll never be able to completely understand everything about this very big universe. Everyone knows this deep inside, but sometimes people find it more comfortable to try and convince themselves and others that they have it all together and know what's happening.

Two kinds of ignorance

No matter what you're trying to learn, you can gain a new skill or absorb new information only if you first admit that you don't already know everything about that particular topic. In the spiritual quest also, a receptive attitude is the first step in opening up to greater spiritual wisdom.

Here I describe two kinds of ignorance: positive ignorance and negative ignorance:

- *Positive ignorance* **is when you don't know and you know you don't know.** This humble awareness keeps you open and receptive to divine guidance and helps you to educate, grow, and improve yourself.

- *Negative ignorance* **is when you don't know, but you think you do know.** This state of mind is really a double ignorance that closes the door to your own growth. Thinking you know when you don't know is like traveling to a party on the other side of town with no idea of where the house is, but being too proud and stubborn to admit it and ask for directions. Negative ignorance makes you drive around in circles and miss the party of spiritual delight!

Once, a university professor went to visit a famous Zen master. While the master quietly served tea, the professor talked on and on about all the intricacies of Zen philosophy. The master filled the visitor's cup to the brim and then kept pouring. The professor watched this overflowing cup for several seconds, until he could no longer restrain himself, and finally blurted out, "It's overfull! No more will go in!"

"*You* are like this cup," the master replied, "How can I show you Zen until you first empty your cup?"

You are a worldview maker

Your *worldview* is the way you see, interpret, and experience the world around you. A simple example of a worldview characteristic would be whether you look at life with a cheerful, optimistic view or a moaning, groaning, pessimistic one.

The process of making new worldviews is not unknown to you — you've been making and changing worldviews throughout your life. Even if you don't think you have a specific worldview, know that this thought is simply part of your worldview. Different people have different ways of viewing the same outer circumstances, and throughout the stages of life, each person travels through many different worldviews.

Can you remember all the years of schooling and effort you had to go through to learn all that you know? Even to be able to read and comprehend these words, many small and large worldviews were created and destroyed throughout your youth. In fact, the human brain is programmed to create new views of the world as we grow.

Here's an example of a worldview change you've already experienced. Jean Piaget, a scientist who is often referred to as the founding father of developmental child psychology, conducted an experiment during the 20th century that demonstrated how a child's brain develops and expands into new world views.

Piaget would sit a young child in front of a tall glass of colored water. Then, right in front of the child, he would pour all of the liquid from the tall, thin glass into a short, wide one. Invariably, every young child would insist that there was less liquid in the shorter glass, even though they had seen the very same amount of liquid being poured with their own eyes.

This incorrect worldview happens, Piaget explained, because these young children have not yet entered the developmental stage that brings a capacity for comprehending what Piaget called *conservation of volume.* If you showed these children the same demonstration a few years later, they would have no problem understanding that the volume of liquid in both glasses has remained the same.

This conservation of volume shift is a good metaphor for the experience of shifting from a materialistic to a spiritual view of the world. The way the children in this experiment misunderstood the value and size of what they were seeing is similar to how many people mistakenly think that worldly accumulations are worth more than spiritual qualities like inner peace, just because the outer objects or positions of stature are more tangible.

The Truth Is Simple, But You Have to Be Ready

Once, a spiritual seeker traveled to a distant town to receive initiation from a highly respected guru. The seeker bowed before the master and asked to be given the secret knowledge that would grant him the state of self-realization. "Oh, guru, please tell me the secret of life that will free me from all bondage."

The guru looked at this seeker and saw that he was not prepared to contain the highest truth. His mind and heart had not yet been scrubbed clean of their tangled webs of memories, desires, misunderstandings, and limited self-identifications. The seeker needed first to be purified by the lessons gained by living an austere, surrendered life of service and contemplation.

Nevertheless, the seeker continued to impatiently entreat the guru to give him that very truth, and so the master compassionately touched the seeker on his head and spoke. "Thou art That." Actually, he said the words in Sanskrit: "*Tat tvam asi.*" In this statement, "That" refers to the unnamable divine source of all, and "Thou" represents all the different facets that make up you.

The seeker sat down and prepared to hear the rest of the master's secret teachings, when he realized the discourse was already over. "That was it? This is ridiculous," he thought to himself, "Thou art That? These three words sound esoteric, but make no sense. Maybe this guru has gotten too old to remember the teachings, or perhaps his respected reputation is, in fact, undeserved."

The seeker politely thanked the master and asked to be dismissed, thinking, "I'm sure I can find a better teacher who can give me an experience of the truth."

For several years, the seeker searched far and wide until he came upon the monastery of another highly respected guru. Again, he bowed before the master and asked to be granted the highest state of realization.

This guru also saw that the seeker was unripe and told him, "First, you will have to offer service in this monastery. Go and work in my fields for 12 years and then come back to me. I will give you the secret knowledge then."

The seeker thought, "Wow, he must be really good to be able to charge so much!" and agreed to the terms. For the next 12 years, the seeker lived in the monastery and toiled in its fields. During this time, inner understandings about the higher nature of life revealed themselves inside his awareness, preparing the soil of his heart and mind for the sacred seed of initiation.

At the end of his assignment, the seeker came once again before the master and bowed with humility. "Oh, guru, I have fulfilled your command and worked in your fields for 12 years, and you have promised to enlighten me. Tell me, master, what is the secret of life that will free me from all bondage?"

The guru now saw before him a shining light — a purified vessel ready to accept and hold the truth. He looked into the disciple's eyes and spoke, "Tat tvam asi. Thou art That."

The seeker was about to think, "Hey, that's the same thing the other guru told me . . ." when his mind stopped and grasped the essence behind these three words. With "Thou art That" throbbing in every particle of his being, the seeker ascended to the spiritual state of the masters, and in that very moment was enlightened.

Don't Forget

Just as words on a page are meaningless to one who hasn't yet learned to read, in the same way, even the highest truths will slip through the fingers of a seeker who isn't spiritually mature and prepared to receive them.

Who Are You?

All my life, I always wanted to be somebody. Now I see that I should have been more specific.
                                            —Jane Wagner

One of the most interesting questions you can ask yourself is "Who am I?" This primordial question is ultimately the foundation for all knowledge and experience. Every aspect of your culture, genetic makeup, life experience, family history, education, and social stature affects the way you experience the world. Therefore, when seeking greater wisdom, truth, and spiritual enlightenment, it is supremely important to first look at yourself and ponder the question, "Who am I?"

This simple question would appear to have a reasonable answer, right? Usually, you're able to ask what something is and receive a satisfactory answer. What is that? My car. Who is that? A friend. Where is that? Two blocks down and turn right. So then, who are you?

You are made up of your personality, your actions, your family, your body, your ethnicity, your religion, your culture, your job, your environment, your expressions, what you feel, what you do, what you say, what you know, what you see, and what you think.

The challenge of spirituality is to see all these qualities and colors of who you are, while also realizing that you are a unique expression of pure spirit, revealing itself as you.

Knowledge of your self brings power

Knowledge is power, especially knowledge of your own self. When you're conscious of who you are, you are also more conscious and aware of how you're thinking, speaking, and acting.

Self-knowledge gives you the objectivity and insight needed to purify and empower your thoughts, words, actions, habits, and character.

Knowing thyself

Why is it important to explore and understand your qualities, including your strongest points and weakest tendencies? Because you have to know where you're starting from.

Self-knowledge is like having the health benefit of knowing what kinds of foods work best in your body. After you discover that certain substances cause allergic reactions or create a bad mood, you can gain greater control over your physical and mental state by avoiding foods that will harm you. At the same time, you can work to strengthen your body so it will be healthy enough to properly digest more types of food.

It is the same on the spiritual path. You need to find out what motivates you and keeps you in a good, healthy, spiritual state. For some, this process may mean adding specific spiritual practices to your daily life (Part II of this book gives examples of spiritual practices for body, mind, and spirit)

Just as you may decide to stop eating greasy junk food or too many sweets to help your body stay in a good physical state, in the same way, you may decide to watch fewer violent movies or go to fewer wild parties to help keep your mind and heart in a good spiritual state.

 **Consider**

Paying attention to your inner state and contemplating your history and personal nature help give you the resources to make better decisions about what works best for you.

Your nature is reflected in your world

Have you ever heard someone say, "Your actions speak louder than words," or "What you are is so loud that I can't hear what you are saying"? These statements are often used to insinuate that someone is acting in a way that is inconsistent with the image he's wishing to present through his words. Yet, these phrases also indicate an important and magical truth about human expression — what you are expresses through everything you do. Therefore, all you really need to do to discover more about who you are is to look at what you've chosen to surround yourself with and ask a few questions, such as:

- What is decorating the walls of your home, such as paintings, photos, or other collections? Is it family? Nature? Accomplishments? Souvenirs? Spiritual icons?

- Do the objects around you represent happy times or sad memories?

- What kind of clothes do you most like to wear — fancy or comfortable?

- What kind of friends do you have — supportive, trustworthy, distant, or close?

- What books do you like to read — mysteries, spiritual, dramas, or romance?

- What kind of television shows do you watch — reality, sitcoms, news, or soap operas?

- What kind of car do you drive — safe, large, small, impressive, or dependable?

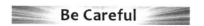
Too much honesty about your mutual tendencies can sometimes be damaging to a friendship. Be honest but kind in your assessments of each other, and remember that the goal of this process is to explore honestly *and* with a focus on uplifting your self-images and expressions. As with every other powerful practice, the key is moderation.

Discovering your tendencies

To discover your personal tendencies, observe how you react and respond in certain situations. How do you handle stress? How about criticism? Do you do well or poorly with tight deadlines? How do you respond when you're waiting to hear if you got the job?

Take a look, also, at the little things, which are just as revealing of your nature. For example, if you have an iTunes or other program on your computer, phone, or mp3 player, do you prefer to program the exact order of songs? Do you let them just play in alphabetical order? Or, do you press shuffle and let the winds of fate be your DJ? Do you prefer having control, or do you thrive on the thrill of the unknown? How much and in what ways?

It's like getting to know other people, only better!

One of the most amazing and wondrous aspects of personal relationships is to experience a deep level of intimacy with another human being. There is something magical about discovering every look and thought of the one you love and sensing how to dance with that person as you move together through the waves and events of life.

Now here's the good news. You can actually find the same level of joy and intimacy within your own mind and heart. You can have the same level of enthusiasm in getting to know yourself as you have when you're getting to know someone else. The key to spiritual awareness is to really know and understand yourself — to love, respect, and honor yourself.

Forget what the spiritual correctness police might say if they think you're being too self-absorbed. The self-absorption you should avoid is the kind of limited self-identification that can make a person inconsiderate toward others. The journey of self-knowledge makes you more considerate of others, because you begin to sense the deep connection of all beings.

You can find more to explore inside every aspect of how you relate to the world. The field for this research into your own nature is wide open and available any and every moment of the day. Here are a few more questions you can contemplate:

- If God promised you an unconditional "Yes" right now, what would you ask for? (Feel free to take some time to contemplate this question, because you never know who may be listening!)

- When someone says they have good news and bad news, which do you want to know first and why?

- When you are in hopeful situations, such as playing a slot machine, being up for a cool prize in a raffle, or awaiting news of a possible promotion, what psychological maneuvers do you use to try to bend the universal flow to your will? Do you feign detachment? Do you beg? Do you ask sweetly or try to make deals with God? Do you surrender by offering it all to God's will? And if so, are you truly surrendered or offering to God's will out of laziness or in hopes that this "surrender" will help you get what you want?

- How do you respond when windfalls of great fortune seem to shower down upon your head or alternatively when everything seems to be going wrong? What are your beliefs during these times? For example:

- During great times, do you feel concerned that the universe is going to balance things out by bringing some rough times?

- During bad luck times, do you feel that God must be angry about something you have done?

This exploration isn't an exercise in making judgments against yourself; rather, it's intended to help you become more self-aware. Just as you have to fully trust friends or a therapist to be able to truly confide in them, in the same way, you must be able to trust that your own love and respect for yourself won't waver. This unwavering self-respect and self-love allows you to safely unravel tendencies that may clash with who you thought you were or wish to be.

Consider

Always be your own best friend.

A side trip into psychology

One of the most fascinating psychological topics I've encountered is that of *Multiple Personality Disorder*. MPD is a condition where extreme trauma has shaken a person's psyche, which then responds by separating into different personalities to block the experience and memory of this extreme physical or emotional pain. Once formed, these subpersonalities can sometimes continue to exist and grow almost as psychic tumors or separate entities living within the same body.

I first learned about this multiple personality condition when I was less than 10 years old. My parents were both psychology teachers who taught all the coolest aspects of psychology to their high-school classes, including attraction/aversion, behavioral psychology, extrasensory perception, and much more. Our bookshelves always had a steady stream of the hottest new psychology books of the 1970s, and I read a good number of them.

The most interesting topic for my young, developing mind was that of Multiple Personality Disorder. In these cases, it would appear that different people were sharing the very same body, either peacefully or not so peacefully. Some would have a wide array of personalities — including boys, teens, women, and men — yet all these very different "people" were actually facets of the same overall person.

Studies have shown that in some cases, different personalities within the same body have even had different allergic responses — such as common allergies to animals, pollens or foods — with some subpersonalities being very allergic to something and others who are expressing through the very same body, having no allergic reaction at all. Some subpersonalities have been shown to have different brainwave patterns, handwriting styles, gender identifications, left- and right-handedness, voice patterns, reactions to different medications, cysts and diseases that appear and disappear depending on the personality, and different levels of visual acuity. Some multiples even have to change to different prescription glasses, depending on who's steering the ship at any moment. It would be hard to find a more compelling demonstration of the amazing and flexible power of your mind and the fluid nature of personality!

Looking at your shadows

One reason many people don't like to look too closely at themselves is because they inevitably encounter their shadows — pockets of action, speech, and attitudes that aren't always in keeping with their highest views of themselves. Therefore, before you delve too deeply into your shadows, you can first adjust your worldview to the forgiving vision of spirituality.

Understand that in your spiritual journey, even mistakes you've made along the way can be transformed into fuel for the fire of spiritual evolution. (This conversion is even better than recycling!) Once you understand this process, you can wave goodbye to those old staples of guilt and shame, along with their friends by the names of anger, greed, and hatred.

If you have habits and personality traits that you or others have judged harshly through the years, now is the time to begin to look at every aspect of yourself with a more objective, kinder, and knowledgeable eye. Ignoring your bad habits doesn't help, nor does overfocusing on them, such as being filled with shame about past actions or thoughts. In fact, trying too hard to get rid of a habit or trait can backfire because the nature of thoughts is to empower whatever they're directed toward, whether positive or negative (see Chapter 15).

Consider

You can even have gratitude for your shadows. Just consider that all your faults, flaws, and past missteps will give you an even more interesting and inspiring testimonial once you grow beyond them into a more spiritual life.

Don't Forget

You can be sure that if an all-intelligent and all-powerful God gave you and everyone else all these different combinations of personal qualities and histories, it's because you're intended to be different. You're unique, just like everybody else, and you're meant to have all your tendencies, conflicts, and complications, along with all your blessings and great qualities. The spiritual challenge behind being you is to take all that you have and all that you are and to raise it up as a joyful toast to the Divine. With this approach, the darker aspects of your nature are naturally lifted up into the light, and you are less likely to do what is harmful and more drawn to creating what is beneficial.—*Teilhard de Chardin*

Appreciating your depths

Spiritual Wisdom

We are not human beings having a spiritual experience. We are spiritual beings having a human experience.
—Teilhard de Chardin

Human personality isn't an item or a stable object. You are a *flow* — a spiritual light that becomes fragmented into the many colors that make up your multifaceted personality.

Therefore, it's possible that you may feel and act a certain way in one moment and very differently at another time. For example:

- If you're in a great mood, you may be extra charitable toward the people around you, tossing out friendly smiles and kind words as you go through the day.

- If you're in a bad mood, you may instead find yourself impatient and angry with the same people in the very same situations.

Your responses to the same situations can vary drastically depending on your mood or personal state of consciousness at the time because you aren't just a single, limited, tangible object. You are the flow of pure spirit expressing itself freshly in every moment as you. Think about your own life and how you act and feel in the following situations:

- When you're playing with happy children
- When you're teaching someone who is eager to learn from you
- When you encounter someone who thinks you're an idiot
- When you feel confused, upset, or fearful
- When you feel the power and light of grace shining through you

Get to know all the facets of your gem, and you'll find it easier to experience the spiritual light that is shining through your gem.

Don't Forget

On your journey of spiritual evolution, each facet of your personality grows and blossoms. You may be very spiritually mature in some ways, while in others, you've still got more work to do. Even the aspect of your personality that gets irritable, and the parts of your mind that entertain thoughts you wish were entertaining someone else's mind, begin to move higher from wherever they are to become freer and lighter.

Once you realize how big and amazing your personality and everything else is, then you can also relax a bit more about the small details of life and have faith in this amazing universe.

Consider

Don't be too upset with yourself if you falter here and there on your spiritual journey. Even the upward flow of spiritual evolution will appear to have some ups and downs.

You are the flowing water

Here's an analogy to help you understand the many levels of who you are: Imagine a rushing stream of water flowing along the riverbanks. In one area, you see piles of rocks that have created a diversion in the water's flow. As you look at this area, you notice the shape of a whirlpool that has been formed by the water rushing across this pattern of rocks.

To an objective eye, the whirlpool shape created by the water flowing around the rocks may appear to be a solid object. To someone who doesn't understand the dynamics of flowing water, this whirlpool shape may appear to be the same water from one moment to another. However, those who understand what is really going on know that this seemingly stable pattern is constantly being animated by fresh flowing water.

The rocks in this riverbed are like all the outer circumstances of your life that have created certain flows and shapes in your character and awareness. The whirlpool shape created by these rocks is like the part of you that others can see — all the appearances and behaviors that make you similar to or different from others.

Nevertheless, spirituality says that what you really are is the flowing water. Your deepest essence is neither the rocks nor the shape of movement, but the fresh stream of divine life force and Holy Spirit that streams through the circumstances of your life, creating this image of you.

In this analogy, what you identify with says a lot about how you experience life:

- **Identifying with the rocks** in the stream is akin to identifying with present situations and past memories, such as what you own, what you've done, or your childhood experiences of having too much of one thing or too little of the other. Focusing on the rocks is like having a materialistic point of view that may lead you to struggle endlessly to rearrange the rocks with hopes of creating changes in the water's shape.

- **Identifying with the whirlpool shape** is also a lower road to go. If you think the personality shape created by the rock circumstances of your life is you, well, then where will you be when those rocks come tumbling down one day? If the whirlpool dissolves or changes, you may actually think you've died!

- **If you identify instead with the flowing water** — with the spiritual energy that invigorates and gives life to the body, mind, heart, and soul of every being that emerges out of the spring of life — then you know a great and wonderful freedom. Even if all the rocks fall down and even if the shapes of water patterns change a million times, you remain identified with the ceaseless flow of water that's unaffected by shifts in the riverbed.

The truth is that you're really all three — the rocks, the patterns of water flow, and the water.

Yes, But Who Are You Really?

This whole universal creation is bigger than anybody can fathom, and guess what? So are you.

In spite of the ultimately indefinable nature of the human soul, sages from spiritual traditions throughout the ages have worked hard to explore and discover what really lies inside themselves and the world around them. Although each religious tradition has its own culture-specific images and doctrines, several themes appear in many spiritual and theological theories.

One common element is a belief in an invisible, divine part of you that lives on in some way even after your body takes its last breath — a spark of God that lives within you, as you.

Spiritual Wisdom

Meditate on yourself, honor yourself, and worship yourself. God dwells within you as you."
—Baba Muktananda

Don't Forget

When you need to remember how special you are

If you ever start thinking that you're insignificant or unimportant, just stop for a moment and look at your physical body. What a miracle you are! Appreciate how the profound complexity of nature conspires to keep you alive — from the unceasing work of your heart and other organs to countless molecular functions and other energy transformational processes.

It simply isn't logical to conclude, upon contemplating these things, that you are anything less than exceptional — and somehow worth all the effort!

Big Self, little self

You can think of yourself as having two aspects: your big Self (with a capital "S") and your little self.

- **Your small self** is an egocentric mass of conditioned responses and defense mechanisms that pulls you to into illusion and keeps you from receiving the wealth of your own inheritance.

- **Your big Self** is the great reservoir of eternal wisdom that's always pulling you toward liberation, freedom, goodness, and divine light. It is also the Self of all.

- **You, as an individual being**, are the juncture point between these two, as they pull your awareness, often in opposite directions.

Don't Forget

The inner effulgence of your spiritual Self shines more visibly when you clear away the clouds of ignorance and delusion that block its great light. You can clear the way for more light to express through your life through meditation, contemplation, purification, and the elevated teachings from those who have gazed long and lovingly at their own shining Self.

Some religions, such as Buddhism, have different worldviews that don't include the idea of a permanent, abiding, eternal self. Rather, they may see the self as a temporary flow of causes and conditions that come and go from a particular body/mind system.

Good news! You already are spiritual

Not only is your essence made of pure spirit, but no matter who you are or how you've lived, I can guarantee that you've already been spiritual, with or without knowing it. Here are some ways you may have been spiritual:

- Remember as a child when you used to daydream during school? Wasn't it a great feeling to get absorbed in your own being and enjoy all the entertainment of your inner creations (until the teacher called on you)? In some cases, your daydreaming may have been a form of meditation, turning your awareness away from the outer world of a boring lesson and into the rich realms of inner creativity.

- When your heart is moved to volunteer your time, finances, and other efforts to a good cause, then you're touching the spiritual practice of selfless service. If you can keep in mind that you're honoring the divine in each person you help, then this practice becomes even more spiritual.

- Every time you go to sleep and every time you wake up, your consciousness passes through a porthole of awareness that scientists call the *hypnogogic state.* Spiritual scriptures refer to these juncture points of wakefulness and sleep as powerful times through which you may be able to grasp the divine presence that exists behind your thinking mind. Don't rush so fast to jump out of bed in the morning. Savor that peaceful yet dynamic space between sleep and wakefulness!

  - While watching a beautiful sunset or smelling the delightful fragrances of flowers in spring, it is likely that you've experienced some spiritual feelings of love and appreciation for the beauty of God's creation.

  - Holidays, weddings, funerals, and birthdays bring opportunities for thinking spiritual thoughts, feeling spiritual emotions, and saying spiritual things. Consider:

    •**Thanksgiving Day:** What are you thankful for?

    •**New Year's Day:** What resolutions are you making to improve your life?

    •**Weddings:** What blessings do you wish upon the happy couple?

    •**Funerals:** Where do you feel your friend or family member has gone? What was the value of his or her life?

Fanning the divine flame

Spiritual Wisdom

Someone inside of us is now kissing the hand of God, and wants to share with us that grand news. —Hafiz

Spirituality is a calling from your soul that ignites a wick that has been sitting inside of you for a long time. The flame in your heart may have glowed at times from the sight of a new lover, the love of your children, or other joyful accomplishments. Perhaps your flame has shined especially brightly during times when you've risen to a challenge with passion and vigor. These kinds of flames can wax and wane depending on outer events and inner interpretations.

However, once the *spiritual* flame is lit and blazing inside you, it becomes like one of those magic candles that you just can't blow out. Oh, it may appear to fizzle here and there, or seem to wane when you blow worldly or negative airs towards it, but your spiritual flame always reemerges to shine as brightly as ever, if you have the spiritual eyes to see its radiance.

Taming the donkey

Each person has a great, wise soul inside. Most people also have a lot of stuff and not-so-spiritual tendencies. The Sufi sages refer to these two aspects of a human being as the soul and the donkey. The higher soul is also sometimes called your inner angel, and the word *donkey* refers to the undesirable qualities of your lower self and is appropriately synonymous with the word "ass". Every person is a combination of donkey and soul, animal instinct and higher divinity.

It is not that all of your animal instincts are bad, by any means. Many instincts, such as self-preservation and maternal concern, are essential to life and the propagation of this donkey/angel species called humanity. However, other animalistic instincts can make you do things that aren't in the best interest of anyone, including yourself.

 **Don't Forget**

One goal of spirituality is to raise all the different layers of yourself into greater realms of wisdom and grace.

Diving into the experience of pure soul

One fine day, you'll come upon the doorstep to your inner sanctum, whether in the midst of your life or at the moment of death. Each soul must enter this space naked and free. No societal expectations can touch this place. No parental advice enters here either. No lover, teacher, student, friend or foe, and no fear, judgment, pride, guilt, attachment, or sadness can exist in this pure space. Your clothes and good looks aren't needed, nor will those few extra pounds keep you down.

No outer events can change or affect your pure soul. It's a whole different ball game from the familiar world of physical qualities. Though your life dramas seem to take years, to that soul, there is only one timeless point of time. Your deepest soul exists in the beginning, middle, and end of everything. This is the eternally happy ending to every story.

Moving Beyond Ego

Question: What is it that makes people forget their true spiritual nature?

Answer: Ego, also known as limited self-identification

When the Indian scriptures tell you to "get rid of your ego," they aren't referring to ego in terms of Freudian theory, or to the common usage of the word for someone who is overly proud or arrogant. In spiritual circles, the word *ego* is commonly used as a translation of the Sanskrit word, *ahamkara*, which comes from two roots:

- *Aham* means, "I am."
- *Kara* is an action verb, which can be translated as "to make."

Your ahamkara is the *I-maker*. It makes the idea that "I am, and I am separate." Ahamkara is the misconception that you are an object — disconnected from everything and everybody else — and that you have to always look out for yourself in this world. This limited ego makes bad decisions and becomes the distorting force in a person's life. This is the ego that spiritual practices and efforts chop away to reveal your hidden gems.

Ego isn't only the part of you that thinks you're better than anyone else, but also the part of you that thinks you're worse or less than another person. It's not the good or bad feelings that decide whether your experience is being tainted by ego; rather ego is the false and limited view of yourself that's creating those good or bad feelings.

Spirituality in Action

To explore what some of your limited views of yourself may be, listen to how you talk to yourself and others about yourself. How do you describe yourself? Do you focus on your talents, gifts, and contributions to life, or on your challenges, human frailties, and other negative descriptions? Do you judge and compare yourself to others? Do you feel burdened by your responsibilities, accomplishments, and failures, or do you remember to identify with the flowing water of spirit that is expressing as the various shapes of your life?

Praising yourself doesn't necessarily mean that you have a big ego — in fact, you may simply be free enough from ego that you gratefully appreciate your individual gifts without the limited self-identification of ego. Alternatively, you may appear to be very humble but still have large pockets of hidden ego. Because ego can be so tricky and difficult to discern, some choose to study under spiritual teachers and guides who have an elevated vision that allows them to see where your ego buttons are and how best to heal them.

Be Careful

In spiritual circles, you'll be sure to find many who will be all too happy to take on the role of "busting your ego," such as those I call the "humility police." Some of these people may be anointed, while others are simply annoying.

Chapter 5 gives you helpful guidance on how to know who and what to follow and listen to as you travel on your spiritual path.

A Sufi poet expressed the ego's condition very well, explaining that "when worldly people don't get something, they are restless; and when they do get it, they become arrogant."

Isn't this the truth? Sometimes good fortune can be transmuted into harmful ego, which is quite a shame. Conversely, difficult times can sometimes push you out of the ego's complacency and limited self-importance, and into something greater.

 **Be Careful**

When you feel an ego-based impulse stirring, such as when people are praising or challenging you, don't fall for the temptation to get swept away by their flattering or insulting opinions. Stop the sense of limited identification before it starts. It may feel good at first to feel special, like a big shot, or even righteously indignant, but those fleeting sensations aren't worth the cost!

Are you really God?

When the great spiritual masters declare that "You are God," they're communicating a truth discovered in the depths of contemplation — in that innermost sanctum of spiritual consciousness and soul communion.

However, if you have an incomplete understanding and image of who you are and what God is, then this statement doesn't really make sense.

After all, if you were God, things would look a heck of a lot different around your world than they do now, right?

Well, not necessarily. You see, it's not the "little you" who is worried about getting to work on time that is Lord and Master over all creation. It is the great, wise you who sees beyond outer appearances and into the heart of life — the YOU that exists within you.

Breaking free from egocentric, limited identifications is the key to spiritual growth. Here are two basic approaches to moving beyond ego:

- **Shrinking your ego:** This approach calls for you to file down all the desires and impulses that arise from wrong identification of yourself as a limited human rather than a divine being. While working to shrink your ego, you become vigilant over any thoughts or desires that come up and may even put yourself into situations that challenge you to let go of limited ego comforts. Saints and sages of many traditions have willingly undergone austerities such as fasting and days of unending prayer to subdue their ego-based instincts and tendencies.

- **Expanding your ego:** With this approach, if someone gives you a huge compliment, you receive it, perhaps agree with it, and continue to move forward without having your ego get puffed up in a limited way that would make you act arrogant or egotistical. Rather, your ego's identification begins to grow and grow, getting bigger and bigger as you realize that you are great and divine — and so is everyone else! In this awareness, the small ego sense bursts into a million fragrant rose petals of universal grace, as you begin to see supreme oneness everywhere.

Being Nothing Isn't So Bad Either

Nearly all men can stand adversity, but if you want to test a man's character, give him power.
—Abraham Lincoln

One day, a rabbi and his cantor walked into their temple together and found themselves overwhelmed by the immensity of God's presence. Both fell to the ground in humble awe and exclaimed, one right after the other, "O Lord, I am nothing!"

The temple janitor was cleaning behind one of the pillars when he saw these two devout men fall to their knees. Moved by their striking display of devotion and humility, the janitor stepped out from the pillar and also fell to the ground , crying out, "O Lord, I am nothing!"

Seeing and hearing the janitor's passionate display, the cantor nudged the rabbi and whispered, "Hey, look who thinks he's nothing!"

But seriously, folks, being nothing can be a very high spiritual state, or admittedly, it can be an excuse for living a shallow life. For a spiritual person, being nothing can open the door to becoming everything. It's one of those funny twists of life: By being nothing, you become everything. How does it happen? What does it feel like?

The following three-part contemplation can help you open to the possibility of living fully while being nothing, walking lightly in your heart even as you walk upon the earth:

1. Imagine what it would be like to have no worries, no fear, no confusion or stress, nothing that you're wishing for or waiting for, nobody to be angry at, and no pressing matters at hand.

Of course, this clear state of mind is easier said than done, right? Nevertheless, just by opening yourself to the possibility of entering this state of inner freedom, you're paving the way to its door.

2. In your mind's eye, invoke an image of yourself as a young child.

You may not have felt a truly deep level of security, comfort, and freedom since your early childhood, before school responsibilities came in and disrupted your little party of being a carefree child — bringing stress, test scores, peers, deadlines, homework, teachers, and all the responsibilities and challenges of being thrust into a large group of other souls. I remember this time as a big shock after a relatively smooth and carefree toddlerhood. Imagine and remember what life was like at age two or three, when your biggest concern was hopefully about which color candy would pop up when it was your turn.

3. Take all that carefree feeling and bring it into the circumstances of your life as it is now.

Imagine what it would be like to live your life with all the things and people that have accumulated around you, but with absolutely nothing to worry about. You're not worried about death, money, or someone else's opinion about you, nor are you afraid of losing anything, yet you're still joyful, caring, vibrant, and involved with everything that's going on. This peaceful state is what it feels like to integrate spirituality into your life.

Chapter 4

Exploring Your Soul's Journey

Topics in this Chapter:

*   Remembering why you're here
*   Gaining benefits from every experience
*   Unraveling the mystery of death

Here you are — in your body and in this world. There's no sense in worrying too much about how you got here, since you're already here. A better approach is to focus on what you should be doing now that you're here. But where is the instruction manual?

Chapter 3 guides you into a greater awareness of who you really are. Here, in Chapter 4, you find more big questions of life:

* Why are you here?
* Is there something specific that you're supposed to do?
* Where will you go next?

The theatre doors are open — come on in and watch the play of your life.

Why Are You Here?

As far as we can discern, the sole purpose of human existence is to kindle a light of meaning in the darkness of mere being.

—Carl Jung

Contrary to what today's commercialized society may say, spirituality says that you are *not* here on earth just to be a consumer of more and more material goods. Rather, your spiritual calling is to look beneath the surface of worldly life to find a spiritual journey that is filled with extraordinary blessings and insights.

Exploring your soul's journey is like having a front-row ticket to the grandest production of all — the story of your life. As you watch all the plot twists and turns, you also come to realize that you are playing the starring role in your movie. If you're funny, it's a comedy; if you're evil, it's a horror show. If you're romantic, it's a chick flick.

Finding your role

One of the greatest blessings is to catch a glimpse of your role and mission. Although your personal goals may shift as you grow and change during the seasons of your life, you can still find great benefit in contemplating and becoming familiar with what your skills are, what your deeper aspirations are, what you like, what you're good at doing, and what comes naturally to you. When these observations about your nature come together to create a vision of your role in life, then you find it easier to act in ways that are harmonious with your greater nature.

Take a few moments and write down the answer to these questions: What is my purpose in life? What do I bring to the party? What can I contribute to this potluck dinner of life?

To help discover your mission in life, look back to your childhood. What were your natural interests and abilities? What kinds of things were you good at doing? What did you choose to do in your spare time? What do you choose to do in your free time now? What kinds of efforts seem to flow naturally through you? What brings a smile of contentment to your spirit? Even if quick and final answers don't pop up right away, the very act of exploring these questions can open doors to discovering more about what you really love to do, so you can follow that bliss into a greater awareness of your role.

Don't Forget

Regardless of the genre of your current life story, the spiritual key is to understand that you are the actor behind the roles, as well as ultimately the director, screenwriter, and audience. (See Chapter 14 for a description of how you are one with the divine consciousness that plays all roles.)

Why are you here? Have you ever asked yourself this question? Certainly, it's an essential query, worthy of deep consideration. After all, if you don't even have an inkling of why you're here, how can you expect to achieve your task?

Imagine a classroom where neither the teacher nor the children have any idea why they are there. What will they do with their time? Maybe they'll spend the semester playing or enjoying cookies and juice. A setup like this may make for a fun time; however, the children wouldn't be prepared for the next grade. They would probably have to return and take the same class all over again next year.

If the teacher still didn't know the purpose of that class, the children again wouldn't learn their lessons, and would perhaps spend their entire lives repeating the same class over and over again.

This scenario is similar to what some spiritual teachers say can happen with the process of reincarnation and soul evolution. If you come to this world with no idea of why you are here, it may take a very long time for you to graduate from your current life lessons into higher and greater spiritual realms.

 Spiritual Wisdom

The entire field of relative existence has a single purpose: the attainment of supreme reality, and the consequent liberation of the questing soul.

—Swami Nirmalananda Giri

Your life lessons may include:

- Remembering who you really are
- Experiencing the flavors of human experience
- Discovering how to respond to the events of your life
- Learning from everything that comes your way
- Staying true to your higher nature at all times
- Remembering to look at your life as a play and to enjoy the show.

You're here to evolve

According to many spiritual traditions, your soul is continually growing, blossoming, and evolving in many seen and unseen ways. Every soul is at a different level of evolution, and even within different levels, each evolving soul is in many grades at once.

For example, you may have learned some life lessons exceptionally well, while other realizations, understandings, behaviors, and transformations may still have a way to go. Even highly evolved spiritual beings can still have significant life lessons to learn, although they may have achieved much in other areas.

Consider

If you're in a three-dimensional body, you probably have more to learn!

Spirit has entered this world through your body, personality, and set of circumstances, where it exists *in* you and *as* you. Through your challenges, efforts, successes, and even apparent failures, you are meant to learn about life and apply what you've learned.

You are meant to evolve into greater understandings and expressions as you become more spiritually aware, happy, kind, intelligent, wise, liberated, and enlightened.

The process of spiritual evolution is not about trying to become something other than who you are; rather, your spiritual journey ultimately brings you back in tune with the great soul that you always have been and will always be.

Spiritual evolution takes place right in the midst of all the experiences and circumstances of your life. Regardless of who you are, where you are, and what you do or don't have, you are on a spiritual journey. Within this journey, your responsibility is to uplift and refine what you think, feel, and give in response to whatever experiences are given to you

Spirituality in Action

A contemplation of waking up

Imagine that you're in the middle of a dramatic dream, in which you have completely forgotten who you really are. In the dream, you're a criminal, wanted by the law in 12 states. You're on the run as thousands of lawmen and civilians try to secure a big reward that has been placed on your head, "dead or alive." How are you going to escape? How are you going to become free? Will it help if you work really hard to study all the maps and research data in the dream library within your dream world? Will freedom come through prayer to a big statue that has appeared in the dream under the name, "The Great Wazzoo?" Will you be able to buy your freedom with more dream cash? Not necessarily.

What is most needed in this seemingly impossible situation is for you — the you that you think you are in the dream — to wake up. You have to let go of those dream-bound thoughts, identifications, habits, desires, and attachments, and awaken to your true nature. In fact, one could even say that your dream-self will make the ultimate sacrifice and face total dissolution and "death" in the process of waking up.

After you awaken, safe and snug in your bed with your dog fast asleep at your feet, you contemplate: "What was that all about?" Did the criminal and all those circumstances really exist, or were they just a symbolic illusion, perhaps representing a subconscious desire to feel more "wanted"? The circumstances certainly *felt* real, but everything is so different now as you rest safely in your bed. It's almost as though you've been re-born from the false dream into a higher waking world where you realize, at last, who you really are. (At least until you awaken from *this* dream!)

Life is a school for the soul

If two angels were sent down from heaven — one to conduct an empire, and the other to sweep a street — they would feel no inclination to change employments.

—Isaac Newton

Spirituality views this world as a school for the soul, filled with events and experiences that can bring spiritual growth. Each person lives within a tapestry of lessons: societal lessons, cultural lessons, family lessons, and personal lessons.

You've taken birth as a human being in today's world with your individual circumstances, thoughts, emotions, and perceptions, because these conditions are the ones you need to experience in order to learn lessons that are necessary for your personal evolution.

A "soul lesson" isn't something that a conglomerate of educators has conspired to force you to do so that you'll pass some kind of standardized "no human being left behind" test. Regardless of whether you get the answer "right" or "wrong" on your soul tests, you can still achieve spiritual growth, which is the greater goal of this school for the soul called life.

Don't Forget

From a spiritual point of view, the circumstances and lessons of your life are designed by this intelligent universe to teach, test, refine, strengthen, purify, bless, and enlighten you.

The immediate outer result of a life test is less important than the inner transformation and growth you experience by going through it. Even so-called "failures" can end up being fruitful tests when they inspire you to explore your personal nature and become more aware of universal laws.

For example, if you meet apparent failures with a combination of self-respect, remorse, and a resolve to improve your responses in the future, then those apparent failures may become the seeds of great success.

Sometimes the best spiritual growth comes from circumstances that challenge you to respond in increasingly higher, clearer, and better ways than you may have in previous situations. Therefore, even if you appear to fail a particular life test, you can still be grateful to the test for revealing what you have to do in order to grow and move on. After all, you can't fix a leaky pipe until you find the break.

The basics: Be good, be happy

You already know the basics of living a good spiritual life: Be a nice person, help others, do unto others as you would have them do unto you, respect yourself, be loving, be happy, have fun, let your kindness shine forth, act with integrity, be honest, say what you think and mean what you say, don't be too serious, appreciate everything in life, don't succumb to boredom, greed, jealousy, or the other inner enemies, realize that every moment is sacred and filled with amazing and infinite wonders, be content with your share, give generously to others, be free with yourself, see everyone as a spark of God, give your all to everything you do, and always chuckle inside at the whole cosmic joke of it all. Okay, you can put the book down now.

Just kidding — I'm only getting started! Be nice to your spouse and children, have compassion for those who are suffering, respect the great ones who have given their lives to serve God, eat healthy food, don't indulge your senses too much, spend some time alone with your own thoughts, make decisions that will benefit all concerned, and last but not least, seek ye first the kingdom of God and all things will be added unto you.

Of course, the challenge is to seek ye first the kingdom of God when it's November 1, and you don't have the money for November's rent yet! You may wonder, "Where are all those things that are supposed to be added unto me?" And believe it or not, it can be just as much of a challenge to seek ye first the kingdom of God when everything has already been added unto you. You may be feeling a bit overindulgent, overly secure, and perhaps not quite so humble and may not really think you still need to seek first the kingdom. This play is so mysterious and complex, with twists and turns all along the way!

Finding the hidden gems

Spirituality in Action

Here's a chance to contemplate how to learn the soul lessons inherent in challenging situations, using the example of a situation that is challenging you right now.

1. Start by thinking about a circumstance that is currently challenging you.

Remember and think about all the details of the situation.

2. Try to imagine yourself in God's place.

Rise above your own limited self-concept and move into a bird's eye view of your life. See the patterns and lessons you've already been through, your goals and aspirations, and your various personal qualities, and ask yourself this question: If you were the omnipotent, benevolent lord of the universe, why would you be creating this scenario for yourself? What lessons could you be trying to teach this beloved person (you)?

3. Remember other similar challenges you've had in the past.

What benefits came from those difficult times? What changes did you make based on lessons learned? What strengths did you gain from persevering through previous obstacles? It's not always easy to see the possible benefits of a difficult situation while you're in it, but memory and hindsight are two of the great gifts of human life. You may even want to write about these previous experiences to help you distill more insights from them.

4. Imagine your current troublesome circumstance as a piece that fits perfectly within a great puzzle and consider how this challenging circumstance may fit in with the rest of your personal history and future goals.

Are there parallels to situations that have happened before, even during your childhood? Could the current challenge be giving you one more opportunity to tap into deeper resources of courage, faith, strength, intelligence, humility, or discipline? Approaching your challenges with a positive attitude may also help to improve them.

5. Ask for grace in whatever context this is comfortable for you — from your own self, from God, Allah, Krishna, Jesus, the Higher Power — you get the idea!

Asking for grace is one of the most powerful tools you have for attracting blessings to yourself and others.

Where Will You Go Next?

When we have done all the work we were sent to Earth to do, we are allowed to shed our body, which imprisons our soul like a cocoon encloses the future butterfly.

—Elisabeth Kübler-Ross, M.D.

Have you lived before? Where will you go next? Will you still exist when your body dies? If so, will you remember then who you are now? Is there anything you can you do now to prepare for your inevitable time of departure?

Most religious theories suggest that after the physical death of your body, your soul continues on in a purer form of some kind. Some traditions teach that you will either go to heaven or to hell after you die, depending on how you've acted or whether you've declared a specific kind of commitment to the prophet or teachings of that religion.

Spiritual Wisdom

Pope John Paul II beautifully described heaven as "neither an abstraction nor a physical place in the clouds, but that fullness of communion with God, which is the goal of human life."

The Pope then went on to describe hell as, "the state of those who freely and definitively separate themselves from God, the source of all life and joy."

Many traditions, including Hinduism, Buddhism, Kabbalah, and Greek Orthodox Gnosticism, say that after death, your soul — the background of who you really are beneath the appearances of who you seem to be — goes through various stages and levels of other worldly planes before returning back to earth and taking birth once again in a human form, or perhaps even into other nonhuman realms.

In most of these reincarnation theories, your soul is said to carry with it subtle impressions that have been created by your thoughts, experiences, and actions from this and previous lifetimes. These impressions are said to travel with your soul from one life to another, where they affect every aspect of your life until they're balanced or dissolved through a combination of right action and divine grace. (Find more about these subtle impressions and the laws of karma that create them in Chapter 15.)

Group lessons

One example of a group lesson for today's cultures, countries, and the whole of humanity is to be living on a planet upon which so many fellow human beings are starving and suffering. With all the wealth circulating in this world, there is no logical excuse for having so many people starving to death. According to World Bank statistics, nearly half of the world's population lives in poverty, earning less than two dollars a day. And according to a United Nations report, on this very same planet, 2 percent of all adults own half of the world's household wealth — with many storing away much more money than they could ever possibly use, even in many lifetimes. The lessons and tests inherent in this situation are obvious once you look at them with a bit of objectivity.

Imagine hearing that a planet has been discovered where a small percentage of the inhabitants had an abundance of tangible properties and massive amounts of wealth that they left unused in electronic bank storehouses, while their planetmates — brothers, sisters, mothers, fathers, daughters and sons around their world — were dying of starvation, drought, and easily curable illnesses. What would you think of such a planet?

Befriending death

Spiritual Wisdom

One definite thing in life is that everyone is going to die. No one can escape this reality. The only difference is that some people die a little sooner and some a little later. The doctor dies as well as the patient. The king dies as well as the servant. This is a place where everyone dies.

—Sri Ravi Shankar

The death of your body is inevitable. Therefore, the truly intelligent thing to do is to acknowledge and contemplate that which you know is going to happen one day. Thinking about death isn't a gruesome task, but a realistic one! Remembering that your journey in this world will end one day does the following:

- Helps you to see beyond the materialistic level of life

- Inspires you to be generous with whatever you have while you're here

- Makes it easier for you to let go of ego and false pride

- Inspires you to bring more spirituality to your life

- Allows you to appreciate the preciousness of each moment

Once you've accepted the cycles of life and death, you also don't feel too upset when your body starts to age. Instead of thinking of them as "gray hairs," call them "silvery wisdom hairs". Look at those budding wrinkles as beautiful mountain ranges forged from the bounty of your life. When the time comes that your body isn't able to do all it once could, spend more time in quiet communion with spirit. As death approaches, make peace with everyone and everything in this world and pack your bags for the next journey, wherever it may take you.

Consider

Remembering that your loved ones will be gone one day can also help you to cherish every precious moment you have in their company. Don't wait until people die to appreciate them!

Don't Forget

Many great sages have suggested that seekers of truth should remember their eventual death. Here are more benefits that remembrance of death can bring to your life:

- When you remember death, you're better able to maintain a big-picture perspective that keeps you from getting as easily bogged down by insignificant, temporary details. As they say, you "don't sweat the small stuff."

- When your self-identification has expanded through remembrance of death, the insufferable ego isn't as a big problem anymore. (See Chapter 3 for more about ego.)

- Remembering death ironically holds a secret key to the fountain of immortality, because it urges you to discover and identify with your deeper self — the part of you that can never really die. As you become more comfortable with the idea of death, you may also become aware of an essence within yourself that's beyond birth and death, which is quite a perk!

For these reasons and more, you should make peace with the idea of death. After all, one year must die so the next can come forth. One blossom of a tree must wilt before another can spring to life. The *Bhagavad Gita,* a profound scripture from India, states quite simply that "for the inevitable thou should not grieve." Doesn't this make sense? What better way to set yourself up for unhappiness than to fear and despise what is unavoidable? What if death ends up being the best thing that has ever happened to you — a fulfillment of dreams you never even dared to dream?

The most amazing thing

Once, in olden times, a king asked his prime minister, "What is the most amazing thing in this world?" You see, kings actually had wise men in those nonpartisan days, of whom they could ask such questions.

The king probably expected his prime minister to point to one of the elements that make up this world, or perhaps to describe a more subtle quality like love or beauty as the most amazing thing in this world. Instead, he replied, "O king. The most amazing thing in this world is that every day we see people around us dying, and we know that every single person has to leave this world one day. Yet, each person acts as though he is going to live forever. That is the most amazing thing in this world."

In spite of all this wisdom about accepting and valuing one's death, being okay with death still isn't so popular on the funeral circuit. Of course, when someone you love leaves this world, you will inevitably feel sad. At the same time, while everyone is moaning about how terrible it is that the person is gone, or saying things like, "He was too young to go," one spiritual practice is to stay centered in your higher awareness of universal perfection and to remember that from a universal perspective, nobody is too young to go. In this world, lives come and go like waves moving to the shore and then retreating back into the great ocean of spirit.

Even when someone you love dies and you're experiencing sorrow and grief over the loss, you can maintain a peaceful composure about their death, while still experiencing and honoring your other emotions of sadness and loss.

Also, remember that your feelings of sadness over losing a loved one are really reflections of the joy and love you experienced with the person while they were alive. See the love behind your sadness and feel gratitude for the gift of their presence in your life.

Contemplating what is valuable

What would your life look like if you really acted from the understanding that you will be leaving this world one day? What in your life will keep its value past the threshold of death? What is most important in life? Money? Success? Relationships?

According to sages from a mystical branch of Islam called Sufism, the only things you bring with you into the "next world" are the thoughts, actions, and feelings you have cultivated during this life. Certainly, you won't be able to bring your bank account along!

A great way to contemplate what is most valuable is to imagine that you are at your last moment of life. You're about to leave this world, and with the profound shock and sentiment that often comes at such times, you take a fresh look at yourself and your life as a finite expression that has a beginning, middle, and now, an end.

What did you do during your life that feels most right? How did you help others during your time here? Were you honest? Kind? Did you explore courageously and dance enthusiastically? Did you rise up from mistakes and traumas by choosing a positive approach?

Contemplate what is most valuable in your life, and while you are still here, strengthen, increase, and expand whatever it is.

Spiritual Wisdom

When I arrived in this world, I was crying, and everyone else was laughing; and when I left this world, I was laughing and everyone else was crying!

—Kabir

If you're looking for an intricate spiritual view of death, one classic text is the *Tibetan Book of the Dead*, which is often recited by lamas or Buddhist priests over a dying or recently deceased person.

This text is meant to give guidance on preparing for and going through the various intermediate states of consciousness that a soul passes through between lives.

Spiritual Wisdom

Preparing for your last moment

Some spiritual teachings say that your thoughts and state of mind at the moment of death are what determine where you will go next. In fact, some have suggested that your entire lifetime of spiritual effort is meant just to prepare you to think spiritual thoughts during the "deciding moment" that comes when you reach the threshold of death. The Sufi poet Jelalud'Din Rumi poetically described this moment of decision as, "A century's worth of work, for one chance to surrender."

The Indian sage, Sri Ramakrishna, explains how ongoing spiritual practices prepare you to remember higher spiritual ideas during your important last moment of life:

"The soul reincarnates in a body of which it was thinking just before its last departure from this world. Devotional practices may therefore be seen to be very necessary. When, by constant practice, no worldly ideas arise in the mind, then the god-idea alone fills the soul, and does not leave it even when on the brink of eternity."

Death: Period or comma?

What will happen to you after you die? According to some philosophers, when your body leaves, you will disappear with it. Poof. Gone. Story over.

This possibility is perfectly logical from the standpoint of a materialistic view of life. When an apple falls from a tree and another apple grows in its place, there's no reason to assume that the spirit of the first apple is either enjoying harp music in the land of "apple heaven" or broiling in some big oven of damnation with other bad apples. Nor is there any reason to assume that the first apple has now come back to life as another new apple.

Most religions suggest that where your soul goes after death depends on how you've behaved during your life — with your past actions deciding, for example, whether you'll burn in eternal flames or float with angels above the clouds.

Consider

While many religions posit these kinds of reward and punishment afterlife scenarios, some eastern philosophies suggest that your experience after death may be influenced less by what you've done and more by what you think, or more specifically, what you identify with in your last moments of life.

Be Careful

From the view of this theory, when death comes knocking, your next experience depends on what you are identifying with. If you've lived your life being completely unaware of your greater spiritual nature and identifying solely with your body and outer set of circumstances, well, then, "Buh-bye."

If, on the other hand, you've made good spiritual use of your time here and have traveled one of the many paths that lead to experiencing the eternal nature beyond your personal physical circumstances, then you just may have more to look forward to. Most likely, the experience of expanding into your eternal nature after the physical body's death would feel less like a brand new experience and more like remembering that you've always been eternal and immortal, and that you still are.

Spiritual Wisdom

The Self is not born, nor does he die. He springs from nothing and becomes nothing. Unborn, permanent, unchanging, primordial, he is not destroyed when the body is destroyed.
    —*Katha Upanishad*

Some spiritual teachers describe human life as the universal soul descending from its lofty universal state into form, perhaps to have a bit of human-on-earth-style fun. Maybe the great formless Soul gets an hankering for some delicious food or other sense pleasures, or decides to manifest in human form to see what's going on in this neck of the universe. And a neck it becomes — or more like a noose around his neck.

How death is like leaving a tough job

You can think of leaving this world (a.k.a. dying) as being similar to leaving a really tough job with coworkers you've gotten to know fairly well. You may be happily moving on to a much better job, or you may be upset, thinking that you're being fired or forced to leave and not knowing what will happen next as you leave the security of this steady but tough job.

The people you've worked with may also feel sad or upset about losing your presence and skills, as they hold a goodbye party to bid a fond farewell to their dearly departing officemate.

Now, just imagine that a few weeks later you find yourself preparing to begin a dream job that is better than you could ever have imagined. With the happiness you find in your new life, you may not even want to leave the new job long enough to go back to the old place, even to visit or reminisce with your old friends.

You may experience this same kind of freedom from past attachments and interests when you leave the steady but tough job of living in this physical world. In both cases, you have to let go of the old to welcome the unknowable new.

Some Indian scriptures describe this idea of the divine manifesting as a human being in colorful metaphorical stories of gods taking form as human beings for a specific purpose, but then forgetting who they really are and getting trapped in the usual physical plane illusions that spring forth from ignorance and forgetfulness of our eternal nature. Sometimes spiritual concepts are best expressed through such metaphors.

Here's an analogy that compares your life to the structure of a tree: Imagine that you're a huge tree, but that you've forgotten the bigger picture of yourself as being the whole tree and have instead started to identify with being only a single leaf on the tree. Of course, it's true that you *are* that leaf, but you're much more than just the one leaf.

- If, at the moment the leaf dies and falls to the ground you continue to identify with being only that single leaf, then you'll be gone with the leaf, biodegrading into small particles around the roots of the tree.

- If, on the other hand, you remember — before, or at least right at the moment the leaf is falling off the tree — that you are really the whole tree, including all the leaves, fruits, branches, trunk, and roots, then the leaf's death is no more significant than losing a few hairs during a good shampoo (which admittedly can be traumatic for some!)

Another metaphor for the process of death is the experience of waking up from a dream. During a dream, you may experience yourself as a very different person who is living in circumstances unlike those of your waking state. Yet, when you awaken from this dream, all those people and circumstances that seemed to exist, including the "dream you," exist no more. This common scenario of dying to a dream can give you another way to contemplate your real life death.

Question: When you awaken from a dream, do you die?

Answer:

- **Yes, you die.** If you've become identified with the dream character and circumstances, then however much you've become identified, that's how much you'll cease to exist when the dream is over.

- **No, you don't die.** If you stayed lucid during your dream and remembered that you are actually the one having the dream rather than just the characters and circumstances appearing in the dream, then you continue to exist within and beyond the dream.

Now, you can apply this dream identification scenario to the death of your body from this world:

- As much as you identify with your body, that's how much you'll disappear when it dies.

- If, through spiritual efforts and grace, you experience yourself as existing beyond the limited identification with your body — to that degree you continue to exist.

Reincarnating all over again

Spiritual Wisdom

It is absolutely necessary that the soul should be healed and purified, and if this does not take place during its life on earth, it must be accomplished in future lives.

—Saint Gregory of Nyssa

Do you want to come back again?

How do you feel about the possibility of coming back to earth again and again in different forms and circumstances? Does it sound exciting? Exhilarating? Exhausting?

Buddhist and Hindu sages suggest that the ultimate goal of life is to achieve a state of enlightenment where you don't have to keep coming back and going through all this rigmarole of lifetime after lifetime. The idea is to transcend the cycles of birth and death, which are fraught with limitation and suffering, and to move on to a higher level that is somehow better, more pure, and more complete.

As with any theory, this one can also be distorted by human tendencies to simplify and emotionalize spiritual topics with the usual approaches of desire and greed. When I lived in an Indian-based ashram, people would often say things like, "I'm not coming back!" meaning that, within the context of reincarnation, they were not signing on for another tour of duty in this world (clearly forgetting that the "rebirth draft" is alive and well!) One fellow ashramite who was a free-spirited video producer from Canada used to buck this trend and say, "I can't *wait* to come back! I'm having so much fun here. I want to have more fun."

I thought this fellow sounded a lot more enlightened than the people who were so insistent on moving out of the human realm of experience, although I also identify with the desire to move into higher realms. Still, instead of defiantly declaring, "I'm not coming back!" I tend to think more along the lines of, "I do my best, and God's will be done."

Some religious traditions describe a person's life as being one card within a much larger hand of cards. This idea of reincarnation has been prevalent in many cultures, including most eastern religions and some early forms of Judaism and Christianity. Reincarnation has also been researched in scientific studies of young children who seem to have reported accurate details of previous lives.

The basic idea of reincarnation is that a soul takes birth in many increasingly evolved levels of form, beginning perhaps with a rock or plant and moving through the kingdom of life until that soul is lucky and evolved enough to score a human form. Then the soul takes form as a series of increasingly evolved human beings until it graduates to the next level. Most philosophies aren't too specific about what happens after this point due to the inherent difficulty in knowing or writing about nonmaterial realms.

Generally, this idea of finishing up one's time in this world and moving into the next realm is considered a good thing. In the mundane perspective, there are good days and bad days, pleasure and suffering. As Einstein has pointed out, everything is relative. To a spoiled person, a broken fingernail can be the cause of great emotional distress, while to a starving child, a small crust of bread can bring incredible happiness.

However, from the perspective of some spiritual sages, this entire realm of human existence is inherently painful. It's based on ignorance of one's true nature. It's a prison for the bird of the soul that longs to fly free, unencumbered by the chains of worldliness.

In esoteric Judaism, the concept of reincarnation is called *gilgul hánéshamot,* which literally translates as the recycling or transmigration of souls. This teaching describes reincarnation as being like the flame of one life candle lighting another.

The essence of the second flame comes from the first, and contains imperfections inherited from the initial flame that are meant to be corrected. However, the second flame is also an independent entity that is separate from the first.

Some have asked me whether I believe in reincarnation. In my personal philosophy, I tend to hold many theories in my mind, without subscribing fully to any one of them.

I "know that I don't know," and prefer to contemplate and consider different ideas that may even seem contradictory unless you see them as puzzle pieces in a big, multidimensional universe.

From that bigger picture, I tend to think of reincarnation theories as being useful but almost as limited as the usual one-life-per-person scenarios. The idea of reincarnation can be valuable in contemplating the nature and experiences of your life, and at the same time, it is also bound by materialistic limitations of separateness and time, portraying a separate soul as moving forward in time on the same planet, dimension, and level of species.

Reincarnation theories also don't address the spiritual descriptions of this world as being an illusion or dream of the great universal dreamer. In that theoretical view, even the apparently solid histories of people and events in this life dream are made of nothing but illusion. Therefore, any attempts to determine exactly how this illusion of life is structured from within the illusion are inherently incomplete at best.

A Jewish story about reincarnation

Once, on Rosh Hashanah night, the soul of a dead man came to Reb Yekhiel. The apparition appeared exactly as the man had been on earth, and Reb Yekhiel immediately recognized him as the soul of the cantor who used to chant so beautifully from the Torah scroll during the Sabbath services in Reb Yekhiel's town. "What are you doing here on this most holy of nights?" the rabbi asked the dead man.

"Surely the holy rabbi already knows," the soul replied. "On Rosh Hashanah, God himself opens the Book of Life, and judges the whole world. All of the deeds of everyone on earth are clearly written in that Book, in every tiny detail. God looks at our sins and our good deeds and weighs them both in the balance. Who shall live and who shall die? Who shall be born — and to which family? During this night, souls are also judged to be reincarnated once again. I am just such a soul, about to be reborn."

"So tell me," the rabbi asked, "why are you being sent down into the physical world again?"

"It is written in the Zohar that when God desires to take back a person's spirit, then all the days that he has lived in this world pass in review before him," the soul replied, "and this is exactly what happened to me. Just before my death, I recited the confessional, as every Jew is supposed to do, and I thought over everything I had done. Then my entire life passed before me — and I saw that in every instance, I had acted in exactly the right way. My whole life had been totally kosher and totally good. When I realized this, a great feeling of egotistical pride came over me. As luck would have it, right in the middle of this feeling, I died, with no time to repent of that sinful pride.

"When I arrived at the Heavenly Court, that sin of pride was still clinging to me like a soiled coat. And because of that sin, the Heavenly Court decreed that I must return to earth once more, in order to atone for my pride." With that, the apparition vanished.

A guided tour through an experience of death

Spirituality in Action

Try this contemplation, but don't really die while reading it!

You're sitting, reading a wonderful book about spirituality, when suddenly, unexpectedly, you feel a pain in your chest and fall to the ground. At first, you have a sense of shock, but then a warm comforting feeling comes over you. You feel light and buoyant, as you rise up softly from the ground without making any effort to move your muscles.

This sensation feels somewhat familiar, yet you're experiencing some confusion about what exactly is happening. Floating above your physical body, you realize that you have stepped out of that body as you may have disrobed after a long night of dancing. The body that you thought was "you" is now lying on the ground, without you.

The most amazing part of this experience is not the realization that you're not the body, but realizing that you weren't aware of this fact throughout your life. You — the you that you are right now — know this as the most obvious truth. You aren't the body, and you never were. You have known this before. How did you forget again and again? You almost want to laugh at yourself for being so silly. You're now able to understand so much more about life than you had ever imagined.

You feel as though you've awakened from a dream that was filled with delusions and misunderstandings. "How could I have forgotten again?" you cry — not out loud but with your entire being. You no longer have the use of your physical body's organs of expression or perception, yet you're still able to perceive and express.

You don't know whether to laugh or cry. You look down at your body and see it lying there, unconscious. You have a tenderness toward it — a recognition of the heart, a reminiscent interest that one would have upon seeing an old childhood house or a favorite toy of the past that you've outgrown.

Your soul begins to rise higher and higher, passing easily through floors and ceilings of so-called density. The atoms of these physical obstacles are filled with space through which your subtle body flows like airy liquid flowing around rocks in a babbling brook. You move higher and higher into the sky, through the atmosphere, and into the black of space. You understand that this blackness is the same dark space of consciousness that has always existed within your being.

You're able to see so much light and energy scintillating through this so-called blackness. As you move into this mass of light, you feel the particles of your being pulled apart as they expand to fill the entire space. This happens so quickly and smoothly that you would never have imagined how naturally you could fill the entire universe.

For the first time, you truly understand spiritual teachings that you'd heard during your time on earth: "I and my Father are one." "Thou art That." "I am Brahman (the universal absolute)." "The Kingdom of God lies within you."

Your knowledge expands to fit into the universal knowledge, just as a hand fits into the perfect glove. Your limited powers expand back into their universal powers. Your limited ability to do or not do some things expands into perfect omnipotence. Your limited knowledge becomes omniscient universal awareness. The time and space you had lived in is now revealed to be merely a construct of the mind, as you become all-pervasive and eternal.

Famous last words

Here are some inspiring words spoken during the last moments of life by insightful folks:

* "The hour I have long wished for is now come."

    —Teresa of Avila

* "I have been dying for twenty years, now I am going to live."

    —James D. Burns

* "Let us cross the river and rest in the shade."

    —Stonewall Jackson

* "If this is death, it is easier than life."

    —Robert Louis Stevenson

* "I go from a corruptible to an incorruptible crown, where no disturbance can take place."

    —Charles I of England (last words on the scaffold)

* "Dying is a wild night and a new road."

    —Emily Dickinson

* "This is the last of earth! I am content."

    —John Quincy Adams

* "I shall hear in heaven."

    —Ludwig van Beethoven (who was deaf)

* "I am going to that country which I have all my life wished to see."
    —William Blake

* "If I had the strength to hold a pen, I would write down how easy and pleasant it is to die."

    —William Hunter

* "It is very beautiful over there."

    —Thomas Edison

Without ears, you hear divine music — the music of the spheres — being played inside of you. Your will is merged and enfolded into the Universal Will, just as a drop of maple syrup merges into a full glass of water. One drop fills the entire glass. You are free! You fly unencumbered, moving through the space of universal consciousness without moving at all, because you already fill the entirety of creation. This experience is what the Indian scriptures refer to as *Sat-chit-ananda*: perfect existence (*sat*), consciousness (*chit*), and bliss (*ananda*). Sat also means truth — truth and existence. You now know that ultimate truth flows, and forever has and will flow through all existence. Existence itself is truth.

You have become the great power and truth of this universe. All is well. All is as it should be right now — and right now is all there is. There is nothing to ask for, nothing to do. There is only the awareness of *I am*. Instead of the pulsing of blood running through your veins, there is a throb of "I am, I am, I am," pulsating through your entire universal being. Take a moment and rest in this infinite space.

Now, remember that you are still here in this physical world, reading this book and quite alive in your body.

Look at your life and your priorities with this heightened understanding. Infuse your life with the existence, consciousness, and bliss that you were imagining just moments ago. Bring the light of this higher awareness into the situations you face. Bring detachment and reality back into the circumstances of your life. Bring your free spirit back with you. Know that you can soar through these high spaces even within your own body.

Never forget: That higher experience is you. Thou art *That* — no matter what! Thou art That even if you get into an argument with someone or make a mistake and then feel guilty. Thou art That even if you have bad habits and bad manners or good habits and good manners. Those are just mental images projected onto the movie screen of this world. The truest part of you can sit back and watch, enjoying the show — laughing with yourself, crying with yourself, but always knowing that when the show is over you get to come home.

Chapter 5

Finding Your Spiritual Path

Topics in this Chapter:

*   Exploring your spiritual options
*   Being guided from within
*   Steering clear of traps
*   Opening to wisdom and grace

Today more than ever, people are searching for meaning in their lives. Yet, many who search find a confusing array of spiritual teachings and traditions and end up wandering through their entire lives without ever breaking through into the great realms of spiritual awareness. That's like going to a store and forgetting to buy the one thing you needed most. (Don't you hate when that happens?)

Today's world offers many people an impressive freedom to create and follow their dreams, spiritual and otherwise. For example, even kids who grow up in terrible financial situations in today's world still have opportunities to become incredibly successful in any and every possible field — if they have the right ambition, vision, perseverance, karma, luck, and grace. "Where there's a will, there's a way" rings truer today than ever in terms of individual possibilities, including spiritual growth.

Yet so many questions arise as you look for the right spiritual road to travel. How can you find the right path? From where can you draw the inspiration and information necessary to transform and uplift your life?

What teachings can guide you to uplift your spiritual perception?

How do you keep from being snookered by "spiritual" frauds?

Who can you trust?

With whom should you travel?

Should you practice alone or in a group?

Should you read ancient texts or modern bestsellers?

How much does it cost to be spiritual?

This chapter gives you tips, tools, and guidance for seeking and finding the wonderful and vibrant spiritual path that you deserve.

You're here for a reason

According to spiritual sages, you didn't just arrive here just by accident or as a fluke. Rather, you are here because it is in the circumstances of your life that you are able to experience what you need in order to learn the life lessons you are meant to learn.

The universal intelligence has arranged all the circumstances of your life, including the time and place in which you have been born. You are living on this planet at this time because you're meant to be here.

Part of your spiritual calling is to learn how to not only survive but to spiritually *thrive* in the 2midst of all the pretense and illusions of modern day life. In a world filled with falsehood, your calling is to grow into greater truth, just as a beautiful lotus flower grows and even draws nourishment from the muddy waters in which it grows.

Searching for Truth in a World of Pretense

Spiritual Wisdom

I do not believe in the collective wisdom of individual ignorance.

> —Thomas Carlyle

Today's world is an amazing time and place for seeking, discovering, and nourishing your spirituality. As they say, it's the best of times and the worst of times. Most people have the freedom to explore and seek higher spiritual truth in ways that were unavailable in previous times and cultures. Yet, at the same time, authentic spiritual teachings and practices can be hard to find amidst the busyness and noise of modern life.

Never before has this world seen anything like the massive scale of illusory commercialization and pretense that floods today's modern cultures. In recent years, the media have done their best to turn audiences into obsessive-compulsive gossipers, as they shamelessly pound out each salacious detail of celebrities' personal lives for hours, days, weeks, months, and even years — for what? Bigger ratings and more revenue.

Advertising and commercialism pervade every corner of today's urban landscape, with little care for the sanctity of people's right to a peaceful environment. Millions of dollars are spent to research how to trigger and draw your subconscious attention to all kinds of products you don't even need, without regard for the side effects of these mental manipulations. If advertisers could figure out how to beam their commercials directly into your head, you can be sure that many would jump at the chance.

Your calling is to find truth and spirituality in the midst of all this worldly pretense. However, to complicate things further, spirituality today also tends to be compromised by the same motives of greed, ignorance, and sensuality that pervade other areas of society.

 **Consider**

In a way, today's world of pretense can actually benefit a spiritual seeker who is proceeding with open eyes. The glaring chaos of commercialized illusions can drive ripe spiritual seekers to become even more vigilant about absorbing themselves, mind, heart, and soul, into the peaceful presence of the divine. The key is to take full advantage of the spiritual benefits of this time (see Chapter 2) while steering clear of potholes along the way.

Consider

Tips for reading divine texts

Some religious followers insist that texts such as the Bible, Koran, Torah, or Bhagavad Gita are the actual, unblemished Word of God. Others see these scriptures as records put together by spiritually inspired but potentially fallible and culture-based human beings. Many religious records have been translated, edited, and re-translated by other perhaps not-as-divinely-inspired, fallible human beings through the centuries. To get the most when reading spiritual scriptures, you may want to:

- Give extra focus to the parts of a text that are supposed to be actual spoken or written expressions of the divine sage(s) who sparked that particular religion or philosophy. For example, if you're reading the New Testament, focus on the words of Jesus.

- Keep your attention on the parts of scriptures that make sense and resonate with your current interests and understanding. Putting other sections aside doesn't mean you are dismissing them forever, but that you are paying attention first to what connects with your soul's journey. Focus on the spiritual teachings you grasp, and they will take your hand and guide you from where you are now into greater awareness and understanding.

Being a good editor

It is the mark of an educated mind to be able to entertain a thought without accepting it.

—Aristotle

One secret to benefiting from spiritual teachings is this: Be a good editor! Drink the nectar and leave the dishwater. Eat the peanuts and throw away the shells. Use the good film footage and cut out the shaky shots. Choose and digest what makes sense and rings true and leave the discards respectfully in a bin for possible future consideration.

You have to be a good editor when it comes to reading and hearing anything in life, but especially with spiritual teachings. Be open-minded, but not naïve. The greatest teachings often come along with other ideas that appear to be less than great. However, if you completely avoid these teachings because you disagree with certain elements, then you may miss out on some of the greatest spiritual guidance for your spiritual journey.

Be careful about reading health books. You may die of a misprint.

—Mark Twain

Following your intuition

Your intuition is a great friend. It's like having a wise guide, mother, father, brother, sister, and comrade, all inside of you. Intuition helps you to find and recognize what you want in life..

Remember the game you played as a child, where you look for something that has been hidden? The other children who know where the item is will say, "You're getting colder," or "You're getting warmer," or if you're lucky, "You're getting *really* warm," or "You're super-hot!" Following your intuition is similar to playing this hot or cold game, except the communications are not spoken aloud, but whispered from the universal mind into your personal mind.

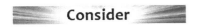 Consider

Even if the communication lines between your intuition and personal awareness have become blocked or ignored, you can still train yourself to open up more to intuitive guidance.

Steps you can take to improve your intuition include:

- Asking for guidance and being open to receiving it

- Trusting that the inner wisdom already guides you, whether you've been aware of it or not

- Acting in accordance with whatever intuitions come, as long as they don't seem to be wrong or harmful in any way

- Staying peaceful when some intuitions don't always appear to pan out as true, with an understanding that the spiritual journey is a learning process

- Being aware that you can't always know whether the results of an action are beneficial or harmful without seeing all its future repercussions and underlying effects

- Remembering to have gratitude and appreciation when your intuitive guidance is successful

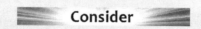 **Consider**

Sensing your heart's recognition

The best way to find your spiritual path is to be guided by your heart's recognition. If you don't know what this recognition feels like, then you may not have found the right path yet. It is a sense that you are in the right place for growing in a positive way.

In the late 1970s, while attending the University of Michigan, I discovered my main spiritual path during a college field trip to a local ashram. I had almost skipped the trip because I wasn't too interested in religions after my nonreligious upbringing. I also thought the place might be some kind of strange cult because it was headed by a swami from India.

Although the ashram *was* somewhat exotic in appearance — with Sanskrit chanting, swirls of incense, and pictures of Indian saints along the walls — it surprisingly didn't feel strange at all. In fact, the strangest thing about the experience was that it didn't feel strange! Through this sense of comfort and recognition, my heart was gently pointing toward this path, which then rocked my world, awakened my spirit, and transformed my life. This gentle sense of familiarity is an example of what it can feel like to be guided toward a spiritual path, teaching, or teacher.

Spirituality Is Not One Path Fits All

The truth is that spirituality is not "one size fits all." Many roads lead to one great destination, and your assignment is to find the right pathways for you. Start by looking at your tendencies and what naturally appeals to you.

Have a delicious spiritual life

If this world didn't have such a variety of religious and spiritual expressions, it would be like a really boring food court with just one restaurant. Including more cultural foods helps to make a better food court or restaurant row.

In the same way, experiencing a variety of spiritual flavors can help you to have a more delicious and colorful spiritual life.

Here are several pathways that can lead to spiritual growth:

- **Self-control:** Some seekers dissolve their small self through disciplined practices that diminish their lower, unspiritual thoughts and tendencies, such as denying themselves sense pleasures. (Note: This is not the most fun way to go, although it can be very effective.) When the clouds of ego and self-identification disappear, a seeker can see the divine light that has always been shining behind those clouds, as the *Bhagavad Gita* says, "brighter than a thousand suns."

- **Devotion:** Some seekers prefer to jump into the deep and intoxicating waters of devotion, worshipping whatever form or forms they consider to be an expression of God. This approach is a special gourmet variety of spiritual experience that is not familiar to most.

To get a sense of how powerful devotion is, just think about how strong the effects of regular, ordinary, human love can be. People have sold their lives, careers, ambitions, and even souls for just a taste of ordinary love or lust. They give it all to attain oneness with the object of their desire, and are sometimes shocked to find that their loved one is not so different from other people, and that he "poops" just like everyone else. But God never "poops" - or cheats on you with your best friend, for that matter. God belongs equally and fully to everyone, and God is always great. The nectar of devotion connects you to this divine greatness in amazing, tender, and inexpressible ways.

- **Study and practice:** Some seekers find spirituality by studying teachings and performing spiritual practices of whatever tradition they're following. If done right, these efforts help you to experience the divine spiritual treasure of life.

Consider

You can and should combine elements of different approaches to create your own vibrant spiritual journey. Today's spiritual environment offers a wide variety of avenues and styles that seekers can choose to highlight, based on their personal preferences and inner guidance. Some seekers prefer traditional religions, while others want to go out of the box. Some like to worship, others to philosophize, and still others like to focus on quietly practicing or serving. Some want spirituality to be a family activity, others join large communities, and still others prefer the solitude of resting in a peaceful inner communion with spirit.

Be Careful

Please remember that choosing what's right for you doesn't mean that what's right for you must be right for everyone else.

Finding the right spiritual diet for you

Finding the right path of spirituality is like finding the right food diet. Different people stay healthy on different kinds of nutrition sources. Some benefit from following low-carb diets or raw food diets. Some take a lot of vitamins and energy drinks, while others just eat whatever comes and trust in their digestive system to sort it all out. Some prepare foods according to ancient principles, such as Chinese medicine or ayurvedic cooking, which outline the medicinal benefits of different ingredients and spices for different body types.

Just as you have many options in choosing the right food diet, you also have many options in choosing the right spiritual diet for you. Some foods make you feel healthy, while others make you feel sick. In the same way, some thoughts, practices, and communities can make you feel emotionally or spiritually healthy or sick. In both health and spirituality-related cases, you have to observe your body, mind, heart, and soul and listen to your own inner guidance.

As with chemically processed junk foods, you may also find a lot of toxins in certain types of spiritual teachings. These spiritual fads may be beneficial for some, or they may be harmful to everyone. The best way to protect yourself from both food and spirituality-borne disease is to use your intelligence and intuition to research and assess what is helpful or harmful.

If eating a big greasy meal gives you indigestion, then you may find it best to avoid eating more greasy meals. If certain spiritual approaches give you spiritual indigestion, making you feel less empowered, peaceful, and happy, or more anxious, arrogant, and depressed, then consider that these spiritual practices may not be the right ones for you.

Young people need spirituality too!

Young children are inherently and naturally spiritual. They're still fresh from the "mill" where spirit becomes human beings, and the world of spirit continues to echo through their experiences and expressions. Yet, along with having a natural sense of spirituality, children today also have a unique combination of spiritual challenges.

Many families today live without the kind of religious focus that families of old used to share. Children today are pulled to focus on outer events of life. Some may focus on playing video games or being shuttled about from one after-school activity to another. Almost universally, today's children are showered with negative and violent words and images from music, television, movies, and other media. This is not the Brady Bunch culture that I grew up in, to be sure.

In most cases, schools are forbidden by law from giving spiritual education, due in part to a confusion in discerning between spirituality and religion. Many kids today don't discuss religion, spirituality, or God with their teachers and peers in school, and in many cases, they're receiving little or no spiritual guidance at home or anywhere else.

Indeed, today's world can be a uniquely challenging time and place for young people to discover and nourish their spirituality. Still, with so many spiritual resources available through the internet, books, and courses, parents and others who take care of children have the opportunity to rise to the occasion and give more spiritual nourishment to yourselves and your children.

Be Careful

Finding the right food or spiritual diet doesn't mean just looking for what is comfortable. You have to also use your intelligence and intuition when deciding what is helpful or harmful. For example, exercising and eating well are not always comfortable in the moment, but can bring long-term health and comfort. In the same way, meditating, studying, and keeping your awareness focused on higher consciousness thoughts and actions may not always be as fun as letting lose and "goin' down with the devil." Nevertheless, even if spiritual efforts are not always pleasant or exciting in the moment, they can bring wonderful, exciting, and even blissful benefits to your life.

Exploring today's spiritual buffet

If you're not yet settled into the perfect spiritual path for you — and even if you are — you may want to sample some of the many expressions of spirituality that are available to taste from cultures throughout time and around the world. I mean, even if you like pizza so much that you want to eat it for every meal, you may still find value in eating other kinds of food every now and then — even if only to remind you of how much you love pizza.

Just think, every week, free spiritual gatherings take place all around the world, with magical music, teachings, and all kinds of other spiritual entertainment from bell ringing sonatas to children's' plays.

Every weekend, many people skip their chance to sleep in so they can attend services in their favorite house of worship.

Every week, hundreds of thousands of pastors, ministers, rabbis, monks, and priests prepare and give inspiring talks.

Across the globe, choirs meet to join their voices in divine song, communities gather to help those in need, priests lead elaborate ceremonies, and great numbers of devoted staff and volunteers offer their time and energy to create and maintain each of these mini-Broadway shows known as spiritual and religious services.

Just imagine waking up on Sunday mornings and deciding which spiritual meal to order, which flavor of worship to attend that day. This is what I did for several years — sampling today's spiritual buffet by going to a different religious service nearly every Sunday.

Sometimes I would also attend spiritual services and gatherings on other days and times, but for the most part, these explorations were a Sunday morning event for me. I thought this practice would be good for my spiritual journey and also support my wish to be as inclusive as possible in my writings and other works.

Most of the Sunday services I attended were Christian-based, which seems fair, because I've already experienced quite a bit of eastern religious practice. The services I attended include Catholic, Presbyterian, Hindu, Buddhist, Quaker, Methodist, Mormon, Theosophist, Rosicrucian, Church of Religious Science, Christian Science, Baptist, Evangelical, Church of Christ, non-denominational, Unity, Unitarian, New Age, gay New Age, and even a place called "Dance Church."

Some of the pastors or ministers I met assumed that I was looking for "a place to land" or was wanting to find a church to belong to. But actually, I'd already landed into a personal relationship with the Divine and was enjoying celebrating that connection in diverse ways through all these different venues.

I do want to add a cautionary note about indulging in this spiritual buffet. Even if you are fortunate enough to enjoy great "spiritual meals" at these various "spiritual cafés," still there is something to be said for delving deeply into one good path at some point in your journey.

If you only stay on the surface of many different paths, then you may miss some of the important spiritual growth that comes from digging into one path with full focus and consistency. If you dig lots of shallow holes in the ground, you won't ever strike water; but digging one deep hole with steady perseverance allows you to create a well that refreshes yourself and others.

Growing as a group

Participating in spiritual and religious groups and gatherings, can bring many benefits to your spiritual journey, including:

- Whenever you have a large group of people singing, worshipping, and growing together, the whole is often more powerful than the sum of its parts, helping to uplift each participant's spirit.

- When you follow a particular religion, you're usually given a ready-made template worldview of spiritual teachings, conventions, traditions, beliefs, folklore, and wisdom, which is usually based, at least in essential substance, on greater truths.

- In a spiritual group setting, you have a chance to learn and grow from interactions and discussions with people who share a similar worldview and are familiar with the same spiritual figures, philosophies, and terminology.

Even if their religious information or group beliefs aren't completely accurate, spiritual groups still give you a chance to delve deeply into one heritage and approach with the support of a community of spiritual seekers and teachers.

 **Consider**

Even if you find an organized religion or group that resonates with your soul's journey, you still have to keep your wits about you and remember that your spiritual journey ultimately takes place inside yourself.

Intuition and intelligence continue to be essential comrades, no matter where your journey takes you. If you're looking to grow with a spiritual community:

- Do your best to find a group of people whose practices and understandings are in keeping with your views.

- Learn from others in your group without blindly accepting everything they believe or say.

Some groups are good; some aren't as good. Some act with altruistic motives, while others are trying to fool people. Some are welcoming your great soul, some are welcoming your great wallet, and some are welcoming both together. Most spiritual groups are a combination, just as with pretty much everything else that involves human beings.

The best way to tell the true nature of a group is to keep your eyes open and look to see how the spiritual teachers of the path behave — not only when they're speaking publicly, but in less formal situations. You can also look at how the adherents of the path behave, although people have their own tendencies that they bring along wherever they go, in spite of what the teachings of a path may be.

Being aware of possible group pitfalls

Keep these following points in mind if you choose to be involved with a spiritual community:

- Group-think exists even in spiritual groups — in fact, *especially* in spiritual groups. When people work together under an umbrella of spiritual commonality, they are likely to form certain agreed-upon views of the world and tend to share many of the same words and phrases. Some of these views, words, and phrases may be very useful, however, group beliefs can also become limiting, because God and spirit are beyond any one particular view of life.

- People are still people, even in spiritual groups. If you think that everyone who participates in a spiritual group is a perfect saint, you may be in for a surprise!

Be Careful

While observing the behaviors of people on a path, also remember that your assessments are personal opinions that may not be perfectly correct in all ways. Not all spiritual people are going to fit into the same mold, and strange are the ways of certain genuine spiritual beings!

You can also do some research on the path by searching on the Internet. However, please keep in mind that every spiritual and religious path has dissatisfied customers, some of whom may become very vocal in spreading partial truths mixed with unsubstantiated gossip about whatever religion they've "divorced." Some smaller groups and a very few select spiritual teachers have completely avoided negative publicity, but most larger groups or religions will tend to have detractors, as well as defenders.

Educate yourself and use your intelligence, intellect, and inner guidance to decide whether the reality of a group — which usually exists somewhere between the extremes of public reports — sounds like something that will be helpful for you to experience. Learn from others without blindly accepting everything they believe or say.

If you find that a path or group you've joined is not really working for you, then bid a fond farewell, give thanks for the freedom you have to make changes in your life, and move forward with a positive feeling.

Exploring with friends

One way to expand your journey is to explore different spiritual experiences, places, and events with friends. Consider starting a spirituality group where you get together with a friend or several friends and choose a different place of worship to visit each week or month.

After the service or event, you may want to have tea, lunch, or dinner together and discuss what you've experienced, observed, and learned from that week's service.

Creating your own spiritual community

You can either grow as a group through attending an organized religious or spiritual community, or you can create your own not-so-organized spiritual community.

Spiritual Wisdom

Where two or three are gathered together in my name, there am I in the midst of them.
        —Jesus

You can come together with friends and meditate together, read and discuss spiritual teachings of whatever traditions interest you, sing devotional songs, or perform personal rituals. You can share your triumphs and challenges within a spiritual context of friendship, or share chosen inspirations from your personal journals.

Here's a sample schedule for a spiritual gathering of friends:

- Participants greet one another and begin with a ritual, such as lighting a candle or reciting a short prayer or meditation.

- Either one, some, or the whole group shares in an experience of singing devotional music.

- Each person brings a quote or selection to read, either every week, or on assigned weeks, or as guided from within.

- Have a discussion and sharing of spiritual and personal insights and experiences you've had during the week or previously. If the gathering is more informal, other participants can join in and help to interpret and understand some of the underlying blessings or lessons in these experiences. Have some simple rules about not just venting or going on and on, but seeking to give and receive good spiritual energy and wisdom while sharing with one another.

- End with a quiet meditation that will allow each person to absorb the experience and enter the depths of their soul within the group energy.

- You may want to continue the gathering informally with a meal together or some refreshments and a peaceful social time if that is wanted. This post-meeting communion can be good for bonding your spiritual friendships. Just try not to leave the meditative space and jump back into too much loud, worldly chatter!

 **Consider**

When gathering with friends, create a schedule and style that works for you.

Separating the Wheat from the Chaff

The goal of pursuing your spiritual search within a group or tradition is ultimately to find the essence that exists within and beyond all groups and traditions. While the intention of spiritual groups may be to assist you on your quest, in practice, the outer expressions of religious and spiritual paths, teachers, and communities can sometimes become skewed away from this essential goal and pointed instead toward dogma or greed.

How dogma is created

Here's a story that illustrates how certain dogmas can muddy the waters of a spiritual path.

Once there was a spiritual teacher whose lectures mesmerized and inspired the many monks and seekers who would gather every evening at his monastery to receive his teachings.

The monastery had a cat that liked to hop around on people's laps during these spiritual gatherings, disturbing the peaceful focus of the space. The teacher told one of the monks that every evening at 6 p.m., the cat should be tied with a rope to a post outside the monastery and released when the gathering ended.

This schedule went on for many years, until the teacher passed on, leaving his foremost disciple to give the lectures, as was the practice in his tradition. More years went by, and eventually the cat also passed away. The monks immediately got another cat for the monastery and continued to tie that cat to the post outside the monastery every evening during the spiritual discourse as part of the daily protocol.

More years and then decades passed. Within 100 years, the doctrine of this path was set down in writing, and one important spiritual practice was that a cat had to be posted outside the lecture hall during all programs. If a monastery didn't have a cat, it would have to get one, because tying a cat to the post was essential to the sanctity of the place. This metaphorical tale shows how dogma, or in this case, catma (sorry), creeps into spiritual teachings, practices, and doctrines.

Sometimes spiritual paths and religions fall into behaviors that are similar to politics. The pure purpose of politics may be to support the quality of life for human beings in this world or in a particular country or state. However, in practice, many politicians bring a club mentality and greediness into their work.

Sometimes politicians in one party will consider attacking a rival party as their most important goal, above improving the greater good of the people whom they were elected to serve. A politician's campaign promises can sometimes be put on a back burner, with other greed-based concerns getting top priority.

In the same way, the purpose of a church, spiritual path, or house of worship is to create an atmosphere for its members to commune with God. Yet, just as with politics, these religions and spiritual paths are headed and run by people, and people can sometimes be thrown off their purest intentions by a few threads of greed, ego, or rivalry.

Even as you love and respect the teachers and members of your spiritual community, the purpose of any group, temple, church, or spiritual teacher should be to give you the resources needed to attain your own great spiritual wealth. A good spiritual group should help you to find your own individual spiritual path of growth and service, and not try to make you dependent or codependent on outer forms.

Don't Forget

When you approach spiritual teachings and paths, keep both your heart *and* your eyes open! The best tools you have for discerning the nourishing spiritual wheat from the useless chaff are your intuition, intelligence, integrity, and your spiritual practices and studies (see Part II).

Be Careful

Bumper-sticker spirituality

It is very easy to jump on today's "spiritual phrase" train, saying things like, "We're all one!" "God is Love!" "Everything is perfect!" "Our path is the way!"

I've been amazed to see many spiritual teachers just repeating the same fluffy phrases, sometimes without much evidence of personal application or understanding. What use is a parrot that has learned some lofty words and can sound very spiritual while repeating them over and over? Does the parrot really make use of the words it speaks?

Being in the company of this kind of bumper-sticker spirituality has the potential to dull your mind, heart, and intuition, and box your journey into the same level of mediocrity of those who espouse these undigested one-liners.

Just as a mother bird chews and predigests the food to feed to her baby birds, so a good spiritual teacher should predigest spiritual teachings with their own experience and contemplation, so they can present these teachings in ways that are easier to grasp, understand, and apply in your own life.

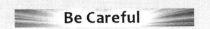 **Be Careful**

Keeping your wits about you

As you encounter different teachings and beliefs along your journey, don't just accept whatever lofty interpretations others have claimed without applying your own intelligence and intuition. For example:

- Just because it's the first time something has been done doesn't mean that it matters or should be done.

- Just because something is ancient doesn't mean that it is true or valuable. One day, today's trash will be ancient.

- Just because someone can perform miracles such as walking on water doesn't mean that they are free from all human faults.

- Just because someone being channeled is on the "other side" doesn't mean that they're not still "a jerk."

All that glitters is not gold

Jesus warned that there would be a time when many teachers would teach falseness in the name of Light. Many of today's paths and teachers are not exactly "false," but may not be quite as great as they appear to be. As the old adage goes, you can't judge a book by its cover, and in spirituality, you can't always judge a person or group by their initial outer appearance or mission statement.

For some, spirituality has become just another business venture. For many, it is a mixture of service and business. With the recent expansion into society of yoga, meditation, and bestselling spiritual books and movies, spirituality has become very lucrative. A whole lot of folks are cashing in on this spirituality boom, so you need to be especially careful before fully entrusting your journey to any particular person or path.

Be Careful

Everything changes, and spiritual teachers and paths are no exception.

Some change by acting differently in front of members than they behave in front of the masses. If you encounter one of these paths, you may end up being the victim of an intentional or unintentional spiritual bait and switch. For example, you may be treated well when you knock on the door, and not so well after you move in. Groups and teachers may also decline over time due to personal issues, poorly guided decisions, the death of a leader, financial successes that breed greed-based decisions, and a lot of other possible triggers. People can mess anything up if you give them enough time and power.

Don't expect things and people to be what they're not, and you won't be disappointed. Keep your focus on the spirit that exists beyond this world of expectations and disappointments.

Consider

Spirituality *cannot* be discerned by noting which groups or people:

- Have more physical beauty
- Own more expensive stuff
- Draw bigger crowds
- Act more confident
- Act more enthusiastic
- Eat a more restrictive diet
- Espouse loftier platitudes
- Wear more spiritual-looking clothes
- Get more press coverage

Spiritual Wisdom

The Sufi poet Jelalud'Din Rumi demonstrates the attitude of a spiritual sage in the following self-description. His words are especially refreshing to read in this modern day, when so many spiritual teachers and others sell out their higher principles for greater fame or fortune.

Rumi says: "They say I tell the truth. Then they ask me to do a puppet show of myself in the bazaar. I'm not something to sell. I have already been bought!" (by the Divine)

If we're all one, then act like it

The road to truth is long, and lined the entire way with annoying bastards.

—Alexander Jablokov

Okay, here I get to give my inner curmudgeon a few moments to have its say. I've met a lot of spiritual and religious people during my journey. Some are wonderful, kind, sincere, and intelligent folks, while others make you shake your head in disbelief.

Recently I attended a church service where the pastor spoke for the entire hour about how the church needed to open up to welcoming new guests. It was almost like being in a membership meeting more than a sermon, although she was very passionate, which was somewhat inspiring.

This pastor enthusiastically spoke about how the church — which was almost half-empty and made up mostly of elderly parishioners — had to push its comfort zone and really welcome new guests and members.

During my journey of going to services in a different house of worship every week, I've also been a new guest pretty much every week. Most of the time, church members and leaders are very friendly, and this pastor certainly seemed like she would be extra friendly, based on her chipper sermon.

When the line forms to greet the minister or pastor after a church service, I usually join in, say hello, and sometimes mention my practice of visiting different churches, or that I'm an author of spiritual books.

In this particular church, after hearing the pastor's enthusiastic sermon about welcoming new guests, I waited at the end of the line for the meet and greet. Right before me was another woman, who turned out to be an old friend of the pastor.

As I stood there, the two women went on and on about how the friend was now a missionary and all that she'd been doing, catching up and reminiscing about old times. I felt a bit like I was intruding in their private conversation, and really had only wanted to say hello to the pastor, praise her enthusiasm, and begin a fairly long drive home.

At one point, I joined in the conversation by offering a friendly comment related to what the two women were discussing and was surprised by the unexpected response. Both women — pastor and missionary — turned and gave me totally dirty looks for interrupting them and then, without saying a word, turned back and continued their conversation. I soon gave up and left. So much for this pastor's enthusiastic sermon about welcoming new people to their church!

Of course, this situation can be chalked up to a single moment of inattention and is only a small but intriguing example of how spiritual people sometimes don't live up to the ideals they espouse.

Don't Forget

It is very easy to talk the talk, and not always so easy to walk the walk.

The spiritual correctness police

In certain New Age circles, you find a whole new breed of word and thought police, who are always ready to judge and call you out for saying anything that doesn't fit the very specific formatting of their belief system. Some humility police will bust you for using the pronoun "I" too many times in your writing or speech, believing that use of this pronoun shows that you have a big ego. There *are* some sages like Papa Ramdas from India, who became so absorbed in universal consciousness that he only referred to himself in the third person. Regardless, personal pronouns remain a convenient and useful part of sentence structure for the purpose of interpersonal communication.

Today's law-of-attraction focus has brought out a whole new breed of positivity police. Anytime you describe anything in less than glowing, positive terms, these positive thought police are ready to pounce and cut you off, preferring, or demanding, that you say what you wish were true rather than what you may have actually experienced. Of course, positive thinking is a great tool for spiritual growth; however, there are times when positive thinkers can become positive stinkers.

Okay, now that I've shared this bit of curmudgeonly advice, I also want to remind you that there are indeed very good paths and avenues for you to travel and experience during your journey. In fact, you can find good growth on almost any path. What matters most is your own intuition, intelligence, and integrity.

Benefiting from Teachers, Thinkers, Saints, and Sages

Spiritual Wisdom

Arise, awake! Approach the great beings and know the Truth!

—Katha Upanishads

Saints and sages are like waterfalls of divine grace and portholes to heaven right in this world. Their inspiring wisdom is like a fishhook that takes you — not to be fried up as a meal — but to be lifted out from what Indian sages call the *ocean of samsara,* the ocean of illusion where you suffer all the pains associated with forgetting your true nature.

This fishhook that pulls you out of the dark waters of illusion and into the light of higher spiritual awareness is a hook that you *want* to clamp onto tightly.

In the company of great spiritual teachers and masters, your own wise, great being can be elicited and awakened, even without your having to do a lot of practices or study all kinds of books. Just be open to resonating with their elevated energy and level of vibration.

Whether you're with a great master in person, or reading their writings, listening to their voice, or thinking about them, their elevated energy and level of spiritual vibration resonates with your own palette of being, calling forth elevated states of awareness that you may have never imagined you would be able to experience — but which have always existed, though perhaps latent, inside of you.

One analogy used for this spiritual alchemy in the company of great ones is of the resonance between one violin and another. If the master violin sings a note, the strings of a second student violin near it will also begin to vibrate at the same note. The second violin's tone won't be as strong or clear as the master violin, but it may be the first time that violin ever experienced that particular note.

In the same way, the presence of a great spiritual being can inspire and invoke in you levels of spiritual insight, awareness, and sensation that you may not have ever imagined. Then it is up to you to keep that note alive if and when the master violin stops playing it outwardly in your presence.

The purpose of a spiritual teacher or guru is to teach you how to be with the Divine, how to relate to the Divine, and how to receive, learn, and grow from your connection with the Divine. From a personal relationship with a spiritual teacher or guru, you should also learn how to relate to the universe or God.

For example, through challenging interactions with your guru, you may discover how to receive criticism in a positive way, or how to continue loving even when that love doesn't seem to be returned, or how to receive an avalanche of love and blessings at another time without becoming greedy or egotistical. You may learn how to keep your trust alive and your heart open without fear of being hurt even when your feelings could be hurt.

Respecting the attainment of a spiritual teacher, pastor, rabbi, monk, or guru doesn't mean that you have to believe they don't have any faults. Rather, you see the sun of divine wisdom, love, and grace shining brightly behind, in spite of, and perhaps even *through,* their apparent faults.

Buddha describes the signs of a sage

In this excerpt from the Dhammapada, Buddha shares some of the qualities of a spiritual master. Even if you don't consider yourself to be a saint or sage (yet!), you can still imagine how it would feel to experience these qualities.

The master looks deeply into things and sees their nature. He discriminates and reaches the end of the way. He moves with love among the unloving, with peace and detachment among the hungry and querulous. He wants nothing from this world and nothing from the next. He is free. He has moved beyond time. He is calm. In him the seed of renewing life has been consumed. He has conquered all the inner worlds. With dispassionate eye he sees everywhere the falling and the uprising. The way he has taken is hidden from men, even from spirits and gods, by virtue of his purity. In him there is no yesterday, no tomorrow, no today. He has come to the end of the way, over the river of his many lives, his many deaths. All that he had to do, he has done. And now he is One.

Living with a saint is more grueling than being one.

—Robert C. Neville

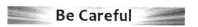
Be Careful

If some spiritual teacher comes along and tells you that they know everything and can tell you without any doubt exactly why you're here, what you're supposed to do, where you've been in previous lifetimes, and exactly where you're going after you leave this world, then this so-called teacher is most likely either a fool or a scam artist trying to fool you. Such overcertainty may be a sign that this person doesn't even know the simplest truth that everything is much bigger and more complex than any human being can know in their mind and express with words.

Good spiritual teachers can be the key to unlocking new levels of your journey. You may learn from personally available teachers, from distant teachers with large groups of followers, or from teachers who have already left this world, leaving behind their teachings for future generations.

In my case, the guru or teacher found me. It happened during a college course I took with one of the guru's followers. This professor brought our class on a field trip to the local ashram in Ann Arbor, Michigan and later drove me to New York to meet the guru.

I encountered my guru just as I was ready to dive deeply into spiritual life, although if you'd told me this at the time, I would have probably balked at the idea. I was right in the middle of my university studies of neuroscience and film-video, and had been delving into all kinds of meditative-style practices on my own, with more of a psychological than spiritual focus. Unknowingly, I had become ripe inside for letting go of worldly interests and jumping into the ocean of deep spiritual immersion.

I could have looked for a very long time and never found a guru who was such an amazing match for my eclectic mixture of interests, qualities, contemplations, and levels of consciousness. Muktananda was a brilliant philosopher with a primo sense of humor, an intelligent grasp of both science and spirituality, and the power to deliver spiritual goods in a way that inspired even world-absorbed students to be naturally drawn into living a disciplined spiritual life.

During my subsequent monastic years, I watched as many devotees would leave their busy lives in every kind of profession you could possibly imagine to spend a day, week, month, or year coming together in our ashram with other incognito spiritual sages to focus deeply on spiritual practices and teachings.

Don't Forget

The path that was right for me is not necessarily the one that is right for you. What's most important is for you to find whatever teachers and teachings are right for you.

As you proceed on your spiritual path and learn from the many good sources available to you, remember that the goal of learning from teachers, thinkers, saints, and sages, and the teachings they have brought forth, is for you to become a fountain of grace and wisdom unto yourself.

Don't Forget

Also remember that ultimately, wherever you are is your spiritual path.

Spiritual Wisdom

People want to run away from where they are to go find their Jerusalem — as if elsewhere they will find perfection. Wherever you are, whatever you are doing there, make that a Jerusalem.

—Lubavitcher Rebbe Menachem Mendel Schneerson

Part Two:

Spiritual Practice

Makes Perfect

Chapter 6

If You're Already Spiritual, Why Practice?

In This Chapter

* Understanding the purpose of spiritual practices
* Choosing practices that appeal to your individual nature
* Uplifting body, mind, and spirit

Spiritual Wisdom

How do you get to Carnegie Hall? Practice! Practice! Practice!

—Anonymous

How do you get to spiritual fulfillment and enlightenment? Practice, practice, practice. Make effort, effort, and effort and receive grace, grace and grace. One spiritual analogy describes the spiritual journey as being like a bird with two wings. One wing is your self-effort, and the other is divine grace. Your sincere efforts on the spiritual path draw grace to you, and that grace makes it easier for you to continue and enhance your efforts.

Growing Through Spiritual Practices

Does butter exist in the milk? Yes, but only with churning does the butter take on its delicious solid form. In the same way, the Divine exists in you and your life, but only with the churning of spiritual efforts and practices does the butter of your delicious higher nature shine forth.

Without churning, you may never know that butter exists within the milk; and without spiritual practices, you may never know your own greatness. With churning, the butter comes up on the surface of milk, and with spiritual practices, the awareness of God arises in your mind.

Even if you are fortunate enough to have a deep spiritual experience without doing any specific spiritual practices, it is your effort, intention, and actions that keep the flame of this spiritual experience burning brightly in your mind and heart.

So many practices to choose from!

The train of self-effort combined with divine grace is one that you definitely want to get on, and you can board this train just by starting to direct your time, energy, attention, and efforts toward spiritual practices. Pretty much any action can become a spiritual practice if you approach it with a spiritual attitude. Some traditional practices from various cultures include:

Meditation Prayer   Scriptural study   Yoga

Rituals   Devotional chanting, choir, and singing

Spiritual art   Martial Arts   Calming your breath

Watching your mind   Joyfulness   Ceremonial dance

Charity   Mantra, rosary, and dhikr recitations

Archery   Flower arranging   Gardening

Spiritual Wisdom

Understand this if nothing else: spiritual freedom and oneness with the Tao are not randomly bestowed gifts, but the rewards of conscious self-transformation and self-evolution.

—Hua Hu Ching

Most New Age and new thought philosophies teach that you are already made of spirit, and that therefore, you are already inherently spiritual. Followers of these paths affirm these beliefs with statements such as "Everything works together for my good," or "I am a radiant light of God."

So the question arises — if you are already a radiant light of God, and if everything is already working together for your good, then why not just sit back, relax, and coast along for the ride? Why put time and effort into practicing spirituality if you're already spiritual?

The answer is that it's not so much that practices make you more spiritual as that they give you the ability to perceive, experience, and reveal your innate spirituality. Spiritual practices help you to perceive, honor, and express your bright, wise spirit that may have been hidden under layers of materialistic distractions.

If you're a multibillionaire but you don't know it, you may find yourself living like a pauper instead of in luxury. Similarly, if you don't know that you're an expression of divine universal spirit, you may think that you're just a world-entrenched person living in spiritual poverty.

Most great skills require not only learning and initial practice, but also ongoing exercise. A great musician practices, a great athlete practices, a great dancer practices, and even a great thief practices. In the same way, you can practice spirituality and become a greater, more spiritual *you.*

Don't Forget

In the spiritual realm, it is not that "practice makes perfect," so much as that spiritual practices *reveal* your perfection. Chapter 3 explains that you are both perfect and imperfect, divine and ordinary. Chapters 4 and 14 show how your spiritual journey is ultimately a path from limited self-identification to elevated awareness.

Spiritual practices help you to move forward on your journey, growing smoothly and steadily, into greater realms of spiritual power.

Spiritual Wisdom

We are what we repeatedly do. Excellence then, is not an act but a habit.

—Aristotle

Consider

While choosing whichever practices work best for you, remember to keep your focus on your greater spiritual goals. Keep your eyes on the prize. What's more important than perfecting every outer practice is for you to approach whatever spiritual practices you do with a good attitude and a clear intention for spiritual growth.

Just as religions often tell their adherents to give a certain percentage of their money as a tithe, so you should give some percentage of your time, energy, and thoughts to spiritual matters for the benefit of yourself and the whole world. Here are some ways that spiritual-based practices help you on your spiritual journey:

- By intentionally doing spiritual practices, you're actively stating to the universe your intention to support your own personal growth. Strong intentions bring strong results.

- Spiritual studies and practices help you make decisions that are in harmony with the greater good.

- If you work in harmony with the universe, your progress will be more fruitful and joyful. When you make efforts to uplift your body, mind, and spirit through the power of spiritual practices, the universe doesn't have to throw unending disasters and challenges into your life to force you to grow.

With a clear intention, it doesn't matter so much which specific techniques you choose to practice, whether big, small, creative, or traditional. Authentic spiritual practices are like different roads that point — with the compass of your clear intentions — toward the same direction of greater spiritual growth.

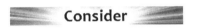 **Consider**

Here are some tips for your spiritual practice:

- If you haven't been living a spiritual life until now, don't feel guilty about what you have or haven't done. Just take steps to move forward in a more positive, spiritual way starting today.

- Don't think you have to be a martyr to do spiritual practices. Although the need for discipline and strength of will power do come into play on the spiritual journey, spiritual growth doesn't have to be "no pain, no gain." In fact, one purpose of spiritual practices is to *remove* your pain!

- Being lazy on the spiritual path is as easy as being lazy in the other areas of your life. You can always make excuses for your lack of spiritual accomplishments, saying things like, "Well, I didn't have this opportunity in life," or "I have too many responsibilities to include spiritual practices," or "The people around me insisted that I live according to their expectations instead of my own guidance," but excuses won't help you to grow.

- Regardless of who you are and where you've been, your spiritual growth is your personal responsibility. You are the one who will receive the benefits that come from your spiritual efforts, and you are the one who will suffer the pain inherent in living a life without the blessings of spiritual awareness, love, faith, and understanding.

- Certain usual ideas about worldly efforts don't quite apply to the spiritual quest. Spiritual efforts aren't just about doing more things or having a full schedule of spiritual events to attend. Sometimes just sitting quietly for a few minutes is the best spiritual effort you can make.

Don't Forget

Spiritual practices can sometimes be uncomfortable, such as when you begin meditating and find it difficult to sit still for long periods of time. Even with such discomforts, you may find spiritual practices to be quite enjoyable. In fact, they can be downright ecstatic!

Spiritual practices are their own reward

Spiritual practices are more than just tools to achieve a certain spiritual state. These practices actually become the reward of practice.

Spiritual practices bring greater happiness and blessings during your times of practice, as well as after you've done the practice. (See Chapters 7, 8, and 9 for specific practices to uplift your body, mind, and spirit.)

Even if you evolve and mature to a place where your spiritual awareness remains steady without doing specific practices, still, you may continue to find great joy and nourishment in continuing to do spiritual practices — not so much with ambitions toward achieving a goal, but as a celebration of spirit.

Just think, even if you didn't need food to survive, you'd probably still like to have a delicious meal now and then, or even very often. In the same way, even if you don't *need* to be doing spiritual practices to maintain your spiritual awareness, you may still like to have a delicious meal of spiritual practices occasionally, or even every day.

Wherever you are on your spiritual path, take refreshing breaks from worldly vibrations by delving into the holy waters of spiritual practices.

Don't Forget

Practices help keep your body, mind, and spirit "machinery" in good working order so that you'll be a better vehicle for experiencing and expressing Divine Spirit.

You can think of your body, mind, and spirit as the support staff for your journey. When one of these areas of your life is out of balance, the momentum of your spiritual journey may be adversely affected. For example:

- **If your body is ill or unwell**, its discomfort can distract your attention away from your spiritual journey. Even though many great spiritual people have shone their bright light in spite of having serious physical problems, for most spiritual seekers, keeping your body healthy and clear helps to keep your mind and heart clear and receptive to spirit, along with giving you the strength and stamina to pursue spiritual efforts.

- **If your mind is disturbed or scattered**, you may not be able to pierce through the outer world into peaceful spirit.

- **If your heart is hardened or closed**, you'll miss out on opportunities to experience the soothing sweetness of divine, universal love.

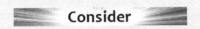

Consider

Getting spiritual is like getting healthy

Saying "I want to become spiritual" is like saying, "I want to become healthy." You need to practice habits that are conducive to achieve your goal of becoming spiritual or healthy. For example, if you want to become healthier, you would want to know which kinds of foods are best to eat, how much water you should drink, and how much exercise will help to keep your body in great shape. In fact, people with different body types can require different diets and lifestyles to maintain their optimum physical health.

Similarly, if you're looking for spiritual health, you have to know which qualities, disciplines, and practices will help you to think right thoughts, make right choices, and take actions that honor and reveal your spiritual nature.

Spiritual practices are essential ingredients for a vibrant and successful spiritual life. Practices give you the fuel to move forward on your journey of personal and spiritual evolution, and also the wisdom to know where to direct that power. Therefore, the goal of spiritual practices is two-fold:

- **Knowing what you want:** Spiritual practices help you gain the wisdom and guidance to make choices that lead in the right direction.

- **Empowering what you want:** Spiritual practices give more energy to direct toward your goals

Both of these aspects must come together for a positive spiritual journey.

Clarifying what you want

You got to be careful if you don't know where you're going, because you might not get there.
            —Yogi Berra

Spiritual practices make all your thoughts and actions more powerful. Therefore, it's important that you clarify and purify your understandings and motives, so your empowered thoughts and actions are focused in the right directions.

Conveniently enough, the best way to gain clarity in knowing what to want is also through spiritual practices for body, mind, and spirit:

- **How practices for your body help you to know what to want:** Keeping your body in good shape will help you know what you want, because the state of your body is reflected in the state of your brain — which is part of that body. And just as the "knee bone's connected to the ankle bone," so the state of your body and brain have a powerful influence on the state of your mind and spirit. (See Chapter 7 for more on practices for your body.)

- **How practices for your mind help you to know what to want:** Clarity of mind is important when you want to discern your best goals. Spiritual practices shine a light on these goals and give your mind the power of focus. This focus helps synchronize all your thoughts and actions, conscious and subconscious, toward your highest spiritual goals. (See Chapter 8 for more on practices for your mind.)

- **How practices for your spirit help you to know what to want:** Spiritual and devotional rituals open your heart to the nectar of devotion and help you stay receptive to receiving divine guidance while moving toward your highest goals. Practices such as prayers and chanting also bring feelings of love, joy, and happiness, which are important nourishment for your spiritual journey. (See Chapter 9 for more on practices for your spirit.)

If you try to access spiritual powers without preparation, you risk making choices that can create more harm than good. For example, certain occult or "black magic" techniques may allow you to access some measure of spiritual power without the proper spiritual preparation. However, powers that are used without the clarity of spiritual discernment can backfire and create harmful setbacks in your journey (see Chapter 16).

How practices keep grace alive

Grace is an unbidden gift of assistance from God or the universe. When grace descends into your life, it is your practice that helps keep that grace vibrant and alive.

For example, one of the most potent ways to experience grace is to be in the presence of holy and enlightened spiritual beings. Just spending some time in the company of high-spirited ones can bring amazing spiritual boosts to your journey, as the vibrations of your spirit resonate with their holy vibrations. One spiritual practice from India is called *darshan,* which basically means to be in the presence of a being who exudes grace.

Still, even if you're fortunate enough to meet great spiritual beings and hear powerful spiritual teachings, all those blessings of grace may end up shimmering up as a fireworks finale, only to expire as they fade back into the night. Your spiritual practices and efforts are what help to keep these spiritual-grace fireworks blazing.

Applying steady effort

Approaching spiritual practices in a disciplined, steady, and ongoing way is like digging a hole to your own freedom. Sometimes you're able to see the light on the other side, while other times you may wonder why you should spend your precious time doing spiritual practices when you'd be just as happy sleeping in or going to a party.

Nevertheless, if you persevere in your efforts, one day you will attain the goal.

A saint is a sinner who never gave up.

—Paramahansa Yogananda

Sometimes the benefits of spiritual practices are felt immediately, and sometimes you don't really experience the benefits until you've practiced for some time. For example:

- You may stand up from a long prayer or meditation session and feel a bit groggy; however in the long run, your mind becomes more awake and clear from the practice of meditation.

- Your body may ache a bit after a yoga session, but in the long run, it becomes more healthy and comfortable.

- Your spirit may feel extra tender and sensitive as you experience feelings of reverence and devotion, but in the long run, you become stronger and sharper than before.

Consider

Practicing the right way

Here are some tips to keep in mind as you learn spiritual practices:

- Be patient and gentle with yourself.

- Don't try to be perfect. You still get benefits even if you can't do a practice fully.

- Your attitude is paramount in any practice.

- Practice cheerfully.

Finding What Practices Are Right for You

As with everything on the spiritual path, there are no hard and fast rules when doing practices. Your unique and individual nature requires a specially customized path to rediscover your own true being. Understanding your soul's patterns and preferences can help you make decisions and take actions that are in harmony with your greatest destiny.

Some seekers find that a very strict schedule of spiritual discipline helps keep them focused and motivated. I certainly loved experiencing this kind of practice during my decade of monastic life in an Indian-based ashram that was filled with spiritual practices.

Early each morning, I would awaken to a cup of piping hot chai tea and an hour and a half session of divine Sanskrit chanting (a great way to begin each day!). And this routine was just the start of our daily schedule. With midmorning, afternoon, and evening times came many more chants, rituals, and meditations, with lots of selfless service in between.

This disciplined environment of spiritual practices gave me a great opportunity to expand my spirituality from being a not-so-disciplined teenager who had been brought up as an atheist to the author of this book. This leap in growth came from a combination of self-effort and grace, blessings and practices.

Taking a disciplined approach to spiritual practices brings benefits and potential drawbacks:

- **Benefit:** A disciplined approach to spiritual practices strengthens your will power and ensures that you keep doing your chosen practices without giving in to laziness and boredom. A strong willpower helps to keep you moving steadily forward on your journey.

- **Drawback:** Some people get so rigid about their spiritual discipline that they lose the ability to receive and act on guidance that may be inspiring changes. As you continue to mature spiritually, you may enter a stage where rigid discipline and imposing your will is no longer best for you. The intelligent force of the universe may want you to be gentler in your practices or to focus on other lessons. In addition, you may start feeling proud or egotistical about your great discipline, which could counteract some of the benefits you receive by doing the practices.

Some seekers prefer to be more spontaneous and guided on what practices to do in each moment. This more spontaneous, "go with the flow" approach also brings certain benefits and potential drawbacks.

- **Benefit:** Approaching your spiritual practices freshly in each moment helps you to intuitively tap into the divine guidance from a state of inner surrender, openness, and enthusiasm. For example, when your body needs a bit more exercise, you can naturally spend more time doing extra physical practices; and when you need to give more focus to contemplation and meditation, you sense that and make the necessary adjustments in your practice schedule.

- **Drawback:** This freelance spirituality mode can also take the edge off your practices. Sometimes you don't feel like doing the very practices you may need the most, similar to how people often crave the very foods that they are allergic to. It may be the same with spontaneously choosing your own spiritual practices. For example, you may not feel like meditating during a particular period, because the deep, peaceful sensations you had previously enjoyed have been interrupted by feelings of jealousy or anger. Yet, this difficult time may be when concentrated efforts to continue your meditation would allow you to break through and become free, once and for all, from those inner tyrants. Or you may not feel like doing physical exercises when your body is out of shape (she says, while pointing at herself), even though those very exercises would help to bring you back into greater physical harmony.

 **Consider**

Follow your inner guidance while still challenging yourself to be disciplined.

Discovering the techniques

So many options are available for learning various spiritual practices, from books to teachers to group meetings, classes, workshops, and retreats. Chapters 7, 8, and 9 suggest some practices to try, and plenty of other resources exist for trying out the practices of different traditions. These days, you can even learn about some spiritual practices by watching videos on the Internet.

My recommendation is to use your intelligence and intuition in exploring the kinds of spiritual practices you like to do. Ask and trust the power of universal grace to answer your sincere call and guide you to whatever and whomever you need to encounter along your path.

Be patient

A martial arts student went to his teacher and said earnestly, "I am devoted to studying your martial system. How long will it take me to master it?"

The teacher's reply was casual, "Ten years."

Impatiently, the student answered, "But I want to master it faster than that. I will work very hard. I will practice everyday, ten or more hours a day if I have to. How long will it take then?"

The teacher thought for a moment, and then said, "Twenty years."

Spiritual practices need to be approached differently from how you approach worldly ambitions. That's because, as explained at the beginning of this chapter, a good part of the spiritual journey comes as grace — blessings that come without necessarily being earned specifically by any efforts you've made. Part of the spiritual path is to lower your personal ego tendencies and increase your receptivity to spirit so a greater beauty, wisdom, and grace can shine forth in your life. Being overly ambitious and impatient on the spiritual path may actually end up blocking the way of grace and keeping you from moving forward.

Don't Forget

You're not alone in this journey of spiritual evolution. Many great benevolent forces exist within and around you, ready to guide your steps and protect you along your way. Through spiritual practices, you learn to be more receptive to the many sources of divine guidance available to you.

After you begin to master specific techniques, you can create your own palette of practices to draw from. You can apply the following tips to whatever practices you encounter:

- **Try the practice to see whether it's one you will like.** Give it a good chance! So many kinds of spiritual practices are available for you to choose from. Select practices that resonate with you, and be open to trying others.

- **Study the practice from those who already know it.** Learn from masters of the practice so that you develop a good foundation of understanding and experience.

- **Allow your own inner intelligence to guide your steps as to when, how, and how much to do a particular practice.**

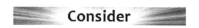

You must listen to your own inner guidance even while learning a practice. For example, if you've had a back injury and your yoga instructor tells your class to move into a backbend pose, you may choose to sit out that particular posture and do your own stretches or take a mid-class meditation break instead of doing that particular exercise.

Be moderate and balanced

Moderation and balance are essential ingredients for a fruitful spiritual life, helping you to enter the flow of spirit. Here are some ways to become more moderate and balanced:

- Keep your mind open to new ways of looking at things, without getting stuck in rigid or dogmatic opinions — and without being dogmatic about not being dogmatic!

- Don't be too hard on yourself — or too easy on yourself!

- Be disciplined yet still open to guidance; loving yet self-contained; successful yet surrendered; and clean yet comfortable.

- Be gentle with yourself and take things one step at a time, as your understanding, awareness, and devotion continue to improve with time and practice.

Letting your practices flow

If you're an automobile driver, think of how hard you had to concentrate when you first learned to steer, brake, and park in different situations. Eventually, after a great deal of practice, you mastered driving and could eventually drive without having to strenuously focus and remember all the rules. Your ability to drive naturally moved from conscious effort to subconscious skill.

A similar process happens when you perfect any skill, such as playing a musical instrument. You may study for many years to learn all the different notes, timings, and techniques. Then, after you've practiced different kinds of compositions and mastered various methods, you eventually arrive at a place where these techniques become tools of your inspired, creative consciousness. At that point, you can begin to create your own personal style of playing and perhaps even compose your own works.

This same shift can happen with your spiritual practices. You make efforts to purify your body, mind, and spirit, and eventually, those efforts become natural and effortless, as you make the practices your own.

You may also experience times when your practices don't seem to be as enjoyable as before. Adjusting your practices to suit your mood and feeling is fine, although persevering with spiritual practices during challenging times can also bring great rewards, including personal breakthroughs and inner strength.

Be patient

A martial arts student went to his teacher and said earnestly, "I am devoted to studying your martial system. How long will it take me to master it?"

The teacher's reply was casual, "Ten years."

Impatiently, the student answered, "But I want to master it faster than that. I will work very hard. I will practice everyday, ten or more hours a day if I have to. How long will it take then?"

The teacher thought for a moment, and then said, "Twenty years."

Spiritual practices need to be approached differently from how you approach worldly ambitions. That's because, as explained at the beginning of this chapter, a good part of the spiritual journey comes as grace — blessings that come without necessarily being earned specifically by any efforts you've made. Part of the spiritual path is to lower your personal ego tendencies and increase your receptivity to spirit so a greater beauty, wisdom, and grace can shine forth in your life. Being overly ambitious and impatient on the spiritual path may actually end up blocking the way of grace and keeping you from moving forward.

You're not alone in this journey of spiritual evolution. Many great benevolent forces exist within and around you, ready to guide your steps and protect you along your way. Through spiritual practices, you learn to be more receptive to the many sources of divine guidance available to you.

After you begin to master specific techniques, you can create your own palette of practices to draw from. You can apply the following tips to whatever practices you encounter:

- **Try the practice to see whether it's one you will like.** Give it a good chance! So many kinds of spiritual practices are available for you to choose from. Select practices that resonate with you, and be open to trying others.

- **Study the practice from those who already know it.** Learn from masters of the practice so that you develop a good foundation of understanding and experience.

- **Allow your own inner intelligence to guide your steps as to when, how, and how much to do a particular practice.**

Consider

You must listen to your own inner guidance even while learning a practice. For example, if you've had a back injury and your yoga instructor tells your class to move into a backbend pose, you may choose to sit out that particular posture and do your own stretches or take a mid-class meditation break instead of doing that particular exercise.

Letting your practices flow

If you're an automobile driver, think of how hard you had to concentrate when you first learned to steer, brake, and park in different situations. Eventually, after a great deal of practice, you mastered driving and could eventually drive without having to strenuously focus and remember all the rules. Your ability to drive naturally moved from conscious effort to subconscious skill.

A similar process happens when you perfect any skill, such as playing a musical instrument. You may study for many years to learn all the different notes, timings, and techniques. Then, after you've practiced different kinds of compositions and mastered various methods, you eventually arrive at a place where these techniques become tools of your inspired, creative consciousness. At that point, you can begin to create your own personal style of playing and perhaps even compose your own works.

Be moderate and balanced

Moderation and balance are essential ingredients for a fruitful spiritual life, helping you to enter the flow of spirit. Here are some ways to become more moderate and balanced:

- Keep your mind open to new ways of looking at things, without getting stuck in rigid or dogmatic opinions — and without being dogmatic about not being dogmatic!

- Don't be too hard on yourself — or too easy on yourself!

- Be disciplined yet still open to guidance; loving yet self-contained; successful yet surrendered; and clean yet comfortable.

- Be gentle with yourself and take things one step at a time, as your understanding, awareness, and devotion continue to improve with time and practice.

This same shift can happen with your spiritual practices. You make efforts to purify your body, mind, and spirit, and eventually, those efforts become natural and effortless, as you make the practices your own.

You may also experience times when your practices don't seem to be as enjoyable as before. Adjusting your practices to suit your mood and feeling is fine, although persevering with spiritual practices during challenging times can also bring great rewards, including personal breakthroughs and inner strength.

Consider

Even if you don't specifically set aside time to do practices, you can still find ways to sprinkle spiritual practices throughout your day. You can take moments, even during the busiest of days, to pause and focus your attention within, remembering who you really are (see Chapter 3). Even one moment of shifting your focus from outer events toward inner spirit can be like taking a spiritual vitamin that nourishes your journey. Do it now — close your eyes for a moment and enter the experience of spirit.

You can also bring spiritual elements into situations that may not be considered inherently spiritual. For example, while you're driving to work, you may want to play a tape with some spiritual music or devotional singing as you relax your body and mind into the meditative focus of driving. Or you can play audio of spiritual lectures and teachings to fill your mind with positive, uplifting words during your morning commute.

 **Be Careful**

If you're playing audio of spiritual teachings and the voice tells you to relax and close your eyes, this instruction is *not* good to follow while driving!

Practicing according to your individual nature

Look at small elements in your life to find out more about your nature and how you can best learn spiritual practices. Do you prefer to follow rigid rules, or are you more intuitive and self-guided?

Do you always rinse and repeat? Do you carefully measure ingredients while cooking? For example, suppose that you're going to mix a drink of some protein powder or healthy greens powder. The label says, "Add 3 level teaspoons to water." Do you do it? Do you carefully measure 3 level teaspoons or just plop in a couple of heaping tablespoons? Either way or someplace in between is fine; however, you can use these simple, daily examples to explore questions such as how you like to follow instructions.

What kinds of guidance and training help you the most? Do you prefer to learn from books? From teachers? In a large group where everyone is doing the practice in the same way? On your own?

As a complex being, you'll probably find that some mixture of different approaches will suit you best.

Doing practices for body, mind, and spirit

Spiritual practices help to purify, strengthen, and elevate your body, mind, and spirit:

- **Practices for your body:** These practices include yoga postures, breathing exercises, martial arts, spiritual dance, and energy balancing — all for the purpose of making your "temple of God" (that is, your body) a worthy vessel to contain and carry the great energy of Holy Spirit. See Chapter 7 for an array of practices for your body.

- **Practices for your mind:** These practices include meditation, contemplation, repetition of mantras, study of spiritual teachings, and affirmations — all of which help to polish the mirror of your mind so it can reflect divine light more clearly and brightly. Check out Chapter 8 for a selection of practices for your mind.

- **Practices for your spirit:** These practices include rituals, prayers, chanting, singing of hymns, and other devotional efforts that inspire love, surrender, and faith. Flip to Chapter 9 to check out some practices that nourish your spirit.

Consider

Spiritual practices do more than just nourish and guide your own journey. Through you, your practices also radiate a spiritual vibration to other people. You become a force of blessing to this world. Doesn't that sound great?

Strengthening your will power

Spiritual disciplines test and strengthen your will power. For example, you may decide to meditate for a half-hour every morning — but then some mornings you want to sleep in or are thinking about quitting meditation early to go have a nice breakfast (I know this one!). These will-power struggles give you a chance to increase your power of self-control.

Consider

Self-control is like a muscle that you strengthen through meeting challenges with your willpower. Gaining more self-control in one area also gives you the strength to free yourself from other harmful habits you may wish to drop in the future.

Suppose that you're considering ending your meditation early to have breakfast. You're sitting quietly, repeating your mantra, watching your breath, watching your thoughts, and quieting your mind, when suddenly you see in your mind's eye an image of eggs . . . with toast and a piping hot cup of tea. Yum. You try to push the image aside, but you can almost smell it, as your mind gets drawn into the imagined, tantalizing odors, flavors, and textures.

At this point, you may think, "Well, I'm not exactly focused on meditation right now anyway. May as well end it early and get on with my day." That part of the game is where your mind makes excuses to convince you to fulfill your immediate desires rather than to complete the spiritual practice at hand.

The important thing to notice is that point where your will meets the pull of the desired object. Your will is saying, "Hey, I made a commitment to myself to meditate for a half-hour every morning, and I'm going to do it." But the eggs are saying, "Come here . . . you are getting hungry." This uncomfortable but magical moment is when you can use your will power and intention to create a new pattern and strengthen your resolve.

In the midst of your inner struggle, there comes a time when you may be just about to give in. In that moment, you can take control, using the force of your will to say "No" to the desire. You can stay focused in your commitment to meditate for the full half-hour. This practice is just like exercising your muscles or your mind. Every time you conquer the pull of your senses, you become more in charge of how you live your life.

Changing your habits

Spiritual practices help you in two important ways:

- Getting rid of bad habits
- Making new, good habits

You have the power to transform your life, and spiritual practices are tools that can help you achieve your highest goals.

 **Consider**

Even if you sometimes give in and lose the battle, whatever efforts you've put into confronting that desire or habit still bring you greater strength the next time. However, giving in to desires and habits without even making efforts to overcome them can weaken your will power.

This same technique can be applied to other will-power situations, such as quitting smoking or maintaining an exercise program. The key is to make a decision and honor it, keeping your word to yourself, which means remaining steady even over the many hills and mountains of temptation that may arise to test your strength.

Practicing being happy

You can develop the habit of being happy just by practicing feeling happy. This habit is not about deception or fooling yourself or others but, instead, tapping into an amazing spiritual law of life. Your inner being and outer expressions reflect one another:

- If you feel happy inside, it shows up in everything you do. (See Chapter 3 to explore how your inner feelings and tendencies express in your surroundings.)

- In the same way that your inner feelings are expressed outwardly, expressing happiness outwardly also affects your inner state of mind, thereby creating greater happiness inside yourself.

During good times, allow yourself to smile; and during difficult times, still do your best to smile. It doesn't even have to be a big, outer smile. Just think, "Smile." Think "Contentment." Sense what it would feel like to have a spontaneous, sincere smile playing on your lips. (Try it now!)

Be Careful

I'm not suggesting that you disregard your grief or sadness or that you walk around with a fake, plastic smile to hide what you feel inside. In fact, certain states of sadness or melancholy can be part of the spiritual growth process. Still, even in such cases, you can go through the grief or sadness while still lifting yourself above the dramas of your mind through spiritual practices. You can experience a sense of happiness that remains steady beneath whatever stormy waves may be pulling you into choppy waters.

Chapter 7

Spiritually Energizing Your Body

Topics in this Chapter:

* Appreciating your body's natural intelligence
* Understanding the benefits of physical practices
* Experiencing the power of your breath

Have you ever really thought about what your body is? Is it you? Is it a part of you? Does it represent you properly? Does your body do what you want it to do, or does it make you do what *it* wants to do? Is your body the boss or a tool of your soul? Is your body a big mass of blood, flesh, bones, fluids, and other components, or is it a temple of God?

This chapter helps you to contemplate these questions and suggests some practices that can help energize your body.

Taking Care of Your Body Temple

Even though your spiritual essence exists beyond your physical body, the body is nevertheless very much a part of spiritual awakening. Your body is the temple within which spirit dwells; it is the tool through which your spirit paints and expresses its glory into this world.

Don't Forget

The spiritual reason to keep your body healthy is to keep your body and mind clear and energized so you have the stamina to focus on higher spiritual matters. A healthy body allows you to sit comfortably for meditation and enables you to enjoy spiritually elevating physical practices such as yoga, dance, and martial arts.

In your body, you experience the three-dimensional world. Yet, while living in the body, you also grow into a spiritual recognition that you are more than the body; you are the soul. While living in the body, you grow into the realization that you are much more than just your body.

Adding spiritual touches to physical activities

Let them praise his name with dancing.
—Psalm 149:3

Physical practices help to calm, focus, and strengthen the energy in your body, bringing its vibration in harmony with your higher nature. Physical practices for your spiritual journey include tai chi and other martial arts, hatha yoga poses, Zen archery, breath exercises, and spiritual dances from nearly every religious culture and traditions.

By maintaining a spiritual focus in your mind and heart, even nonspiritual activities can be spiritualized. You can do everyday activities, such as playing sports, gardening, cooking, taking care of your children, working at your job, or walking the dog, with a spiritual approach.

Consider

You can also infuse spirit into usual physical exercises by adding spiritual touches. For example, you can turn an ordinary walk into what is called a *japa walk* by repeating a mantra as you walk.

Japa is a Sanskrit word for the practice of repeating a mantra — a potent spiritual word or phrase — over and over again. People who practice mantra repetition often synchronize the mantra repetitions with their breath's inhalations and exhalations.

To go on a japa walk, you coordinate your mental mantra repetitions and breath together with your footsteps as you walk with a peaceful, energetic, and steady pace. With a japa walk, your entire body, mind, and spirit are walking together in harmony, infused by the power of the mantra.

Different religious traditions offer different mantras, names of God, or scriptural phrases that can be used for a japa walk. Jewish and Arabic traditions call these sacred phrases *zikhr* or *dhikr*, which translate as "mind protector." Some mantras are longer verses, but for the purposes of a japa walk, you may find it best to use shorter phrases that can be easily repeated in your mind and synchronized with your steps. You can also come up with your own positive phrases in your native language. Here are some holy words and phrases from different traditions that can be used in a japa walk:

- **Buddhist:** Om Mane Padme Hum, Om Vajrasattva Hum, Buddha, Quan Yin, Avalokitesvara

- **Jewish:** Shalom, Elohim, Adonai, Ehyeh Asher, El Shaddai, Ha Shem, Shekinah, Barukh Ata Adonai, Ruach Elohim, Moshe Yeshua Eliahu

- **Hindu:** Om, Shivo'ham, So 'ham, Hare Krishna, Om Sri Ram Jai Ram Jai Jai Ram, Hari Om Tat Sat, Om Shanti, Sat Nam, Aham Brahmasmi

- **Islamic:** Allahu Akbar, Bismillah Al-Rahman, Al-Rahim, Ya-Rahman, Ya-Salaam, Ya-Mutakabir, Ya-Ghaffar, Ya-Fattah, Ya-Hafiz, Ya-Sabur

- **Christian:** Jesus Christ, God, Holy Spirit, Amen, Ave Maria, Jesus, Mary, and Joseph

 **Consider**

You can also repeat positive mantras and words while doing various physical exercises and efforts, including household chores and other tasks that don't require a lot of mental decision-making.

Your body is a precious gift

Some spiritual sages have said that even the gods and angels long to take form as a human being, suggesting that it's only the human body, heart, mind, and soul that can experience the unknowable, supreme reality in a tangible form.

The Indian poet Surdas asked: "*This human birth is like a precious diamond. Why have you let it go to waste?*"

Remembering your physical needs

Sometimes spiritual people get so focused on the spirit that exists beyond the external world that they don't take good care of their bodies or physical needs. I'll have to raise my hand and admit to occasionally taking that mistaken approach. Others are excessively focused on what they put in and do with their bodies, whether by undergoing extreme health regimens or following rigid dietary rules. Some religious zealots have even harmed their bodies in the name of subduing the flesh and exalting the spirit, although the popularity of these extreme mortification practices has fortunately dwindled in recent centuries.

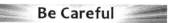

Harming your body in an attempt to honor spirit is taking a low approach to seek higher awareness. With a greater spiritual view, you come to see everything as a form of spirit and worthy of reverence — including yourself and your body.

Spirituality in Action

Thank your body

Take a pause to give thanks to your body right now. Close your eyes and feel the vibrations and energies that flow throughout your body. Put your hands on your head and heart and bless this divine vehicle of spirit. Let your healing energy flow from your hands into your body to wherever it is most needed.

Take in a deep breath of life energy and feel the energy spreading throughout your body — into your fingers and toes and to the tip of your nose.

To illustrate a good attitude spiritual people can have toward their bodies, my guru used to quote an elderly sage who was on his deathbed and preparing to leave his body and this world. The sage first said goodbye to his family and then began speaking to his own body, saying, "Oh, my dear, beloved friend. With your help, I have been able to pursue different things in my life and realize the Divine Self. You have always tolerated everything I have done to you without complaining. You have cooperated with me in my sorrow and misery as well as my joy. I beg your forgiveness for all the wrongs I did to you. Now I must leave you." And with that, the sage took leave of his body.

Remember, it is your precious body that allows you to live and breathe on this beautiful planet, interacting with all the people and things you love.

Exploring food choices

Many religious traditions have rules that dictate what you should or shouldn't do with your body. Some traditions have dietary guidelines about what you shouldn't eat at specific times, or combined with certain other foods, or ever.

Some who practice yoga and meditation do without certain foods that are said to either excite their senses (such as onions, garlic, and coffee), or that can lower the vibration of their energies (such as meat, poultry, or alcohol). Others may find the same foods that are prohibited by some traditions to be fine or even beneficial for their bodies.

Different health traditions also suggest different dietary choices. Just as with spirituality, conflicting ideas about health abound, with no clear-cut path that has been proven to work for everyone. Ultimately, you have to decide what is best for you. Your body is your responsibility, and it is your job to maintain your own body as best you can, given the information and resources you have available, along with your genetic and environmental circumstances.

An old man

A traveling salesman was passing through a small town when he saw a little old man sitting in a rocking chair on the stoop of his house. The old man looked so contented that the salesman couldn't resist going over and talking to him. "You look as if you don't have a care in the world," the salesman told him. "What is your formula for a long and happy life?"

"Well," replied the little old man, "I smoke six packs of cigarettes a day, and I drink a quart of bourbon every four hours plus six cases of beer a week. I never wash, and I go out every night."

"My goodness," exclaimed the salesman. "That's just great! How old are you?"

"Twenty-five," was the reply.

To indulge or not to indulge

Some spiritual traditions suggest that adherents lessen activities that diffuse their energies and take them away from higher spiritual goals. One of the biggies that apparently causes difficulty for some swamis, monks, and priests is the practice of *celibacy* — which basically means to refrain from sexual activity.

Many reasons are given for practicing celibacy. For Buddhists and Hindus, the goal may be elimination of desires or the preserving of spiritual energies. Some Christian monks have wanted to imitate the life of Jesus by taking on vows of abstinence, poverty, and obedience.

Different traditions also have different rules about this topic. Some advocate total abstinence from sex for dedicated practitioners, priests, and monks. Some suggest general abstinence except for the purpose of conceiving children. A few obscure spiritual traditions actually turn the sexual act into a spiritual practice with the intention of lifting it from the lower levels of usual animal instincts into an expression of higher spiritual energies.

Be Careful

Asceticism is not for everyone! This universe has created a wide variety of flavors because it likes to taste all these different flavors through its experience in and as each unique form. Trust your inner wise soul to guide your steps, and you'll be guided to do what's right for you.

Staying natural

In general, I suggest that you stay as natural as possible when it comes to what you put in, on, or near your body. In the case of food, nature has combined many important elements in the earth's bountiful produce that can't be perfectly replicated in artificially produced foods. Human bodies have been living well on only the nourishment supplied by nature from the beginning of the species until recent times.

With modern science, production, and distribution avenues in place, the world has suddenly become filled to the brim with artificial everything. Kids are drinking juices made with 0 to 3 percent real juice, and eating plastic candy products made with "artificial fruit flavor" that give the instinctual impression of eating nature's healthy foods, but with little nutrition and a lot of chemicals.

Do you really trust that big corporations and government committees always make the right decisions about what should be allowed in foods? I've seen even committees with altruistic motives and no lobbyists make lots of mistakes and poor decisions. I wouldn't assume that something is safe and healthy just because you see it on a grocery store shelf.

Take time to research so that you can choose what to eat based on intelligent information. Check out books, Web sites, and newsletters that focus on keeping your body healthy and free from toxic substances.

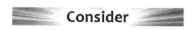

Consider

Most studies agree that natural fruits, vegetables, grains, and legumes lead to good health, and suggest striving, in general, to stay as natural as possible in food and everything else.

Here are some more ways to stay healthy by staying natural:

- **Do your best to stay away from poisons.** Look carefully at what you use to clean your counters and bathrooms. If you spray it, you breathe it! You can find natural alternatives to most chemical cleaners and poisons in health-conscious stores, and many common household items, such as vinegar, water, and baking soda, can be used as perfectly good cleaners.

One of the most bizarre scenes I've seen took place during a Thanksgiving dinner with friends where the owner of the house started spraying poison all over their kitchen to get rid of a few ants. The living room we were all sitting in was right next to the kitchen, so the fumes were clouding out into our breathing space. I quickly and kindly asked him to stop, but was really surprised that this intelligent fellow hadn't thought twice about spraying poison.

Now, I don't like having ants in my kitchen either, but I'm not willing to poison myself to get rid of them! Look online to find out different natural methods that people have discovered and tried. Some use boric acid to get rid of insects, and others even swear by drawing a line with chalk, saying that the ants won't cross the line (I haven't personally tried this one yet). If you must spray with usual products, do it sparingly or preferably outside, near the area where they're entering your home.

I suggest steering clear, too, of defogger cans that fill your home with poison for an hour or two. Does it sound like a good idea to fill your living space with poison? Of course, extreme situations may require extreme measures. However, poison has become a fast-food type of solution to problems in today's society, with little consideration of how that poison is going to affect your body or the bodies of those you love.

- **Don't take too many medications.** Business-based medicine has turned today's world into a world of drugs. I've consulted doctors who've zipped off all kinds of potent prescriptions for minor ailments. Each time I've had prescriptions filled, the pharmacist inevitably hands me a list of potential side effects for that drug — side effects that are often much worse than whatever I went to the doctor for. One list was a whole page long and had some of the most disgusting-sounding possible side effects you could imagine!

  Obviously, if you have a serious illness, you should use whatever means are available to cure it, including medicines. I'm not suggesting that you should never take medicines, but to appreciate that your body is your responsibility. Be aware and do your research. Sometimes, even with doctors in white lab coats, you have to "just say no."

- **Read the labels of anything you're going to put in, on, or around your body.** Inquire about natural alternatives when possible. Remember that your skin is also a breathing organ — check the labels of what you're putting into your body through the pores of your skin. Health-food stores often offer natural options, and many of these simple products are as good or better than chemical conglomerations, but without as much of the bad stuff.

Don't bathe your body in toxins just for convenience sake.

Stretching, Exercising, and Hatha Yoga

Spiritual Wisdom

In the practice of Yoga, every cell is consciously made to absorb a copious supply of fresh blood and life-giving energy, thus satiating the embodied soul.

—B.K.S. Iyengar

One field of spiritual practice in India is called hatha yoga. Hatha yoga includes the physical postures and exercises that prepare your body for meditation and the ultimate yoga, which is a conscious experience of union with the divine. (*Yoga* means union, and *hatha* refers to balancing the sun and moon energies within your body.) Hatha yoga consists of various movements, breath control exercises, and physical postures that can produce a profound state of inner union, vitality, and harmony.

The ancient wisdom of hatha yoga has trickled into modern-day life mostly in the form of exercise videos and health-club courses that help you lose weight and get your body in better shape.

Yes, these positive effects are available through practicing hatha yoga, however many hatha yoga practitioners lack a solid understanding of the deeper spiritual purpose of hatha yoga. One yoga magazine reporter told me that the hottest thing around the hip Hollywood crowd is to get what they call a "yoga butt" — proving that modern society can make a junk-food version of anything, including sublime ancient wisdom!

Don't Forget

The deeper purpose of yoga exercises is to uplift you spiritually. One yoga scripture describes those who practice exercises without a higher intention as "mere holders of bones." Hatha yoga postures are intended to be a support for your journey to the *real* yoga — union with the divine!

Where hatha yoga postures come from

How did ancient hatha yoga researchers know that specific postures could heal kidney weaknesses, back injuries, hormonal imbalances, mental agitation, circulation sluggishness, brain, thyroid, and digestion disorders, and so many other physical maladies? They had no books. They didn't learn it in school. They didn't have instruction manuals and videos to explain it to them.

The ancient hatha yoga sages discovered all these postures and exercises with their subtle intellect, through intuitive insight and divine inspiration.

Volumes can and have been written about all the exercises and theories behind hatha yoga. Some postures are called by the Sanskrit names of the animals they resemble, such as *koormaasana* (the tortoise pose), *matsyaasana* (the fish pose), or *bhekaasana* (the frog pose). Most are based on the idea that certain positions relieve tensions and allow your blood and energy to flow more freely in your body. Some stimulate your immune system; while others create or strengthen specific patterns of energy flow in your body.

Spirituality in Action

Being moved from within

Your inner Self is filled with intelligent wisdom. Here's a chance to tap into its healing guidance:

1. **Sit or lie down quietly, and bring your focus inside.**
   Take a few moments to quiet your mind and soften your breath. Become aware of your body from head to toe.

2. **Invoke the intelligent energy in your body and invite it to move through you.**

3. **Let your body gently begin to stretch.**

   See what feels good and relax into whatever postures come up. Allow yourself to be guided from within. Your body can go into so many different kinds of movements. Stretch gently or dance enthusiastically. Feel the intelligent energy of spirit moving through your body as it guides you on how to move your body.

Sometimes different postures are put together into a flowing sequence. One common series of poses is called *surya namaskar*, or "sun salutations." This sequence takes you from a standing pose into various push-up type lunges and back bends that flow naturally into one another, and then back into a standing pose to begin the cycle again.

Many hatha yoga postures work on your spine — carefully stretching, opening, elongating, twisting, turning, and bending your spine this way and that. Popular postures for the spine include the cobra back arch, the forward bend, and various spinal twists. Your spine has a very special spiritual significance. It is not only the backbone of your physical body, but also of your energy body.

Be Careful

Hatha yoga postures are extremely powerful, and you should learn them in person from a teacher who can make sure that you are doing them correctly.

Remembering to rest

One of the most important elements of a good hatha yoga workout comes at the end, when you go into what is called *shaavaasana* (the corpse pose), one of my favorite postures.

Spirituality in Action

Lie on your back with your hands out just a bit from your body, palms gently open and facing up. Keep your feet slightly separated. Relax your entire body, either bit by bit or all at once. You may want to tighten and relax different parts of your body — your toes, hips, stomach, chest, arms, hands, throat, and face — or you can just relax everything together right away. Allow your breath to become deep and steady.

As you lie in shaavaasana, you may also want to practice something called the *full yogic breath,* where you breath in deeply, filling first your stomach area, then your chest area, and then your upper ribcage area. Then you pause for a moment before releasing the breath, starting again at the stomach area and again moving up to flatten down the chest and upper ribcage areas. This breathing exercise can come to feel like a wave of healing energy.

After doing full yogic breath for a while, let your breath return to its natural flow and relax completely into the pose. Some teachers say that if you don't include this resting shaavaasana time at the end of your hatha yoga routine, you won't receive as many benefits from the exercises. This relaxing yoga pose is one more example of how spirituality is not about doing more, but doing what is best.

You can also apply the philosophy behind this pose to your life, understanding the importance of adding moments of deep rest to your activities. Perhaps you'd like to go into shaavaasana for a few minutes before you go to sleep at night.

Living longer versus having fun

A man approaching retirement went to see the company doctor for one final checkup. To his horror, the doctor said, "I don't know quite how to put this, but your heart is on its last legs, and you have only six months to live."

"Is there nothing I can do?" asked the shocked man.

"Well," said the doctor, "you can give up alcohol and cut out smoking. Don't eat rich foods, don't go dancing, and don't even think about sex!"

"And this will make me live longer?" the man asked hopefully.

"No," replied the doctor. "It will just seem longer!"

Practicing Spiritual Breathing

Your breath is much more than just the simple movement of oxygen in and out of your lungs. Your breath is a vehicle for not only the physical oxygen that's necessary for your body functions, but subtle energies as well. The air has its own aura or energy field. Sometimes, you can even see these tiny scintillating particles of light filling the air around you. (Please don't tell me I'm the only one who sees them!) Indian scriptures use the word *prana* to describe this life force and their word for breath exercises that increase your life force is *pranayama*.

You've probably noticed that your state of mind affects the way you breathe. For example, when you're agitated, your breath tends to get shallow and fast. When you're feeling happy and peaceful, your breath becomes slower and deeper.

Just as your state of mind affects the way you breathe, so also the way you breathe affects your state of mind. Because your breath mirrors your mental state, you can create an intentional feedback loop where you guide your breath to become calm and slow, little by little. Calming your breath also calms the thoughts in your mind. As the agitation of your mind begins to subside, your breath naturally becomes even calmer, thereby making your mind even quieter.

Consider

Breathing slowly and deeply can lead you into more peaceful spaces within your mind, heart, and soul.

Spiritual Wisdom

The soul is the divine breath. It purifies, revivifies, and heals the instrument through which it functions.

—Hazrat Inayat Khan

Spirituality in Action

Here's a way to experience healing life-force energy through breath control:

1. **Sit quietly in a meditative space, allowing each breath to get longer and longer, deeper and deeper.**

2. **Slowly increase the length of each inhalation, as well as the pause at the peak of your inhalation while holding the air in.**

3. **Let the air out slowly with each exhalation, pausing again at the end of each exhalation as the air is retained outside.**

You may have an easier time doing this exercise while counting mentally. You can begin by breathing in to the count of three, gently retaining the breath for a count of three, releasing the air to the count of three, and resting on the point of exhalation to the count of three. After the count of three is comfortable, you can add a number, and do the same cycle to the count of four.

Continue to add numbers to your breath rounds until the point where it would become uncomfortable. If you feel a need to take a few ordinary breaths here and there before continuing on, that is fine. Trust your inner guidance.

Be Careful

Breath exercises should give a bit of challenge, but no discomfort. Be careful not to force the breath, while gently guiding your breaths to become longer and deeper.

Various teachers give different suggested ratios of breath inhalation, retention, release, and rest, where your count for inhalation is different from retention or exhalation. As someone who likes to do my practices with minimal bookkeeping, I suggest starting with this simple straight-across count.

The important elements in this practice are your focus on the breath and on consciously expanding and softening your capacity to receive and release air and life force through your breath. Breathe in and feel that you're breathing in light and filling your body with light. Breathe out and shine that light into the world.

Chapter 8

Empowering Your Mind

Topics in this Chapter:

*   Exploring the value of your mind
*   Clearing the clutter of your thoughts
*   Integrating meditation into your daily life

Of all the tools you have to work with in your life-journey, the most important is your mind. Without your mind, you wouldn't even remember the people and experiences that have been most important to you or the valuable experiences you've had. Without your mind, you wouldn't even be able to contemplate who you are.

The clarity of vision in your eyes is important. Your ability to speak is important. All the functions of your body and senses are useful. Nevertheless, your mind is the No. 1 tool for any endeavor in life — including on the path of spiritual evolution.

The Amazing Value of Your Mind

Ancient spiritual scriptures and modern neuroscientists agree that what you know, see, hear, taste, and feel is experienced in, through, and with your mind.

Neuroscience says that even an object that you perceive as being outside of yourself is not experienced outside yourself, but in your own brain and mind. Even a pain you feel in a part of your body is not being experienced in that part of your body, but again, in your brain and mind.

Here's a simple scientific explanation of the electro-chemical brain processes that come together to create the experience of pain in a stubbed toe:

1. **Nerve impulses that signal pain travel from your toe through the branches of your nervous system.**

2. **These impulses move up through your spinal cord and into the parts of your brain that deal with pain, as well as to areas of your brain that represent that particular toe.**

3. **This combination of electric and chemical activity culminates with you experiencing brain patterns that communicate a feeling of pain in your toe.**

   And voilà! Stubbed toe pain.

Don't Forget

Just as the experience of a stubbed toe is taking place in your brain and not your toe, so all of your experiences of the physical world are also taking place in your brain and mind.

Be Careful

This example isn't intended to limit the process of personal experience to only what scientists know of the brain and mind. Certainly, whatever is creating your experience of the world is far more amazing than modern science can capture.

Opening up your creative mind

Even if you don't consider yourself to be an artist, improving your creative skills will inevitably improve all the different areas of your life. Whether or not you choose to take up specific arts such as painting, cooking, writing, photography, garden designing, crafts, or singing and playing music, you knowingly or unknowingly are already an artist of the amazing creative artwork that is your whole life.

Because you're already an artist, why not strive to be a great one? Whether you're setting up your living space, cooking a meal, or teaching your children right from wrong, doing whatever you do with a creative and spiritual flow enhances all your actions and helps turn whatever you do into a spiritual practice. Every activity in life is enhanced by doing it artfully or creatively.

One way to improve the creative artistry of your works is to keep your focus on what you are doing and not on what material benefits you may receive from it. For many people, the initial impetus to do something is sparked by hopes of increasing their income or receiving other benefits, which is fine (unless you're a renunciant).

However, when you're actually in the midst of doing an action — writing the book, designing the recipe, sewing the costume, or building the structure — your creativity tends to flow more smoothly when you remove your focus from the desire or greed that may have motivated you to begin the action and shine the light of your focus on the action itself and on staying open to a creative flow through your connection with the universe.

In recent decades, nearly every field of creativity — including science, music, philosophy, the arts, and even spirituality — has unfortunately turned into one more avenue for commercial profiteering. Today's greed culture became especially obvious to me when I started offering my creative spiritual works, including an extensive Web site of writings, video, music, and other spiritual multimedia resources, for free.

During my vibrant decade of monastic-style ashram living, I became very comfortable with the idea of offering creative service without looking to receive anything in return, other than the honor and joy of being able to do it.

When I left the ashram to go to Hollywood, I found a very different culture that was still creative and artistic, but often focused on material benefits and "getting ahead." Friends would invite me to come to meals or parties so that I could meet people who "could be a good contact for you," instead of thinking about who would be interesting or uplifting for me to meet. One coworker in my early years of news editing gave me a stern lecture about how the union rules said that I had to request overtime pay for working through a missed lunch even if I hadn't been hungry when asked to work through the hour. This focus on hourly wages was very new for someone like me who hadn't counted an hour for pay in ten years.

Therefore, after my Hollywood years, when my life shifted into a more reclusive time of writing, singing, producing uplifting videos, and creating Web site offerings, I decided to go back to my more comfortable tradition of approaching my creative works as freely offered service. Although this approach brought some lean financial years that were somewhat out of balance, still it was worth going through these challenges to be able to offer spiritual resources as I thought they should be offered — freely.

During my monastic years, I'd been blessed to have access to an abundance of inspiring videos, audiotapes, and spiritual teachings, and now I wanted to share my spiritual resources in the same free spirit through these online offerings. The "google gods" were kind in giving my pages good rankings, and many guests have come from around the world every day to enjoy the free multimedia spiritual resources.

However, some acquaintances, colleagues, and book marketing experts seemed to be upset by the idea that I was wasting all this Internet traffic flow without capturing e-mail addresses or pushing products and advertising, especially when they knew I was living on meager funds. For some, their concern was based on wanting the best for me, and for others, it seemed that my commitment to sharing rather than selling broke some kind of unspoken business law about the importance of maximizing financial profits. More than one person became angry when I refused his moneymaking suggestions and explained that my goal was to give these works freely, without capturing anything from guests other than hopefully their enjoyment and upliftment.

In truth, my commitment to keep these works freely available was not only altruistic, but also a way to tap into greater creativity. Many artists, scientists, and philosophers throughout time have discovered this secret — that divinely inspired creativity often flows best when you work with full focus and freedom from materialistic desires and intentions.

Even on a neuroscience level, parts of your brain that deal with creative, holistic, and spiritual consciousness issues tend to be on the other side of the aisle from the parts of your brain that deal with business or bookkeeping tasks. Certainly, some people have achieved a good combination of these abilities, but others whose priority is focused on spiritual awareness or creative expression may prefer not to get too bogged down in too many contracts and business deals — and thus you have the archetypal "starving artist" syndrome. Some artists find that focusing too much on selling can eventually turn into selling out.

Adversity reveals genius, prosperity conceals it.
   —Horace

If you want to open up your mind's creative abilities, one suggestion is, if circumstances permit, to move forward with your artistic endeavors without worrying too much about how to sell what you do, but with a higher intention of wanting to use your time on earth to express something wonderful. Through the efforts of many poor but prolific artists came the great renaissances of philosophy, arts, and music, along with world-shattering scientific and philosophical paradigms. These productive artists focused on inspiring audiences with their wisdom, talents, and spirit, above merely looking for a way to cash in for big bucks.

With an artistic mindset, you can create your own renaissance in whatever fields of expression inspire you. With a creative approach, you can even craft your view of the world into one that will transform and uplift your experience of the world. You may still receive big bucks from your creative works, but either way, your focus will be on the spiritual creative flow as you dance a glorious dance of being you.

Change your outlook, change your life

It sounds simple, doesn't it? Change your outlook, and you change your life. In reality, however, it isn't always so easy to change your outlook from within that outlook. As Albert Einstein said, "The significant problems we face can never be solved at the level of thinking that created them."

This is the challenge of spirituality — to move beyond common, materialistic world-views into a greater vision that will create a greater world. You can also call this optimistic approach *higher possibility thinking,* where you're imagining the best of what could be. In many cases, it is your imagination that holds the key to envisioning and creating a more wondrous life (see Chapter 15).

Many spiritual teachers and philosophers, east and west, past and present, have declared that your mind actually *creates* your reality.

Spiritual Wisdom

All that we are is the result of what we have thought.

— Buddha

The act of contemplation creates the thing contemplated.

— Isaac D'Israeli

According to your faith, be it done unto you.

— Jesus (Matthew 9:29)

If you think you are free, you are free. If you think you are bound, you are bound. For the saying is true: You are what you think.

— Ashtavakra Gita

The greatest discovery of my generation is that human beings can alter their lives by altering their attitudes of mind.

— James Allen (1864-1912)

Attributing the creation of the outer world to your mind can sound silly, narcissistic, and even ridiculous. After all, if you were in control of this world, things would look very different, right?

Well, this topic is one that you have to entertain and consider without becoming hard-nosed about the details. Yes, you're creating the world, and no, you're not creating the world. If you expect spirituality to fit into neat little boxes and labels, then you're going to have a very limited experience of spirituality. Give yourself the freedom to imagine and explore the meanings behind teachings such as, "Your mind creates this world," and, "It is done unto you as you believe."

In spirituality, you can be divine and limited at the same time. This universe is simultaneously perfect and imperfect, formless and in form, and eternal and bound by time (see Chapter 14).

This theory that your mind is creating your world suggests that:

- **Your limits and obstacles in achieving your goals are exactly what you think they are.** If you think that you have to follow the same path that others in your family or culture have taken, or if you believe that you don't have the ability, resources, or good karma to achieve your deepest heart's desire, then you won't even try to move beyond the limitations your mind has put into place. You may not even begin to consider what your true goals should or could be.

- **Everything you see and know is colored by the glasses of your memories and thoughts.** Some Indian scriptures demonstrate the idea that everything you see and experience is being interpreted through your mind, memories, and thoughts using the simple analogy of seeing a snake in a rope. If you see a plain old useful rope on the ground but think it is a poisonous snake, then your internal experience of fear is the same as it would be if that rope were an actual snake. Your outer actions would also reflect this projection as you stop what you're doing and run away in fear, perhaps never to even discover that it was only a rope.

- **Your destiny unfolds according to the thought-seeds you've planted.** Clear intentions focus your conscious and subconscious mental energies on creating a destiny that reflects your intentions and beliefs. So many famous celebrities and artists tell of making efforts throughout their youth to practice and develop the skills that became their future success.

- **You are who you think you are.** Your thoughts and actions are inherently guided and limited by your self-concepts. If you identify yourself as being a kind and generous person, then you will rise to the occasion to express these qualities in situations that arise in your life. Your expressions of kind and generous qualities through your thoughts and actions are in harmony with the kind and generous person you think you are.

Who you think you are often comes from who others think you are, so unless you use contemplation to discover more about who you really are, you may take on the opinions of others as your own and limit your view of your current and potential greatness through their limited views of you.

- **Changing your vision literally changes the world.** Imagine that! Seriously — imagine it right now!

One Indian scripture goes so far as to boldly declare that "The world is as you see it." The Sanskrit of this phrase has a nice ring to it, so I'll share it with you: "*Ya drishti, sa srishti.*" Literally, this phrase means, "As your vision is, so this creation is," or more simply, "The world *is* as you see it."

This phrase doesn't just refer to some pop psychology, "I'm okay, you're okay" kind of concept. This "*Ya drishti sa srishti*" means that the world is flexible and inherently molded by how you see it — that your perception is also your reality. This ancient spiritual concept of "the world is as you see it" is also echoed in the science of quantum physics, where scientists have discovered that the very act of observing the world affects what you are viewing. You can find out more about how your mind is a cocreator in Chapter 15.

Be careful not to fall into a guilt trip as you begin to realize how responsible your mind is for all the situations in your life. Along with your increasing awareness of your mind's power, be sure to include a sense of trust that everything is fine, as you learn and grow in your journey through life.

Taking steps to refine your mind

Refining your mind gives you the clarity to create a better outlook and improve your life. Three ways to refine your mind are contemplation, meditation, and communion with spirit.

- **Contemplation** includes cleaning up, organizing, uplifting, and taking control of the thoughts in your mind — watching, directing, and guiding your thoughts to find greater awareness and understanding. (For more on contemplation, see the section "Contemplation: Clearing the Clutter," later in this chapter.)

- **Meditation** is a practice of peaceful introspection that helps you increase your mental strength and clarity by focusing your mind and quieting your thoughts. (I cover meditation in the upcoming section "Meditating: Silent Mind, Holy Mind.")

- **Communion with spirit** is not really a practice that you do to refine your mind as much as a gift that comes when your mind has become more refined. Through your contemplation and meditation efforts and the magical sprinkling of divine grace, you come to feel near, within, and in an ongoing interaction with spirit, God, or universal Consciousness. (For more on this topic, see Chapter 9.)

Saying it another way

Here are quick descriptions of contemplation, meditation, and spiritual union:

1. First you focus your mind — contemplation.
2. Next you quiet your mind — meditation.
3. Then there is no mind — spiritual union.

Recognizing and Clearing Your Mental Clutter

Arrange whatever pieces come your way.

— Virginia Woolf

Imagine that you are walking around all day, picking up every object you see. Several things happen:

- Your pockets become full and heavy.

- Your hands are occupied with holding all kinds of things.

- Your ability to walk and maneuver is impaired due to carrying so many objects.

- If you need to find a particular item in your pockets, you have to empty a big messy pile and sort through it until you find the desired object.

- You'll likely become tired and irritable from the inconvenience of carrying so many things around with you everywhere you go.

Now, imagine that these objects are the thoughts in your mind. Day in and day out, you think this thought: read this book, have this conversation, wish this, wish that, fear this, fear that, think, think, think about what, who, where, when, why did this happen? How can you make that happen? Who do they think they are? Do they like you? What was it you were supposed to pick up after work? You've got mail, void where prohibited, please stand behind the red line, details at 11, ring! ring! Who's there? Are you ready to make a commitment? Tell me what you think, tell me what she thinks, when did you first notice the swelling? Can I help you? Can you help me? Do you know what that person did years ago? Who does he think he is? Does she, he, it really love me? What is that supposed to mean? Did you call to confirm your appointment? Did you get those reports done? Did you buy gas on your way home? Did you take out the trash, do the dishes, feed the dog, pay the bills, pick up the kids, mow the lawn, buy that gift, cash your check, go to work, go to school, go to the store, to the recital, to the movies, to dinner? Did you do this, do that, go here, go there, be this, be that, go, go, go, go, do, do, do, do, be, be, be, be. Aaaarrrggghhhhhhhhh!!!! Welcome to a cluttered mind!

Sending your mind to the naughty corner

When you're misbehaving and acting in ways you know are not helpful or right, you can follow the example of television nannies and send your mind for a time out in the "naughty corner."

Just as with a child, you should do this gently and firmly. When you've misbehaved in some way, find some time to sit by yourself, quietly. Consider what you can learn from the situation that would improve your actions in the future. Observe your feelings — it doesn't really feel so good when you do something you know is wrong, does it? This uncomfortable feeling of having caused harm through your words or actions can certainly be punishment enough to inspire you to change. Think about ways you can make amends or improve things next time around. Ask for blessings and give thanks to divine spirit for giving you the opportunity and guidance to take one more important step on your big, universal, spiritual journey. Then give yourself a loving hug and move forward into a new day.

Spirituality and common sense both say that if you can learn to keep your thoughts in their proper places, you won't have to walk around holding such a big mess of thoughts. A clear and uncluttered mind leaves you free to accomplish all that you really want to do.

Start cleaning up the clutter of your mind and heart just as you would straighten out your garage or organize your office space. Here are a few examples of the kind of clutter that you can toss out (no tax deductions for these donations, though).

You can throw away your:

- Unresolved anger toward someone from a long time ago

- Guilt and shame over things you have done or said in the past

- Fears and paranoia about what may happen in the future

- Feelings of hopelessness and depression — these emotions are like thieves that sap your energy and joy

- Unimportant goals that are in conflict with your greater goals

You can't hire a maid service to do this kind of cleaning – it's up to you to clear the clutter in your own mind. In the next section I give you tips on how to clear different kinds of mental and emotional clutter.

Using contemplation to clear your mental clutter

I went to a bookstore and asked the saleswoman, "Where's the self-help section?" She said if she told me, it would defeat the purpose.

— George Carlin

The basic idea behind contemplation is to become the director of your mental movies and the conductor of your symphony of thoughts.

You don't have to just sit back and be at the mercy of all the unnecessary or even harmful thoughts that pass through your mind. The spiritual practice of contemplation helps you let go of unproductive thoughts and neutralize their effects in your life.

Instead of letting your mind do every random thing it wants to do — thinking about this person or that problem, and obsessing over and over about the same details without ever finding a solution — you can begin to take control of your own mind. Just as with an undisciplined child, you can guide your mind with loving and gentle direction when possible and a firm hand when necessary.

Uncluttering your outer life — your environment, relationships, schedules, and communications — also helps to bring more inner peace. Less clutter outside can mean less clutter inside!

It's natural for negative feelings and emotions to come into your mind. What you need to do is to learn how to clear them away. The following sections offer ways to get rid of cluttered, harmful thoughts through contemplation and applying a spiritual point of view.

Get rid of anger

Instead of letting anger fester for months, years, or decades, you can contemplate exactly why and with whom you're really angry. Is your anger based, in part, on some earlier experiences in your life? Sometimes unresolved angers from the past can project unfairly on people in the present.

If you're angry at someone, try to understand the other person's point of view. Are they just a total jerk with utterly unredeemable qualities, or is it possible that they think they are acting correctly? Consider what you'd like to say to the person and imagine how they may respond – try to put yourself into their shoes.

Don't Forget

Remember that whatever anger you're feeling is in you, and not in anyone else. Your state of mind and actions are your responsibility; other people's state of mind and actions are theirs. Even if you need to address someone else's actions outwardly to protect yourself or others in the future, you can still strive to do so without getting entangled in the gnarly webs of ongoing anger.

A great way to release anger is to move your awareness and understanding into the spiritual realms of trusting that a benevolent universe is bringing exactly what you need to experience. Remember that every person in this world is a spark of the divine. Every experience is a pleasant or unpleasant gift from a friendly God who loves you and wants to help you grow on an eternal, spiritual level, even if this growth requires you to go through some challenging times. Look at the person you're angry with and remember that ultimately it's not about them, but about your relationship with the divine.

Even while honoring and feeling your emotions, you can simultaneously know that you and every person, place, and thing are part of a grand universal dance of creation — the divine play of life. Consider that the person who has made you angry may have been hand-picked by the divine director to play their role in your life movie, and enjoy the show.

Unravel feelings of sadness

Getting rid of sadness can be tricky, because sometimes you may feel sad even while things are going pretty well in your life. At other times, you may be sad because your life is especially difficult. Your sadness may also be part of a "dark night of the soul" experience that is preparing the way for greater happiness in the future.

In some cases, sadness may indicate a chemical imbalance in the brain, or it may be a response to allergens and toxins that are so prevalent in today's world. In this section, I'm referring to more common forms of sadness such as those that come from boredom, disappointments, or dissatisfaction with the circumstances of your life.

When you're feeling sadness, instead of rushing off to distract yourself with sense indulgences or numbing yourself with drugs, overwork, or shopping, you can use contemplation to search inside yourself and discern why you're experiencing sadness. Is it based on not getting what you want? Is it a sign that something is out of place in your life? Is this sadness an inevitable part of the process of growing up and remembering who you really are?

 **Consider**

If you're feeling overwhelmed with sadness, sit quietly and allow your mind, heart, and spirit to settle into the hand of grace that always exists within each moment — if you but take the time to stop and remember. Honor your feelings of sadness, but be ready to let go of them as you move back into greater happiness.

Doubt your doubts

If it's true that your thoughts create and reflect in the world around you, then what do you think doubts do to your life? They keep you from having, being, and doing what you want. Doubts sow the seeds of failure in your mind and heart.

I'm not talking about the kind of doubt that makes you reconsider whether something or someone is in the right place in your life or whether your actions are correct. These beneficial kinds of doubt are called *discernment,* which is a good spiritual quality and a great tool for the practice of contemplation.

Doubts are rascals that make you fear that you aren't what you hoped you were or that something is going to go wrong in the future. Doubts keep you from raising your hand to answer the teacher's question even when you think you know the answer. Doubts hold you back from telling someone that you love them. Doubts keep you from pursuing your dreams. Doubts create fears, and fear often creates whatever is feared.

Be negative toward your negativity

Negative thoughts are like dark, heavy clouds that cover the sky of your soul. Your negative thoughts may be directed toward a particular person or experience, but guess what? Negative thoughts color everything else in your mind, too.

Negative thoughts are like viruses to your mental state of well being. Understanding the effects of negative thoughts should give you greater motivation to hold yourself back from jumping into the abyss of negativity.

If someone betrays you, insults you, or steals from you, and you go around thinking negative thoughts all day long, then you're likely to see more negative experiences pop up in your life. When you understand the effect that negative thoughts have on your spirit and the world manifesting around you (see Chapter 15), then you find it easier to replace your negative thoughts with positive ones.

Unmask false contentment

If you're spending a lot of energy covering up your sadness, anger, or pain so that you'll look happy to others, the apparent contentment you project may actually be keeping you from finding true peace and contentment.

Through contemplation, you can look at whatever is keeping you from true contentment. You can sort out how you really feel and what you really think, and find ways to create real contentment instead of presenting a facade of pseudo-contentment. Why spend so much energy trying to *look* happy when you can spend the same energy and actually *be* happy?

Give up greed

When you want more, more, and more, you create a state of constant discontent inside yourself. It's like the idea that if you clench your fists to avoid giving, your closed hands are also not able to receive anything. Do it right now. Open your hands wide and hold them in front of you, palms up. Now, live your life with that same state of openness.

There's no good reason to give in to greed during this short journey on earth. If you're greedy, no matter how many millions of dollars you have, you will always want more. No matter how big your TV, how new your car, or how nice your clothes, you'll always want something bigger and better. Greed is the enemy of contentment and satisfaction. Greed makes you tense and unhappy.

It's fine to have hopes and desires, but greed keeps you running on the hamster wheel of unending desires and can even convince you to take advantage of someone else to get more for yourself, which is a spiritual no-no! After all, with spiritual insight, you realize that ultimately there is no other.

Contemplate to see whether you have areas in your life where you're feeling greedy. Look for ways to transform that greed into contentment, gratitude, and generosity. Don't accuse or judge yourself, but gently open your inner hands and trust that God will give you everything you truly deserve and need.

Contemplating daily events

Contemplation is one practice that you can truly practice anytime and anywhere. Suppose while you're driving to work tomorrow, a car brazenly weaves in and out of lanes and cuts right in front of you, causing you to have to brake quickly. You honk at the car, and life goes on. This situation is a great opportunity for you to contemplate your response to the situation. Obviously, your adrenals will have reacted to the imminent danger, but how quickly are you able to calm down? Within a moment? An hour? Does this one disturbing event color your whole day?

Also, think about why you honked. Did you honk from anger? Did you honk while shouting an obscenity to that idiot? Did you think an angry thought, wishing that the inconsiderate driver would be taught a lesson? Perhaps you would have been happy to hear some police sirens going after the rogue driver. Or did you honk out of kind concern, hoping that your commentary would remind the driver to practice safer driving skills? (Yeah, right.)

This contemplation isn't meant to create a judgment against yourself, but to use an outer event to stimulate greater self-awareness and self-control. At the same time, this situation is a good opportunity to remember that whatever you wish for others may come back to you in some way and form. If you create sirens with your mind, those sirens just may arrive when the other driver is long gone, and *you* are the one who is speeding!

Heal your hatred

Here's the thing about hatred: No matter who or what you hate, that hatred turns into self-hatred, because it lives inside of you. Even if you hate a very bad person, *you* will be the victim of your hatred, not the bad person. Here are three ways you can move beyond hatred:

- Have a deeper understanding of universal justice. Trust that everyone ultimately receives the results of their actions now or in the future, whether these results are visible to others or only experienced by the person performing the actions.

- Feel compassion for everyone who is bound by ignorance. Understand that every-one does the best they can with the resources they have, and that those who act badly are often misbehaving as an outer expression of their inner suffering.

- Increase love, which can turn hatred into fragrant flowers. Shining the light of spiritual love on any situation inherently removes the darkness of hatred, just as the rising sun dispels the darkness of night.

If you can turn hatred for even one person into love and compassion, you help to build a beautiful road to paradise right here on earth.

Eliminate your impatience

Impatience creates dissatisfaction. Impatience is a sign that you're not fully focused on the present moment. You may be trying to squeeze more into a 24-hour period than is possible and become frustrated when obstacles keep you from rushing forward. You want things to move faster and happen more quickly than they are. Even in youth, impatience makes you drive your parents crazy while they're driving the car by asking over and over, "Are we almost there?" Youthful impatience makes you pull out that loose tooth before it is ready to let go, making a big mess (one of my childhood specialties).

The truth is that time is an important element for the lessons you have to learn here in the physical world. Growth takes time, patience, and steady effort. When you plant seeds in your garden, you have to have enough patience to keep nurturing those seeds, seedlings, and plants until their fruits and vegetables are ripe and ready to eat. If you're impatient, you'll plant the seeds and check the next day to see whether you have enough vegetables for a nice salad. Then you'll either give up on watering your garden or destroy the plants by pulling them up to check their status. Can you tell how well I know this kind of clutter?

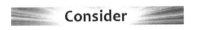 **Consider**

Patience is necessary on your spiritual journey, because your growth is not always out-wardly obvious or tangible. Sometimes you may experience immediate positive effects from your spiritual efforts, and other times you'll have to keep your practices going for a while before you start to notice the benefits. Sometimes you may even seem to be going downward on the spiritual evolutionary scale, but don't let your impatience over apparent setbacks discourage you from continuing your efforts to evolve spiritually.

One way to naturally heal the clutter of impatience is to focus on the present moment while remembering the eternal nature of the universe. This combination of remembering the present moment and the eternal nature simultaneously can help free your mind from the prison of time so that you can learn to enjoy each moment — from the hills of joy to the valleys of sorrow, and from exciting adventures to times of rest.

Another helpful way to heal impatience is to clean up your greediness. By clearing greed from your life, you also steer clear of the kind of impatience that comes from wanting to have what you want right now.

Jostle with jealousy

It's important to understand what jealousy is and isn't. Jealousy is *not* seeing what someone else has and wanting the same for yourself. Being inspired to improve your lot after admiring what someone else has achieved is fine, especially if what the person has achieved is something that would be beneficial to the world and your life and spiritual journey.

Jealousy, on the other hand, carries a level of destructiveness. You not only want what others have, but you also don't want *them* to have it. You may have a materialistic idea that there's only so much success to go around and that if someone else gets some, there will be less for you. Jealousy is a problem, because everything is made of the same, one, divine light, which reflects our thoughts like mirrors. Therefore, your wish of less for another comes back to haunt you and keep you from achieving your dreams.

Negative effects of jealousy can include being in an agitated state of mind, losing enthusiasm for your own journey, or getting what you thought you wanted but not finding peace and happiness there. Therefore, keep your attention focused on what you want for yourself and not on jealousy over what others have.

Calm your infatuations

Infatuation happens when a single desire or obsession wipes out all your other thoughts. On one hand, you can say that infatuation does bring your mind into a state of focus, which is considered to be a beneficial characteristic to have for spiritual contemplation. However, you have to consider whether what you're focusing so much attention on is uplifting or binding your spirit.

Infatuation is such a powerful intoxicant that it can make you give up what you know is right or best. For example, lustful thoughts often fall under the heading of infatuation. Lustful infatuations can even make you gamble your presidency just to satisfy them. (I'm not mentioning any names!)

Through contemplation, you can look at your infatuations more objectively and consider whether they're helpful or harmful for your overall goals. Separate your mind from the pull of the infatuation long enough to take back control of your thoughts. If you want to be infatuated, be infatuated with the greatness and glory of your divine, spiritual life!

Focus on the positive

When tragedies take place, people naturally try to balance out the negative experiences by keeping their minds on more positive, spiritual topics. For example, after the twin towers in New York City were brought down by terrorists in planes on September 11, 2001, the entire United States moved to focus on the positive, even while being horrified by the ongoing traumas of loss and destruction.

For a time, television stations cancelled their usual violent fare. Scary movies were put on hold. People tried to be kinder to one another. Musicians came together to sing inspiring songs and generate funds to help those whose lives had been turned upside-down. The entire nation came together time and time again to sing "God bless America."

As glorious as this uplifting response was, it didn't last very long. Still, there is hope that if the media can recognize the harmful effects of negative fare during times of tragedy, then perhaps one day they'll also realize that the same negative fare contributes to creating more times of tragedy.

Even if it takes society a while to understand the power of positive and negative images, you can apply this understanding to your own life right now. Don't wait for tragedy to come before you bless yourself, your loved ones, or your country with uplifting thoughts and words. Fill your mind with good, positive, and healthy ingredients that this conscious universe can use to cook up wonderful life experiences.

Focusing your thoughts

Spiritual metaphysics teaches that you empower and ultimately become whatever you focus on the most. Understanding the power of your mind should inspire you to be more vigilant about how you spend your precious personal consciousness. Here are a few tips:

- **Be a focus miser.** Pay as much attention (or more!) to where you're spending your attention as you do to where you're spending your money.

- **Have discriminating tastes.** Feed your mind and heart with good quality thoughts by keeping the right company, both inside and out. Company doesn't just mean the people you're around, but also what you read, watch, and listen to.

- **Don't think junk thoughts.** Just as you have to limit the number of junk food meals you eat to stay physically healthy, you should also limit junk thoughts that have no "nutritional" value and can create physical, emotional, mental, and spiritual diseases in your being.

Putting your desires in order

Spiritual Wisdom

If you only care enough for a result, you will almost certainly attain it. If you wish to be rich, you will be rich; if you wish to be learned, you will be learned; if you wish to be good, you will be good. Only you must, then, really wish these things, and wish them with exclusiveness, and not wish at the same time a hundred other incompatible things just as strongly.
— William James

Imagine a list of every desire you've had since the day you were born. Aren't you glad most of them never came true? If my dreams from age ten had come true, I would right now be a go-go dancer married to David Cassidy! (I can't believe I just admitted that publicly.)

When you have a lot of unclear, conflicting desires popping up all over the place, your personal and spiritual power becomes weakened and diffused. Think of how strong a laser light is — it can even cut through steel. Yet, the only difference between a laser light and a lamp bulb is that the laser light beams are all moving together — completely synchronized and focused on one goal. When you're clear and focused on what you really want to achieve in life, your thoughts and intentions become even more powerful, and you find it easier to let go of all the other less important, perhaps conflicting desires.

Contemplating Spiritual Teachings

Always read stuff that will make you look good if you die in the middle of it.
— P. J. O'Rourke

Words are the threads from which the cloth of your experience is woven. Therefore, it is worth your while to study words, meanings, and ideas that will add beautiful colors to the tapestry of your soul's dance.

Studying spiritual teachings can bring many personal benefits to your journey, including the following:

- Spiritual teachings act as guideposts along your way, helping you to choose what is best to do or not do.

- Spiritual teachings help you to recognize the signs of spiritual progress, giving you greater understanding and appreciation for your journey.

- Spiritual teachings give you new words to use and expanded concepts to consider as you increase your understanding of life.

- Spiritual teachings nurture and bring forth your own ever-fresh spring of spiritual wisdom.

- Spiritual teachings help you realize that you aren't all the things people in this world may think you are — rather, you're a spiritual soul who is finding your way back to wholeness, self-recognition, and remembrance of your true nature.

Even if you don't understand or agree with every spiritual idea that comes your way, the teachings of most spiritual teachers are generally good company for your mind. (Find more tips for studying spiritual teachings and avoiding possible pitfalls in Chapter 5.)

Spiritual teachings can significantly expand your world of possibilities. For example, if you've never even imagined that a particular goal is possible, how can you know that it is what you would really want? Reading the words of great spiritual beings who have reached beyond usual societal complacencies can spark all kinds of new interests, goals, and possibilities in your life.

Don't Forget

Just studying spiritual teachings isn't enough. The important thing about learning higher truths is to transform objective understandings into subjective experience. Unintegrated knowledge is nearly as useless as ignorance!

Here are four steps to expand and incorporate your knowledge of spiritual truths through the stages of study, reflection, application, and integration:

1. **Study by hearing or reading good spiritual teachings.**

2. **Repeatedly reflect on and contemplate the deeper meanings behind the words.**

3. **Apply the teachings to circumstances in your life.**

4. **Awaken to a deeper, more personal understanding of spiritual truth.**

Spiritual teachings are like maps

Spiritual teachings are like maps. They can help guide you on which direction to go, but you still have to travel the way yourself. A map can tell you some of the terrain ahead — that after this river there is a mountain to avoid and then a forest. A map can also help spark your interest in going to visit a certain place. In the same way, spiritual teachings can spark your commitment to personal awakening and help guide you through the paths and obstacles of your spiritual journey.

Nevertheless, when studying spiritual teachings, remember that the map is not the territory!

Unlocking the scripture of your own life

You may read the title "unlocking the scripture of your own life" and wonder how *your* life could possibly be a holy scripture. After all, you're living a more or less ordinary life, and there are so many other people in the world — you're just one more. People live and die every day, so how could your life be special?

According to spirituality, each person is more than special. Each person is a flame of this divine creation. Spirit is in everything, and divinity is everywhere. Therefore, if you're looking to discover and explore this great spirit that exists everywhere, why not start your explorations right at home?

Spiritual Wisdom

Every man's life is a fairy tale, written by God's fingers.
— Hans Christian Andersen

After all, you can know nothing as intimately as your own experiences: your mind, your body, the dreams you have, the deep urges and emotions that sweep through your being, the joys and sorrows you feel, the hopes you carry in your heart, the goodness hidden behind your highest intentions, the confusions you struggle with, and the insights you catch.

Yet, even with all these experiences to draw from, you may still miss many of the subtle and profound aspects of events while you're right in the middle of moving through them.

By taking time to contemplate with an overall view the wealth of lessons that is being offered to you in each moment of your life, you discover and gain more respect for the amazing depths of who you are and all that you think, feel, and believe.

Tapping into the power of contemplative writing

One useful tool for exploring your thoughts and experiences is the practice of contemplative writing – taking time on a regular basis to contemplate and solidify your thoughts in writing. Many seekers find that keeping a spiritual journal inspires and requires them to clarify their thoughts and experiences.

You may choose to write about your past experiences, your present epiphanies, or your hopes and dreams for the future. You may want to contemplate spiritual teachings through writing or to record the visions and intuitions that come when you meditate or pray. Just the action of sitting down to write makes a statement to your wise soul that you are listening.

Consider

Taking notes on your experiences and understandings also gives you a written record that may come in handy during future phases of your journey.

Some days you may write beautiful poetry; other times, sad thoughts, joyful celebrations, petty grumblings, or profound revelations. Contemplative writing can help you to:

- Witness the magnificent and diverse play of your mind

- Get to know all the different aspects that make up you — from your wise soul to perhaps a frustrated inner child.

- Look at life from the artistic perspective of a writer, and come to see your personal dramas as a colorful and divine dance.

- Increase your sense of self-acceptance and self-respect.

Contemplative writing can help you to see your life as a divine and amazing play. Then, whether good or bad events come your way, you can see the events with friendly eyes and say to them, "Thanks for the story."

Ultimately, it doesn't matter whether you plan to publish your writings, although opening yourself to sharing personal thoughts with others can be a powerful experience. Your revelations and breakthroughs may also help readers find greater healing and wisdom in their own lives. Even if it's not your calling to make what you write available to others, it is still in your best interest to take advantage of the power of writing to explore, uplift, and heal your mind and spirit.

Consider

Some people prefer to set strict disciplined schedules for their writing, such as writing a certain number of pages every morning or evening, while others prefer to write only when they feel a need for expression. As with every practice, you have to explore your own nature and decide what style of writing best suits you.

Meditating: Silent Mind, Holy Mind

Spiritual Wisdom

Only when the mind is settled can it become quiet. Only when the mind is quiet can it become still. Only when the mind is still can it see. And only when the mind can see can it reach the mystery of mysteries. This is the process that anyone who practices has to go through. How long it takes is up to the individual.

— Yen-ch'eng

Meditation is the practice of stilling the thought waves of your mind. This practice helps you to:

- Experience yourself as the witness of your own mental processes.

- Turn down the outside noise and inner chattering so that you can hear the voice of God and receive the guidance of your wise soul.

- Understand that you're not your mind — you are the one who is thinking through your mind!

The basic gist of meditation is to plug up your senses by sitting quietly and focusing your attention inside yourself instead of on outer stimulations or mental concerns. Meditation builds a bridge above the choppy waters of your conscious mind, upon which you can reach the higher intelligence within your soul. As this bridge becomes stronger through continuing your practice of meditation, you are guided more clearly by inner wisdom in all areas of your life.

The practice of meditation brings a long list of benefits, from the mundane to the divine (including the attainment of knowing that even mundane things are divine). Meditation helps lower your stress and find greater peace inside yourself. Meditation helps you focus your mind and can make you a better teacher, dancer, artist, singer, engineer, lawyer, mother, father, husband, wife, student, lover, and worker. Meditation helps you to relax, get along better with people, be more creative, make clearer decisions, experience God's presence, and attain supreme enlightenment, liberation, salvation, and nirvana!

And all this can be yours for only $19.95! Just kidding, these benefits are free and available to you just for taking time to sit quietly and focus your attention on the peaceful center of your being.

As you follow a steady practice of sitting for meditation, you'll find that shifting your mind into the state of meditation becomes easier to do. Eventually, you are able to experience the state of meditation even when you're in a crowd and doing whatever usual work or other activities you do. As you continue to meditate, the beneficial state of meditation becomes naturally integrated into your daily awareness.

Meditation: A natural part of life

Most people think of meditation as sitting cross-legged with eyes closed, which is a great way to experience the state of meditation. However, you can also experience the state of meditation through any activity that requires a great deal of focus or peaceful, repetitive actions.

Natural sources of meditation were once built into daily life, before society became as busy and technologically complex as it is today. For centuries, people paid much more attention to nature's magnificent and subtle displays — watching, enjoying, and meditating on her ever-changing beauty and drama.

Bells and whistles:
Spiritual experiences along the way

Some meditators experience various visual, auditory, or other internal visions, sounds, sensations, and understandings when they sit for meditation. These inner experiences may delight your spirit and entice your mind, and can be a great incentive for you to continue your meditation practices. Some meditation traditions suggest that you meditate on these inner experiences, while others tell you to ignore them and rest in emptiness.

Most meditation masters suggest that even if you do enjoy your meditation experiences, you shouldn't get too attached to these inner visions, sounds, and revelations. Being too attached to these enchantments can become a distraction from your greater spiritual quest, as can any attachment to sensory pleasures. Yet, these amazing inner experiences can also fill your heart with inspiration and bring about great spurts of spiritual growth. Brahmananda, one of the great poet sages of India, opens the secret gates to some of these meditation experiences in this poetic description:

No one is playing this delightful song you hear, o dear one. The music within your heart is so sweet, but no one is playing it.

Sit down in a meditation posture and close your ears off from outer sounds. You will hear a soft sound within. Concentrate, and soon you will hear the vibration of a unique kind of music.

In the beginning, you may hear a kind of orchestra, and then each instrument will be heard separately: the bell, conch, flute, veena, and drums.

As days go by, the sound gets louder and the body starts trembling. A drop of nectar will fall into your palate and fill you with great bliss.

Body consciousness disappears and a light dances both within and without. Only a rare saint can confirm what I am saying.

A peaceful, meditative focus was also present in our ancestors' lives through all the daily tasks that have since been replaced by modern technology and convenience, such as churning butter, milking cows, plowing fields, and chopping wood. These naturally meditative actions offered regular times of peaceful repose, steady movements, and communion with nature.

Modern life brings fewer occasions for routine meditative actions. Many people today are rushing from one responsibility to another, having complex interactions with other people, dwelling on fears of job security, preparing for meetings, going through e-mail requests, maintaining their houses, cars, dogs, children, and financial situations, all while thinking about vacation plans, eating schedules, desires for recognition, concerns about weight and hair styles, and so on. Personal energies are pouring out through countless spigots of worldly life, leaving many people feeling depleted and distracted. However, it doesn't have to be this way for you.

Take the floodlights of energy that are going out into your daily life and turn them around, redirecting these energy flows back into yourself through meditation.

Sit quietly and reap the benefits from having all this extra energy in your body, mind, and spirit. Allow the spiritual energy of meditation to carry you into more meaningful explorations of your inner world and soul. Let your mind become so calm that it reveals the peaceful sky of spiritual awareness. Invite the great universal sun of divine grace to shine through everything you think, say, and do.

Spirituality in Action

Here's an example of how to meditate on a spiritual concept. Sit quietly, close your eyes, focus your mind, and dive into the essence of these words: *This moment right now is eternal. Every moment is eternal.* Allow your mind to move beyond the limitations of time and expand into the eternal presence. If you'd like, you can mentally say these lines with your inhalations and exhalations. As you breathe in, think, "This moment is eternal," and as you breathe out, think, "Every moment is eternal."

Relaxing into meditation

The basic practice of meditation involves sitting quietly and turning the energy that usually pours out through your senses back into yourself. You close your eyes and focus your mind inward. From there, you may want to pay attention to the flow of your breath. Its natural rhythm will help keep your mind focused and quiet. If thoughts come up, the best thing to do is to just let them float by and keep your mind focused on your breath.

Spirituality in Action

Here are three steps you can use to meditate:

1. **Watch your breath.**

2. **Let your mind become quiet.**

3. **Become the witness of your mind.** See whether you can watch your thoughts pass by without identifying with them. Remember that you aren't your thoughts; rather, you're the one who is thinking them!

Starting a meditation practice

You may want to start by meditating for 15 minutes or so in the morning. You can start with a shorter meditation and gradually extend the time until you've reached a comfortable but substantial time, such as one hour of meditation each day, or every few days, or once a week.

Don't Forget

Some meditation is better than no meditation. As with every spiritual practice, I suggest that you try different methods and schedules to see which ones work best for you.

Here are a few more suggestions for beginning your practice of meditation:

Consider meditating in the early morning because:

- Your mind is usually quieter when you first awaken from sleep. You've just had a long rest and have also gone through deep inner states of consciousness, such as the dream state and what spiritual scriptures call the *deep sleep state*, where your mind is completely quiet and still.

- The world is most quiet early in the morning. Because your personal energy is connected with the energies around you, meditating in a quiet city or town can help ease you into a more peaceful state.

- The sun represents brightness and activity and affects your brain and internal rhythms. While the world is still dark or when the sun is just beginning to dawn, your mind is biologically programmed to be still.

Consider

Whether in the morning or any other time, it is beneficial to meditate at the same time of day if possible, especially when you're first learning to meditate. Keeping a steady meditation schedule prepares your mind, body, and spirit to be in a meditative state during that time. Just as lunchtime brings inspiration to eat, so meditation time can bring the inspiration to meditate. Your mind is a creature of habit, so you may as well use that tendency for your benefit!

- **You may want to use a special set of clothes just for meditation, as well as a special meditation cushion or cloth to sit on.** Meditating in and on the same fabrics can help your meditation practice because when you meditate, the energy in and around your body becomes more spiritualized, concentrated, and powerful. Although this spiritual energy is invisible and not fully detectable by technological devices, you will likely be able to feel it moving in and around your body. This energy also permeates the clothes you wear and the seat you are using, giving them a special bath in your meditation energy. The peaceful spiritual energy of meditation that gathers in your clothes and seat helps you to glide more smoothly into meditation the next time.

- **If you have the means and space, you may want to set aside a special room or corner of a room where only meditation takes place.** Create your own holy space, either in a room or in the corner of a room. Your spiritual energy accumulates in that area and makes it easier for you to meditate. Meditating repeatedly in the same place is like putting your meditation energy in the bank — except in this case, your balance keeps growing the more you use it.

- **Meditate regularly.** If you wash your hands carefully with antibacterial soap and then go outside and touch unclean things, you can't say, "Well, I cleaned my hands extra carefully this morning, so they don't need more cleaning now." If you eat a big delicious meal and feel completely full, you can't just say, "Well, I'm full now, so I should never need to eat again." If you exercise regularly for a year and then stop exercising for ten years, your muscles will eventually lose their strength. In the same way, even though one meditation session can be greatly beneficial to your spiritual journey, you benefit most from meditation when you practice it regularly.

- **Consider meditating with a group of other meditators.** A room full of concentrated, quiet minds can help you keep your mind still for several reasons:

  - Meditating in a group inspires you to sit still, because you won't want to disturb anyone else's meditation by getting up or moving around.

  - A powerful energy permeates the atmosphere in a place where people are meditating. If you have a group of meditators sitting together — each creating and adding to this energy — the whole room fills with their spiritual energy, making it easier to absorb your mind into meditation.

  - Expert meditators have even more of this powerful meditation energy, and it's contagious. Therefore, meditating in the presence of expert meditators is a good idea.

Even though meditation energies are contagious, don't get caught up in thinking about how much energy you're going to get from others. I know some who have gotten greedy for this meditation energy — and, of course, greed is not a quality you want to cultivate on your spiritual journey!

What is flapping?

Four monks were meditating in a monastery. Suddenly, the prayer flag on the roof started flapping. The youngest monk came out of his meditation and said: "The flag is flapping."

A more experienced monk said: "The wind is flapping."

A third monk who had been there for more than 20 years said: "The mind is flapping."

The fourth monk, who was the eldest, said, visibly annoyed: "Mouths are flapping!"

Sitting correctly when you meditate

Sit still, either on a straight-backed chair with your feet on the floor, or with your legs crossed. Yogis usually suggest sitting in a cross-legged position for meditation. Cross-legged configurations help circulate the energy within your subtle system, making your body like a closed circuit. A lot of meditation energy leaves your body through your feet and hands, so crossing your legs helps to keep the energy from your feet moving back up into your body instead of moving out through the soles of your feet to dissipate into the air.

Personally, I prefer to sit in a posture called *half-lotus,* in which my legs are crossed, with one leg resting on top of the other, and one foot resting on top of the other thigh. Some limber folks are able to sit in what is called *full-lotus* posture, with their legs crossed and both feet on top.

If these fancy positions aren't your cup of tea, you can just sit in a regular cross-legged posture or perhaps kneel with your calves folded under you and your derriere resting either directly on your feet or on a pillow tucked between your seat and your feet. If sitting on the floor is difficult for you, you can also sit comfortably upright in a chair with both of your feet flat on the floor.

Consider

If needed, you can sit on or support the small of your back with a pillow. You can even meditate while lying down in bed, although habit may bring you into a state of sleep instead of meditation.

When sitting for meditation, you want to keep your spine as straight as possible while staying relaxed and comfortable. The spiritual energy is said to move up through your spine, so a steady, straight, and relaxed posture can help create a good space for that energy to flow through your spine.

You may also want to touch your thumb of each hand to the first finger, which allows some of the energy that would normally flow out of your hands to circulate back inward, bathing your body in more of your own meditation energy and spiritual life force.

Spirituality in Action

Try bringing the tips of your thumbs and first fingers together. See whether you can feel the increased energy flowing from your thumb into your first finger and vice-versa. Or you can bring the palms of your hands together in a prayer pose and feel the energy connect there.

If you want to quiet your mind during the day, you can meditate outside in nature or even on a bus, train, or at work (during a break! Signed, your boss). Adding short moments of peaceful pause to your day can help you integrate the benefits of meditation into your daily life.

One of the closest experiences many people have to meditation is when they take a short nap. You know how it feels to just settle down and relax your mind into that peaceful sea of your own inner consciousness during an afternoon nap?

If you're lucky, during a short nap, you'll experience that one moment of shift where your mind is reset and filled with new, vibrant energy. This shift is similar to an experience you can also have in meditation — where you may sit quietly for a whole hour just to experience that one precious moment of divine shift of spiritual rejuvenation.

Be Careful

As with everything else, the key is moderation. You don't want to be extreme by meditating too much or your mind may become a little spacey. Let your practice develop gradually and naturally.

A global awareness meditation

Sit quietly and contemplate all the things that are going on around the earth right now.

You may want to sit outside for this exercise so that you can hear the sounds of nature and feel the gentle rumble of the earth under your seat. Let your thoughts calm into a deep awareness of all that is happening on this planet.

Become gently aware of a world filled with people laughing, crying, yelling, loving, sleeping, dreaming, giving, and taking, with dogs barking, and wild animals killing, being killed, and loving and protecting their young. Remember all the insects, fish, animals, plants, and people that are working, sleeping, eating and starving, living and dying — all on this very earth upon which you sit quietly. Offer a prayer of blessings to the whole world from within your powerful state of meditation.

Chapter 9

Nourishing Your Spirit

Topics in this Chapter:

* Entering the holy space of spiritual union
* Praying for yourself and others
* Honoring sacred images
* Singing with devotion

You are an emanation of spirit that has descended as you into the events and circumstances of your physical, mental, and emotional life. Because of your divine heritage, the material things of this world can never fully satisfy the longings and aspirations of your soul. Only spiritual nourishment will fill the deepest parts of your being.

Be Careful

Don't spend your entire lifetime collecting baubles of this earth that can dissolve and disappear with the slightest gust of karmic winds. Take time to connect with that eternal, loving, divine spirit that exists inside of you and behind the appearances of this world.

If all you do after reading this book is to add a one-minute pause somewhere in your daily schedule for connecting with spirit, then you'll have gotten your money's worth. With a combination of self-effort and divine grace, may you be fortunate enough to enter the holy experience of union with spirit.

Think about spirit. Relate to spirit. Speak to spirit. Listen to spirit. Remember spirit. Feel spirit. Love spirit. Enjoy spirit. Entertain spirit. Receive blessings from spirit. Learn to trust spirit. Learn to see spirit. Learn to be spirit.

Understanding Spiritual Communion

Spiritual Wisdom

I Am That I Am.

— God, Exodus 3:14

Spiritual communion is the experience of being united with the divine. Spiritual communion involves absorbing your limited self-identification into the divine spirit that exists beyond your mind. You move beyond the limitations of your mind and enter into the awareness of your greater self — which just so happens to be one in essence with the great Universal Soul.

Here, the word *communion* is not referring to the Catholic sacramental ritual, but to an experience of spiritual union that arises inside your awareness like a blissful, shining, spiritual sun. This sun of divine presence has always existed inside you in its full effulgence, but for most people, it is hidden by many clouds of restless thoughts, self preoccupations, and worldly concerns.

Once you've cleared the clutter of restless thoughts through contemplation and turned your attention inside yourself through meditative practices, the light of divine presence becomes naturally revealed in your awareness. Of course, getting those pesky clouds of restless thoughts to clear may require quite a few efforts and practices! (See Chapter 8 for tips on clearing the clutter of restless thoughts.)

Here are some ways that spiritual communion can manifest:

- Your heart becomes unfettered by day-to-day worries and tribulations as your self-identification shifts from focusing on the limited details of your life and expands into greater fields of universal awareness (while you still take good care of the necessities and responsibilities of your life.)

- You feel the presence of the divine with and within you – as you sit quietly for meditation and even as you travel through all the twists and turns of life.

- Your sense of being separate from everything else is dissolved as you experience the state of union with the same spirit that pervades everything.

- You take care of the responsibilities at hand while savoring the delicious streams of love and eternal awareness that flow through your heart and soul.

Think of how good it feels to be holding and hugging someone you love very much, with the warmth of love throbbing in your heart. With spiritual communion, you're not only hugging and holding someone you love, but you are hugging and holding love itself.

When you first touch the space of communion with inner spirit, you may have a sense of familiarity, a sense of "Oh, yes, I remember this!" After all, according to the spiritual sages, you've always been one with divine spirit — but like the lion cub described in Chapter 2, you've forgotten your divine heritage.

Create a space to welcome this experience of union with the divine. Open the door of your heart and absorb yourself in prayer and devotional meditation. Sing a song to honor the divine; give thanks as you light a candle; set up an altar; play uplifting music; offer flowers; or burn some fragrant incense. Nourish your connection with spirit through devotional practices, and experience the great blessings of spiritual communion and divine love.

Spiritual Wisdom

Though I speak with the tongues of men and of angels, but have not love, I have become sounding brass or a clanging cymbal. And though I have the gift of prophecy, and understand all mysteries and all knowledge, and though I have all faith, so that I could remove mountains, but have not love, I am nothing.

— 1 Corinthians 13-1-2

Prayer: Touching the Sacred

Think of prayer as a way for you to plug the "laptop computer" of your individual self into the big universal "computer mainframe" of Divine Grace. Prayer is an active communication with God through whatever form or formlessness you relate to on your personal journey.

People pray for different reasons, including:

- Asking for something you want for yourself
- Asking for something that will benefit others
- Giving loving thanks to God for what you've already received
- Asking and listening for divine guidance on what steps you should take
- Offering your mind, heart, life, and soul into the sacred presence of spirit

Prayers are declarations to God and yourself that powerfully affirm the connection of your individual soul with the divine soul, and your individual will with the divine will. After all, if you didn't think your prayers had any impact, you probably wouldn't pray, right? If you didn't think your blessings were actually going to help someone, why would you bother to give them?

God does respond to your prayers

A fellow was climbing a tree when suddenly he slipped and grabbed at a branch that caught him and held him out so he was hanging over a huge cliff. Soon the man felt himself getting exhausted and unable to hold on. He looked up to the heavens and cried out: "God, help me, please, help me."

All of a sudden, the clouds parted, and a voice boomed out from on high. "Let go!" said the voice.

The guy paused, looked up at heaven once more, and asked: "Is there anyone else up there?"

Spiritual Wisdom

As long as you believe that God is only in heaven and does not fill the earth — let your words be few. Only when you come to know that you too contain His presence — only then can you begin to pray.

—Hasidic prayer

Spiritually aware prayers are kind of a "Thy will be done," plus a little extra. You enter into an active state of open communication with your image or sense of God and speak to that image or sense of the divine in words and feelings. You may have a special request — for yourself, for a friend, or for the entire world: "O Lord, please help my friend, please heal this world, please protect me, please guide me to find the right career, please take away my sadness, please help me to gain a spiritual vision, please take care of this person who has just died, please let things go smoothly and in accordance with everyone's best interests."

When you pray, always remember that God knows best, and that what you ultimately want is whatever is best. In true prayer, you'll find beneath every request the whisper of "Thy will be done." By keeping your prayers centered in faith and surrender to "Thy will be done," you're allowing the universal will to use your positive thoughts, intentions, and energies in the best way.

Connecting through prayer

Asking God for the needs of life is one more way to connect with the divine. Even if you have a surrender and trust that God's will is done regardless of whether you ask for anything specific, you can still communicate your needs and ask for blessings with a spirit of faith and surrender. Communicating with the great universal creative Consciousness is a good thing to do, whether you're asking for help or giving thanks.

Regardless of the specific words and thoughts you use in prayer, taking time to connect with the divine presence is likely to bring good energy and positive effects into whatever situations you're praying for.

Consider

Don't just pray for some limited concept of what you think is available in your life. Give spirit a chance to surprise you and outshine your expectations.

After all, how can anybody really know exactly what to pray for? (See Chapter 3 for details on knowing what you don't know.) What if you pray and ask that you or someone else gets a particular job when there's a much better career opportunity for you or the other person just around the corner? With hindsight, you would thank God for not answering that prayer. (Well, technically, the prayer was answered, but the answer was "No.")

Therefore, the best way to improve someone's lot in life, including your own, is to send positive blessings while trusting the divine universal perfection to use your blessings in the best way.

Spiritual Wisdom

That prayer has great power, which a person makes with all his might. It makes a sour heart sweet, a sad heart merry, a poor heart rich, a foolish heart wise, a timid heart brave, a sick heart well, a blind heart full of sight, a cold heart ardent. It draws down the great God into the little heart, it drives the hungry soul up into the fullness of God, it brings together two lovers, God and the soul, in a wondrous place where they speak much of love.
— Mechthild of Magdeburg

Do you pray for the world?

When you hear about an earthquake or other disaster around the world, do you pray for the people involved? When you hear that a hurricane may hit the coast and cause devastation, do you pray for nature to be gentle?

There's no need to feel guilty if you don't pray to keep disasters away, but it gives a good chance for self-examination to contemplate why you don't.

- Do you choose not to pray because you don't realize your own power of prayer?

- Or do you choose not to pray because you trust God completely and feel no need to petition to change His will?

Giving blessings to others

Spiritual Wisdom

It is one of the most beautiful compensations of this life that no man can sincerely try to help another without helping himself.

— Ralph Waldo Emerson

Scientists have spent millions of dollars to research whether prayer has a statistical, measurable effect upon those who are ill. Although these kinds of experiments are tricky due to uncontrollable variables, many of them do indicate some beneficial effect of prayer upon an ill person, even if that person doesn't know whether they're in the group being prayed for or the group not being prayed for. Of course, one can assume that even patients who were in the group *not* being officially prayed for by research assistants probably still had loved ones praying for them – this variable is one example of the uncontrollable elements that can throw a cog into scientific studies of spiritual phenomena.

Nevertheless, the generally positive data on the efficacy of prayer suggests that you have a lot more power to give blessings than you may realize. Even if you don't have enough money or medical knowledge to help someone in need, you can still give blessings through your power of prayer. You can even give blessings to others in the secret, sacred space of your heart — without anyone knowing.

Now, if you were to realize your own power and give prayers and blessings to the world, and if every other person did the same, just imagine what a paradise this world would be!

Spirituality in Action

This exercise can help you explore your ideas about bestowing blessings: Practice walking around town or a shopping mall for an hour, imagining that you have the power to give blessings to anyone you choose. Who do you bless? Why? Because they look happy? Because they look troubled? Because they smile at you? This exercise is an opportunity to explore your concepts about who you believe deserves blessings and also to consider whether some of those concepts may be blocking you from receiving all the blessings you deserve. A good way to go is to bless everyone (including yourself!).

Be your own house of worship

Religious priests, pastors, ministers, and monks often perform rituals and ceremonies to bless the events and milestones in the lives of their congregations. But you don't have to wait for a priest to bless the events and actions of your life. Bless yourself and the world right now and anytime.

Spiritual Wisdom

Here's a Buddhist blessing that is also a prayer for peace:

May all beings everywhere plagued with sufferings of body and mind quickly be freed from their illnesses.

May those frightened cease to be afraid, and may those bound be free.

May the powerless find power, and may people think of befriending one another.

May those who find themselves in trackless, fearful wildernesses — the children, the aged, the unprotected — be guarded by beneficent celestials, and may they quickly attain Buddhahood.

Bring the power of blessing to all of your daily activities. Before you send a resume for an important job possibility, or make an offer on a house, or mail your proposal to that book agent, or e-mail someone you'd really like to get to know, first pause and bless what you are sending. Invoke spirit and ask that whatever happens be best for you and all concerned.

Worshipping God in Form

Ultimately, God is beyond this physical world. Yet, here you are in it. How can a person who is in a physical form relate to the nonphysical nature of divine spirit?

People who have physical forms are used to relating to things that have form, and are not so used to contemplating something as nebulous as divine spirit. Therefore, spiritual seekers throughout time have worshipped God through forms. Some have worshipped God as the sun or mountains or through archetypal, symbol-laden forms and figures such as the Hindu and Greek pantheons of gods and goddesses. Some worship the cross that represents the sacrifice of Jesus, and some worship people who have attained great spiritual stature.

 **Consider**

Worshipping images and figures that represent Divine Spirit can help teach you how to relate to and communicate with the sometimes-elusive Divine Spirit that exists within and beyond everything.

Creating a sacred space

Not only can you add touches of spirit to your home atmosphere by including artwork, candles, rituals, incense, devotional music, and natural elements, but you can also set up an altar or mini-temple that can represent the sacred space of your devotional heart. This sacred space can be a shelf or table of any size, perhaps covered with some decorative cloth.

Place on your altar objects that carry spiritual meaning for you. These items may be statues, paintings, icons, photos, candles, holy water, sacred oils, bells, crystals, gems, flowers, and whatever other personal or symbolic objects help to open your heart and focus your mind on spirit.

Consider

One great way to begin each day is to stand or sit before your altar and to fold your hands, bow your head, or otherwise honor the forms and representations of divinity you've chosen to include. Some like to wave a flame clockwise around each image – a common tradition in Indian temples. Offer the day to grace, ask for a specific blessing, or just give thanks for all the blessings you already have.

You may also want to set up a meditation space right in front of your altar so that you can sit in front of these representations of spirit while turning your attention inward toward the spirit that also exists inside of your own divine form.

A potential downside to worshipping divine forms

The ashram I used to live in was filled with representations of the divine in form. Its beautiful gardens included statues from many different spiritual and religious traditions, and inside the buildings and temples, you'd find reminders of the divine around every corner, with photos, statues, candles, and other representations of gods, gurus, saints and sages.

After leaving the ashram and moving to Los Angeles, I continued this practice of worshipping the divine in form by covering the walls and shelves of my apartment with photos and statues of divine forms. I also placed a photo of my guru in my car, in an elegant metal frame that I superglued to the dashboard. For several years, this photo was a natural part of my daily drive.

One day, I took my car to a car wash and was surprised to have it returned with my guru's photo frame broken off the dashboard. As I drove away, my mind was racing, thinking about how I would have to get a new frame as soon as possible.

At that point, I remembered to center myself and looked at my thoughts with a more objective view. I saw that I was feeling less protected in that moment than I had felt just a few minutes earlier when my guru's photo was still glued to the dashboard. At that moment, I decided that if I was basing my trust in the divine on whether or not a photo was on the dashboard of my car, then I shouldn't have one there at all.

Therefore, if you do choose to practice worshipping forms, be sure not to get into the same trap that I was in. Don't allow worship to become just one more way to get attached and snared by the expectations and fears of this world. Use a divine image to bring out the best, the greatest, and the most sublime in yourself. Feel devotion for the greatness of God through whatever form you worship; and understand that the divinity you see in any form is always your own divinity shining forth and reflecting back through the many mirrors of this world.

Singing to the Divine

Just think of the blissful, peaceful harmony that comes from good spiritual music. When you sing to the divine, you're using your voice as an instrument to make a beautiful offering from spirit into spirit. The divine universe has given you this instrument of your body and voice, and you play it to express love and respect for that divine presence of God.

Even if you don't think you have a great singing voice — perhaps certain talent judges might critique your tone or call your singing "pitchy" — don't worry about their real or imagined assessments. Sing to spirit with openhearted love and enthusiasm. In "Devotional Idol" singing, the most important points are given for your sincerity, devotion, love, focus, and surrender into the blissfulness of spirit.

Traditions around the world have sung their scriptures, from the Koran to the Torah to Psalms, the Bhagavad Gita, and many other texts. Whether you prefer to sing Latin hymns, Native American chants, Sanskrit mantras, Gregorian chants, or gospel songs, the practice of devotional singing opens your heart and mind to divine and joyful experiences.

Why I love devotional singing

When I lived in an Indian-based ashram, many hours of our daily schedule were devoted to singing to God — with fast chants, slow chants, and elaborate texts scattered throughout each day, from early morning until bedtime.

While following this schedule for many years, the transformational power of chanting became evident to me. I could feel the mantra power tangibly during each chant and could also see beneficial long-term effects that chanting and devotional singing had brought in soothing, invigorating, and empowering my mind, heart, and soul.

During those years and since, I've found devotional singing of various kinds to be a great way to connect with spirit, and an amazing bridge to achieving spiritual happiness.

What's more beautiful than hearing a mother sing a lullaby to her child? What's more potent than a group of men singing together in strong deep voices filled with conviction? What is more heart opening than singing from your soul to the omnipotent and omnipresent God?

When you sing to God, you're loving God. You're making a statement that with all the other things you could be doing with that time — working on your career, cleaning your house, going out with friends, or watching television — you're choosing to spend time to offer a devotional song to the Divine.

Singing with a group

Where two or more are gathered in my name, there am I in the midst of them.
— Matthew 18:20

Inspiring words about the power of divine song

Singing is a universal way to praise and connect with God. Here are some examples of the importance of spiritual singing from several traditions, beginning with a message for those of you who think you can't sing:

- If you can walk, you can dance. If you can talk, you can sing.
    — Traditional African saying

- There are halls in the heavens above that open but to the voice of song.
    — The Zohar

- I will sing thy name, I will drink thy name, and get all drunk, oh, with thy name.
    — Yogananda Paramahansa

- O God, I will sing a new song to you; with a ten-stringed lyre I will chant your praise.
    — Psalms 144:9

Group devotional singing or chanting is a powerful practice to support and nourish your spiritual quest. You can find devotional singing in various church and temple programs, from singing Latin vespers at Catholic churches and monasteries to the ever-growing popularity of Indian kirtan chanting in yoga studios.

The group dynamic is especially helpful for releasing the joyful spirit of spiritual singing and chanting. There is something about group singing that creates a uniquely sweet power. When you have a group singing or chanting together with devotion, the entire room becomes filled with a great spiritual energy.

Singing and your breath

Another side benefit of chanting is that it gives you a natural *pranayama*, or breath control exercise (see Chapter 7). When you sing devotional texts, phrases, or stanzas, your breathing becomes naturally deep and harmonious as you regulate your breaths to support the singing.

Try group chanting at least once, in whatever traditions appeal to you. Singing together with love to honor the Divine — what could nourish your spirit better than that?

Part Three:

Living a Spiritual Life

Chapter 10

Cultivating Spiritual Virtues

Topics in this Chapter:

*   Improving your life from the inside out
*   Letting virtues arise naturally
*   Unfolding your honesty, compassion, and humility

Spirituality is not just about learning new ideas or doing spiritual practices. It also requires applying what you learn to your daily life. Spiritual is as spiritual does.

Thoughts and actions that bring your soul and the world higher are called virtuous. Hold your decisions and actions up to the light of spiritual wisdom and ask: Is this action right? Is it kind? Is it helpful? Is it just? Is it harmonious? Is it educational? Is this action or decision taking into consideration the bigger picture of the world? Is it enlightened, intelligent, beneficial, honest, humble, and compassionate? Do your actions express the best in yourself rather than the lower pulls of the senses or base emotions? Are your actions being guided by spirit? Are they offered with a clear mind and a pure heart?

Don't worry if you haven't always been virtuous in the past. Today is a new, fresh day. If you weren't spiritually virtuous yesterday, you can be spiritually virtuous today. If you didn't act with spiritual wisdom yesterday, today you can be spiritually wise. If you were a thief, today you can stop being a thief. If you've done something wrong in the past, today you can do things right.

Discovering How Spiritual Awareness Brings Virtues

Although you can and should make efforts to act in a virtuous way, the good news is that spiritual awareness itself inspires you to be naturally virtuous.

The more you understand the spiritual nature of this world and the deeper unity of all things, the more it makes sense to act with honesty, compassion, surrender, and humility. With a more universal vision, spiritual virtues are not so much qualities that you must force yourself to express, but are seen as the best and perhaps only way to respond to the world.

Here are some initial tips for increasing your spiritual vision and virtues:

- Take time to contemplate and consider your priorities and always strive to put first things first.

- Do your best to be more helpful than harmful – not only to yourself or to people you like, but for every single person and living being on this planet (including this living planet!) Stay loyal to the ultimate good.

- Move beyond black-and-white thinking to a bigger, more inclusive awareness. Big-picture thinking is part of spiritual "growing up." Realize that not everything fits into neat little boxes.

- I'll let Buddha give the last of these virtue tips, as he taught his followers quite simply to, "Abstain from evil, do good, and purify the mind."

Jesus also offered advice to his followers about the importance of not just being a groupie but also putting his words into practice and building a strong foundation for their spiritual journeys:

Spiritual Wisdom

Why do you call me, 'Lord, Lord,' and do not do what I say? I will show you what he is like who comes to me and hears my words and puts them into practice. He is like a man building a house, who dug down deep and laid the foundation on rock. When a flood came, the torrent struck that house but could not shake it, because it was well built. But the one who hears my words and does not put them into practice is like a man who built a house on the ground without a foundation. The moment the torrent struck that house, it collapsed and its destruction was complete.

— Luke 6:46-49 (Jesus)

Watching virtues arise naturally

Once you understand, realize, and experience the greatness that is your divine birthright, spiritual virtues come naturally. Therefore, the easiest path to cultivating virtues is to stay focused on your life as an expression of pure spirit. With an expanded spiritual awareness, you naturally speak, think, and act with greater strength, confidence, self-respect, and integrity.

Spiritual awareness guides you to move in harmony with this conscious universe. A solid spiritual nature protects you from the muddy waters of desire, greed, and other not-so-spiritual qualities that can bring you down.

One way universal guidance increases your virtues is by presenting you with situations that challenge you to rise into greater levels of honesty, goodness, generosity, and purity. When your intention is focused on spiritual development and growth, life's challenges also come along with the grace to benefit and evolve from them.

Your inner peace, spiritual happiness, and self-respect are powerful tools for growing into new virtues. Have you noticed how when you're feeling happy and full of love, you're naturally kinder and more generous with the people around you? In the same way, when you develop greater respect and love for yourself, you discover, day by day and year after year, that you naturally become more virtuous. And these virtues will be real — not plastic, manufactured, or ready to fall apart at the first gust of the winds of challenge and temptation.

Spirituality in Action

Krishna's list of virtues

Chapter 16 of the *Bhagavad Gita* offers a powerful list of spiritual qualities to contemplate and cultivate. You can use these positive words to create an empowering affirmation. Go through this list of virtues and say, "I have fearlessness; I have purity of heart; I have steadfastness in higher knowledge," and so on:

"Fearlessness, purity of heart, steadfastness in higher knowledge, charity, control of the senses, sacrifice, study of scriptures, austerity, straightforwardness, harmlessness, truth, absence of anger, renunciation, peacefulness, absence of crookedness, compassion towards beings, freedom from covetousness, gentleness, modesty, absence of fickleness, vigor, forgiveness, fortitude, purity, absence of hatred, absence of pride."

Recognizing the signs of a sage

Spiritual sages tend to live by their own rules, or more accurately, by divine rules that have been revealed to them through their inner wisdom, intuition, and deep-souled guidance.

When most people hear that someone is living by his or her own rules, they assume that these personally designed rules would be more lax and easy than common, traditional societal rules. However, spiritual sages generally hold themselves to a higher degree of virtue and discipline than most people do.

Although different spiritual sages have different styles, ideas, and behaviors, certain qualities are usually present in one form or another, including obvious virtues, such as kindness, honesty, and purity of thought and action. An ancient text called *Yoga Vasishta* describes in more detail some of the signs and qualities that often manifest in the ways and actions of spiritual sages.

Even if you don't consider yourself to be a spiritual sage, you can still contemplate these qualities from the *Yoga Vasishta* and hold them as aspirations and signposts in your own unfolding spiritual journey:

- **Although externally engaged in worldly actions, the sage has no attachment in his mind to any objects whatsoever.** He behaves like an ideal citizen and friend of all. Outwardly, he's busy, but at heart, he's calm and quiet. He's free from the restrictions of caste, creed, stage of life, custom, and scriptures. He doesn't work to get anything for himself. His face is never without the luster of cheerfulness on it.

- **In the company of the humble, the sage is humble.** He plays as a child in the company of children; he is a youth among the young; and he acts as an old man in the company of the aged ones. He is full of courage in the party of the courageous people and shares the misery of the miserable ones.

- **There is nothing the sage has to achieve.** He therefore performs and gives up actions without much concern, like children do. In spite of his being occupied with actions appropriate to the time, place, and circumstances, he isn't touched by the pleasure or pain arising from them. He is full of mercy and magnanimity even when surrounded by enemies. He regards his activities as a part of the cosmic movement and performs them without any personal desire. He never hankers for the pleasures that aren't in his hand, but enjoys all those he has. The idea of "I" and "mine," of something to be achieved and something to be avoided, has died within him.

- **No purpose of the sage is served by any activity or by abstaining from activity.** He, therefore, does as the occasion suits him. He's a great worker. He works without any anxiety, egoistic feeling, pride, or impurity of heart. He's a great enjoyer. He doesn't discard the pleasure he has or desire the pleasure he doesn't have. He finds equal pleasure in old age, death, misery, and poverty, and in ruling over an empire.

- **The life of a liberated sage is really the noblest and happiest life.** From him, goodness is scattered all around. Having seen him, having heard about him, having met him, and having remembered him, all creatures feel delighted.

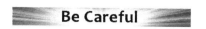
Be Careful

Even as you strive to become more virtuous, don't get too stuck in judging how virtuous your actions are or how unvirtuous other people's actions are. Although virtuous actions are important for a powerful and positive spiritual journey, these virtues shouldn't distract you from focusing on the divine spirit that exists beyond this material world of both virtuous and nonvirtuous deeds. As the poet Jelalud'Din Rumi's invitation says, *"Beyond the ideas of right-doing and wrong-doing, there lies a field. I'll meet you there."*

Spiritual Wisdom

Acting from conscience

Here Swami Sivananda describes some of the common ways people approach situations when they don't have the benefit of spiritual virtues, ending with the right answer coming from the power of self-reflection and assessment that is called conscience. Whenever you're about to make a decision in your life, you can check your motivations against this list:

"Cowardice asks, 'Is it safe?'

Avarice asks, 'Is there any gain in it?'

Vanity asks, 'Can I become great?'

Lust asks, 'Is there pleasure in it?'

But conscience asks, 'Is it right?' Conscience prompts you to choose the right way instead of the wrong and informs you that you ought to do the right thing."

Understanding how one virtue leads to another

As you become more aware of your spiritual nature and the spirituality of all things, you naturally begin to think and act in greater accordance with the higher good of all. Here are some ways each virtue can inspire more virtues, beginning with the search for higher truth that has brought you to read this book:

- **As you seek truth,** your own sense of honesty strengthens, clearing the way for you to see more clearly into your pure, spiritual heart.

- **As you look into your heart,** you discover and appreciate the presence of spirit and become more content with who you are, how you are, and where you are.

- **As you become more content,** worldly attachments and desires naturally dissolve into the light of your peaceful, happy heart.

- **As you become free from limited desires,** your faith and surrender increase, inviting the beneficence of universal grace to guide your steps.

- **As you allow yourself to be moved and guided by divine grace,** your humility keeps the dastardly ego from tripping your steps (find more on this dastardly ego in Chapter 3).

- **When your ego is kept at bay,** your tendency toward dissatisfaction expands into gratitude for the perfection of everything.

- **When you glimpse this universal perfection,** you attain the gem of equal vision, seeing that everything is made of divine spirit.

This list shows how each virtue leads to and nourishes the next. Of course, you can contemplate many more big and small virtues besides those named in this chapter. I simply present a few of my favorites to help get the ball rolling.

Gaining the Power of Truth through Honesty

It wasn't by chance that I chose to put honesty first in this exploration of virtues. In my ever-so-humble opinion (don't worry, humility is next!), honesty is paramount on the spiritual journey. After all, the goal of that journey is to attain the highest truth.

Some people make efforts to appear more virtuous than they really are, which isn't quite honest. This tendency brings up a subtle distinction — the difference between making efforts to become more virtuous and merely putting on an outer show without developing true inner virtues. If you put on a plastic smile to hide the sadness you're feeling, that can't be called true happiness, and if you appear to perform good actions just for show, that is not true virtue.

Some have been tempted to substitute an outer-bandage approach of *appearing* virtuous instead of creating real, deep, lasting, and profound spiritual transformation. Here are several problems with this acting-more-virtuous-than-you-are approach:

- **You can't hide who you really are.** Along with the fact that you live in a conscious, intelligent universe that knows what is and is not truth, your subconscious thoughts are also constantly being expressed to other people through everything that comes out of you, including your body language, subliminal speech patterns, and all the ways you express yourself. Even though others may see only what you want them to see on a conscious level, and even if you may seem to fool others by being dishonest, you can be sure that their inner intuition (and the universe itself) is quite aware of any incongruities between your apparent outer virtues and your perhaps not-quite-so inner virtues.

- **The false can obstruct the real.** If you display outer virtues that aren't based on inner sincerity, you may come to think you're virtuous, and others may think you're virtuous. However, this false presentation can actually keep you from doing the inner work necessary for true transformation. Obviously, you need to act appropriately and keep your thoughts, comments, and actions more or less "in the box" when you're in public situations, such as work environments. However, in the privacy of your own home and mind, you can look honestly at what you really feel and think about things in your life. Otherwise, your false image of peacefulness may keep you from doing the inner work required to grow from that circumstance and find true peacefulness. With a happy spirit, you can see and acknowledge the truth of who you are and what you feel so you can grow steadily into greater fields of virtue. The virtue of honesty in the form of self-examination ensures that when you display virtues, they are real.

- **Only true virtues will be there when you need them.** Of course, acting in a virtuous way is always a good idea and tends to inspire more spiritual awareness in your life. Acting happy and thinking positive thoughts can help bring more happiness and positive actions into your life. However, unless you develop virtues that are real and true, you won't be able to apply them to all the events that come up. Remember, life is going to throw some surprises your way — it's inevitable. If you're honest with yourself, whatever real virtues you have will be ready to guide you through all the intricate mazes of this strange ride called life.

Be Careful

Although honesty is a great virtue, it should come with a measure of kindness and consideration. In the name of honesty, you shouldn't just unleash whatever unsavory thoughts and feelings may be bubbling up inside you upon whomever is unfortunate enough to be the one triggering them. The idea is to be honest and decent at the same time.

Discovering the perks of being truthful

Well, aside from Mark Twain's observation that *"If you tell the truth you don't have to remember anything,"* being honest can also bring other benefits.

Being honest is a powerful statement to the universe that you trust the world around you, and, more importantly, that you trust and respect yourself. For example, if you're upset about something but have heard that spiritual people never feel upset, you should still honor what you are truly feeling rather than hiding your honest thoughts and feelings just to fit into what other people say you should be feeling. Being truthful with yourself and others empowers your self-examination, self-knowledge, self-acceptance, and self-respect. Here are a few quick ways to increase your honesty:

- **If you say you're going to be somewhere on time, do your best to be there.** Don't wait until the last possible minute and then hope and pray that there won't be any buildup of traffic as you race dangerously through streets, only to be late and end up inconveniencing those who were depending on you to arrive on time. Plan your schedule so that you'll be able to easefully meet your commitments without creating unnecessary stress for others, for yourself, or for all the drivers who are unfortunate enough to be in your way.

- **Don't offer to do something for someone unless you really intend to do it.** You may feel really good while offering to do a favor or give a gift to someone. Some people become addicted to the positive feeling of being generous, but are not so enthusiastic about the less comfortable responsibility of following through on their offers and promises. Before you jump into the pleasant feeling of seeing someone's face light up with gratitude for your kind offer, be clear and committed that you are prepared to fulfill what you offer.

- **Make a point of keeping your word to yourself.** Keeping your word to yourself means that if you're not ready to change a habit, you don't begin one half-hearted attempt after another, each one doomed to failure. This half-hearted approach can dampen your power of honesty and resolution. Rather, wait until you know deep inside that the time is right for a change and then make the change fully and with total commitment.

Being honest with yourself

Honesty is not only about telling the truth to others, but also doing your best to tell the truth to yourself. When you are clear and honest inside and out, a more esoteric benefit of honesty comes into play: your words become more powerful.

This teaching is expounded in a scripture called the *Yoga Sutras*. In this text, the sage Patanjali explains that when you become completely established in absolute, total honesty, you also attain a kind of supernatural power: Your words begin to come true. You're able to declare a thing and have it be so.

Although this teaching may sound strange at first, it does make logical sense in terms of both the material and spiritual effects of honesty.

- **Material effects of honesty:** When you're continually honest, you get so used to speaking only truth that you take your own words very seriously. Then, when you make a commitment to yourself, you intend, insist, and make sure to keep it. With the power of intention present in every word you speak, your words become more powerful.

- **Spiritual effects of honesty:** Honesty brings you in harmony with the great eternal truth that pervades the whole tapestry of life. As Mohandas Gandhi observed, truth alone will endure; all the rest will be swept away before the tides of time. Because the ultimate nature of this universe is truth, practicing honesty brings you in alignment with the universal power of truth that exists behind all creation, thereby empowering your words and thoughts.

Leaving a door open for God's will

When you're sincere in your efforts to be completely honest, you may be less inclined to make absolute declarations about what you will or will not do in situations where unexpected obstacles could keep you from fulfilling your promise.

Many spiritual folks like to include with their declarations some form of "God willing" to acknowledge their awareness and acceptance of the power of God to either support or change their plans. Muslims often end declarations of intention with the phrase *Insha'llah*, which means, "As God wills it."

"Yes, I will be at the department meeting at nine o'clock sharp . . . as God wills it." Try that one on your boss!

Understanding Humility

Some think that humility means that you have a low image of yourself, but in fact, spiritual humility is quite the opposite. Through recognizing the awe-inspiring universal perfection of spirit, you also discover your place within that perfection. As one ancient spiritual text explains, "From perfection comes perfection. Even if you take something away from perfection, it nevertheless remains completely perfect."

When you experience an expanded view of universal perfection meeting perfection in yourself, how can there be room for silly feelings of arrogance or pride? Therefore, as with all virtues, the essence of humility lies not so much in adjusting your outer actions and words to appear to be humble, but in shifting your inner state of self-identification so that humility is the only approach that makes sense.

> *Don't be so humble – you are not that great.*
>   *– Golda Meir*

To adapt Golda's humorous statement to spiritual humility, I would instead say: "Be humble, because you are greater than you can ever imagine (and so is everyone else!)" Here are some questions that can help inspire your shift into spiritual humility:

- What if you could acknowledge your great qualities without feeling proud about them?

- What if you knew that only through divine grace have you been blessed with your good qualities?

- What if you felt as happy seeing someone else's positive achievements as you do seeing your own?

Humility allows you to bear the opinions of others without balking or feeling obliged to conform to their judgments. With humility, you have the presence of mind to consider every idea that comes your way, yet your guidance ultimately comes from within — from your blessed state of surrender, faith, and self-acceptance.

Don't take yourself so seriously that you are constantly trying to gauge and compare yourself with how others are. When you don't think about your individual qualities and circumstances too much, then humility comes naturally.

With humble self-acceptance, you gently accept who and what you are, and this acceptance brings you into a greater sense of who and what you *really* are. Humility can be like Popeye's famous line: "I yam what I yam," which, of course, is but a step away from the Lord's famous line: "I Am That I Am."

Be a humble drop of water

Here's an analogy to help you understand the nature of humility, using the common spiritual metaphor of a drop of water falling into the ocean and thereby becoming one with the ocean.

If the drop were to say, "I am the ocean," its assertion would not be false pride, because the drop has indeed merged completely into the water of the ocean, thereby becoming one with it.

However, if the drop were to say, "I'm the best damn drop that has ever merged into this ocean," then perhaps it would not be such a humble drop!

Resting in the humility of your heart

Unlike some of the other virtues, humility can be especially difficult to gauge, both in yourself and in others. I mean, if you think you're humble, what does that say? And if you don't think you're humble, maybe you're right or maybe you're just too humble to acknowledge your own humility.

Spiritual Wisdom

When the light of humility dawns on the soul, the darkness of selfishness disappears and the soul no longer lives for itself, but for God. The soul loses itself in God, lives in God, and is transformed into Him. This is the alchemy of humility. It transforms the lowest into the Highest.

— *Kirpal Singh*

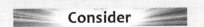

Staying free from harmful comparisons

Here are some tips to help keep you free from the habit of comparing   yourself to others:

- If you see someone who seems to have a better situation than you — such as someone who has better looks, more success, a better attitude, a bigger wardrobe, or more happiness — you can use their example to improve your own situation. You can also transform harmful comparisons into positive opportunities by shifting your awareness into a higher perspective and lowering your focus on outer qualities and materialistic desires. You can strengthen your feeling of self-respect rather than using someone else's good fortune as an excuse for feeling bad about yourself or pulling out the cat claws to tear the person down.

- If you see someone who lacks some of your good qualities, you can keep pride and arrogance away by understanding that the person may have other qualities that are better than yours, by feeling a humble gratitude for the good qualities you are blessed to have, and by sending the person and everyone else blessings to be the best and happiest that they can possibly be.

- Rather than focusing on who is better or worse than anyone else, keep your awareness centered on the divine spirit that expresses through all. A vision of universal unity naturally brings with it the virtue of humility. Far from being a weak stance, true humility is strong, powerful, and grounded in your identification with the highest.

In some cultures, humility is expressed by bowing to one another or by reaching down to touch the other person's feet. I have witnessed some fairly humorous scenes with great beings meeting one another and practically fighting over touching each other's feet first to show their humility. I'm not saying that this behavior is a bad thing, but it's an amusing sight to behold.

True humility can sometimes look like ego or pride to those who don't understand the nature of this virtue. For example, if you know that your talents and achievements have come through divine grace, then you can receive praise for them with a smile, a nod of agreement, and a shared appreciation for those gifts. Still, even if your acquiescence to praise is coming from a pure sense of gratitude and humility, some may misinterpret it as coming from a lack of humility — giving you more opportunities to stay humble under the duress of their incorrect opinions.

Some saints and sages who, through humility, realized and proclaimed their oneness with God were misunderstood by those who had not achieved their elevated awareness, Some sages were punished, crucified, or martyred for proclaiming their higher identification by those who didn't understand their true state of humility.

The humble prayer of an unknown Confederate soldier

The following prayer, appropriately anonymous, shows how humility can fill even challenging times with great spiritual growth and significance:

"I asked God for strength that I might achieve. I was made weak that I might learn humbly to obey. I asked for health that I might do greater things. I was given infirmity that I might do better things. I asked for riches that I might be happy. I was given poverty that I might be wise. I asked for power that I might have the praise of men. I was given weakness that I might feel the need of God. I asked for all things that I might enjoy life. I was given life that I may enjoy all things. I got nothing that I asked for, but everything I hoped for. Almost despite myself, my unspoken prayers were answered. I am, among all men, most richly blessed."

Protecting your virtues through humility

Here are just a few benefits that come from the virtue of humility:

- Humility, like its friend surrender, brings you to a place of greater inner freedom. You're not trying to impress others, but rather aspire to fulfill a greater destiny and be of service to all. With humility, you don't need to rack up huge credit-card debts to buy fancy furnishings and clothes to show off to your friends, but can make decisions from spiritual wisdom, intelligence, and self-knowledge.

- With humility, if you discover you've been doing something wrong, you are better able to see your error and take steps to correct it without being distracted by the ego's defense systems of making excuses and blaming others. For example, if you have failed to fulfill a promised commitment due to being swayed by a more pleasant opportunity, humility keeps you from trying to cover up your action by lying or blaming others. Instead, you can take note of the harmful effects of your selfish actions, take responsibility for your choices, humbly apologize to whoever was harmed by your transgression, and commit to yourself that you'll be more careful about giving and keeping your word in the future.

- Humility also keeps you from being overcome by guilt or shame due to any mistakes you've made in the past. Everyone at some point in their lives inevitably falls short of their greater aspirations. Maybe you took something you shouldn't have taken or said something you shouldn't have said. During such times, humility allows you to confront your erroneous ways without falling into the kinds of extreme self-condemnation, guilt, shame, or low self-esteem that can weaken your resolve and bring about even more failings. With humility, your love and self-respect for yourself stays strong as you focus on doing what is best in each moment.

- With humility, you know that you are an individual expression of spirit and can let that spirit express through you as a flow of creative inspiration. Your focus shifts from the usual concerns people have about what others think of them and moves into an egoless flow of action that opens the door to spiritual guidance and grace.

⊰ Spiritual Wisdom ⊱

Humble words

Here some great spiritual sages describe the importance of humility:

- "Those who aspire to greatness must humble themselves."
  — Lao-tzu

- "It was pride that changed angels to devils; it is humility that makes men angels."
  — St. Augustine

- "The tree laden with fruit always bends low."
  — Ramakrishna

Wishing Everyone Well with Compassion

Compassion is another important spiritual virtue to cultivate. Compassion comes from an amazing ability human beings have to feel empathy. You see something happen to someone else and are able to feel it in your heart and soul. In fact, sometimes you may find it easier to have compassion for others than for yourself.

The spiritual thing to do in any situation is to wish everyone well in whatever lessons and situations they may be going through. Nobody gets it easy in life. Whether rich, poor, beautiful, ugly, intelligent, or ignorant, people have to deal with challenges and problems, regardless of their station and circumstances in life.

Some Buddhist masters go so far as to say that life is inherently made up of suffering. Realizing that everyone has to go through suffering and difficulties helps you create an umbrella of compassion that covers everyone.

Spiritual Wisdom

When we finally know we are dying, and all other sentient beings are dying with us, we start to have a burning, almost heartbreaking sense of the fragility and preciousness of each moment and each being, and from this can grow a deep, clear, limitless compassion for all beings.

— Sogyal Rinpoche

Compassion often comes from digested challenges. For example, you may go through a terribly difficult experience that brings up feelings of helplessness, anger, frustration, grief, or sadness. Then, the next thing you know, your concern for other people becomes stronger.

Perhaps someone doesn't offer you a helping hand when you need one, so you make a commitment to help others in the future when you see them in need. Or someone betrays your trust by breaking her word, and after experiencing the disastrous effects of her actions, you become more trustworthy to others in the future. After experiencing the pain of losing a loved one, you may be inspired to extend your help, care, and blessings to others who are going through the same struggles.

Be Careful

Compassion isn't meant to entangle you unnecessarily in other people's situations or to make you feel angry with whomever or whatever is causing another person to suffer. When you're guided and able to help someone, true compassion allows you to do so with a positive attitude, peacefulness, and a tenderness of the heart.

Increasing your power of compassion through empathy

Through empathy, you have the very precious ability to learn from watching other people's life lessons. You watch someone learn a lesson, and you are able to learn the same lesson without having to go through the same outer circumstances yourself. This ability to learn from other's mistakes is one reason why watching certain reality television shows can actually be beneficial to your journey – if you are watching them with a spiritual focus and intention to study human nature and the laws of nature.

As with all the virtues, increasing your spiritual awareness also increases your ability to feel compassion and empathy:

- **Your compassion automatically expands when you realize that we are all one.** Humanity is one great big family. And, in spirit, all people, beings, and things are one on an even higher level. Therefore, anyone who comes before you is, in a sense, a part of you. Their joy is your joy, their pain your pain, and your compassion for them is ultimately compassion for yourself. It is from this universal view that some Buddhists make the amazingly compassionate vow to save all beings from the ocean of worldly suffering before saving themselves.

- **Your empathy naturally increases when you clear away the inner cobwebs of anger, greed, and jealousy.** Think about the following:

  - Have there been times in your life when you were happy to see something bad happen to someone who you thought deserved the pain?

  - Have you ever seen somebody achieve great fortune and instead of feeling happy for them, found yourself overcome by that not-so-fortunate feeling of jealousy?

 Consider

These kinds of negative tendencies keep you from feeling true empathy for others, and also keep your own good fortune far away. However, after spirituality uplifts your body, mind, and spirit, you become like a clear mirror that is happy to see good things happen to everyone.

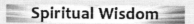

Advice from Patanjali

Here, the ancient yoga scholar Patanjali offers helpful advice on how to respond to the different kinds of people you encounter:

- Be friendly with those who are happy.

- Have compassion toward those who are suffering.

- Have sympathetic joy toward those who are virtuous

- Be indifferent toward those who are wicked.

Being compassionate in today's world

Modern society faces a unique situation regarding suffering and compassion, mainly due to the prevalence of media. People today witness massive amounts of violence and tragedy without necessarily having to be present or involved with the situations surrounding them, as was the case with the wars, famines, plagues, and other disasters of ages gone by.

You sit down to watch a bit of television after a long day at work, and what do you see? On drama shows, you may see graphic shootings and an amazing array of troubles, woes, dangers, and fears. On news shows, you'll see a string of reports and stories about intense, often violent situations. Some tragedies are real, some are fiction, and most of the time it is difficult to distinguish between the two.

How do you respond to so many disasters as you sit comfortably on your couch or recliner? How many people have you watched be killed from the comfort of your home? Do you respond any differently to the real disasters than you do to the fictional ones?

The relatively recent explosion of news media has to some degree numbed the viewing public to their own compassion. I mean, just moments ago I had the television on and heard a quick teaser for news at 11 with a fast-paced professional news-anchor voice rushing to say, "We'll tell you about a local fire where several children were killed."

How can you feel compassion for each situation when you are constantly bombarded by disasters, any of which would have been the talk of the town in centuries gone by?

Watching the news compassionately

I witnessed a concentrated example of how compassion can be numbed when I left a decade of monastic life and began to work as an editor for one of the news stations in Los Angeles. Not only did I see intensely dramatic stories, but I saw them over and over while piecing the video footage together for broadcast. To be sure, this footage was a far cry from the spiritual wisdom videos I had been editing during the previous ten years!

News people have to learn not to let the disasters "get to them." You might say that they have to turn off their compassion to some degree, or they would be crying at every story. As just one of many examples of how numbed news people can become, whenever the Los Angeles police chased a car (which was a fairly common occurrence), our newsroom folks would watch all the angles of coverage on the television monitors that lined the newsroom walls. Several times, someone would go around the newsroom taking actual bets on whether the driver would live or die, as cheering or jeering filled the room, depending on who had won or lost the bet.

When you watch the news, understand that decisions are being made by people who live and breathe news, and who may see a horrific story as just another way to entice viewers to watch their show. Your mission as a spiritually aware person is to not get dragged into complacency, numbness, or anxiety, but to watch, care, trust, and remain anchored in spiritual awareness and faith all at the same time.

Compassion is often a byproduct of properly digested suffering. If you feel a sense of compassion for someone who is suffering — especially from a situation you have previously gone through — you're giving a signal to the conscious universe that you've got the message. You've properly digested your suffering from that challenge and have transformed your suffering into compassion for others.

With this shift from suffering into compassion, you won't necessarily have to go through the same kind of sufferings over and over in your life, as the same lessons come again and again, trying to break the shell of your heart to release the sweet nectar of compassion.

The lessening of suffering for yourself and others is just one of many ways that spiritual virtues help to create a happier life and a better world. More compassion, humility, honesty, and empathy equal less suffering.

Having compassion for those who are suffering doesn't always have to translate into making efforts to relieve them of suffering. Sometimes you're not able to help, and at other times, you may see people who are learning important lessons by going through certain hardships. These occasions are where your spiritual discernment comes in handy, allowing you to look at a situation and decide whether and how to express your compassion outwardly.

Spiritual Wisdom

Wise words about doing unto others

Being helpful to others is one of the primary tenets of spirituality and humanity. Here are some wonderful words of guidance about the Golden Rule:

- "What is unpleasant to thyself, that do not do unto thy neighbor. This is the whole law. All else is exposition."
  — Hillel

- "Try to do to others as you would have them do to you and do not be discouraged if they fail sometimes. It is much better that they should fail than that you should."
  — Charles Dickens

- "Behave to your servants as you desire God to behave to you."
  — Philo

- "Love thy neighbor as thyself."
  — Matthew 23:39

- "If you want others to be happy, practice compassion. If you want to be happy, practice compassion."
  — Dalai Lama

- "We may wonder, whom can I love and serve? Where is the face of God to whom I can pray? The answer is simple: That naked one. That lonely one. That unwanted one who is my brother and my sister. If we have no peace, it is because we have forgotten that we belong to each other."
  — Mother Teresa

Chapter 11

Uplifting Your Whole Life

Topics in this Chapter:

*   Staying focused on spirit
*   Serving with love
*   Finding true abundance
*   Keeping good company

One of the most important aspects of spirituality is to see things from a broader, more long-term perspective. Spirituality connects you with a part of yourself that lives beyond the material world — beyond birth and death and the joys and sorrows of life.

Anchored in your spiritual depths, you're not as easily swept away by the waves of temporary temptations that give joy in one moment, but take away your joy in the next. You won't seek to fill your life with only fool's gold, while neglecting the real treasure of spiritual awakening. You'll be able to approach every aspect of your life with a positive and powerful sense of freedom, generosity, love, and service.

Moving from Worldly Limitations to Spiritual Freedom

Spiritual Wisdom

A boat may stay in the water, but water should not stay in the boat. An aspirant may live in the world, but the world should not live in him.

— Sri Ramakrishna

The Indian sage Sri Ramakrishna also describes the state of a spiritually aware person as being like a nanny in a rich family who brings up the child in her care with the same love as if it were her own, but who knows full well that she has no claim upon it.

In the same way, it is possible for you to live a successful and fully engaged life without being too attached to the specific external details. Whether you like, love, dislike, or try to change the details of your life, you can still experience spiritual freedom from the burdens that come with feeling too much attachment to things.

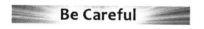

The key to this inner freedom is to look at life with a spiritual awareness that extends beyond your individual temporary circumstances.

Having the peaceful equanimity that comes when you're free from excessive attachments to things of this world doesn't mean that you lose interest in the events and responsibilities of your life, but that

- You ride the waves of life without being drawn underwater by the lows or getting overly elated by the highs.

- You stay inwardly peaceful even while dealing with urgent tasks.

- You remember the eternal nature even in the midst of time deadlines.

- You attain steadiness and contentment – qualities that are great friends for your spiritual journey.

- You remain free from the anxiety of needing to have everything be exactly as you think it should be.

- You act, strive, live, and give whole-heartedly while remembering that your greatest riches exist beyond the physical world.

Be Careful

Enjoying everything in your life is great, but getting overly attached to those things is not so great.

Rising above limited desires

How can you get off this roller-coaster ride of wanting and getting, wanting more and getting more — being disappointed and then relieved; happy and then sad? In answering this question, spiritual sages of many traditions have advised people to do the following:

- Remember the temporary nature of life.

- Loosen your focus on materialistic desires.

- Remember the underlying, imperishable, divine current that eternally flows behind, beyond, and within this topsy-turvy, ever-changing, undependable world.

A 7th century poet-philosopher from India named Bhartrihari wrote a famous treatise called "The hundred verses on renunciation." In this section, Bhartrihari describes how attachment turns even blessings into fears:

With enjoyment, comes fear of disease

With social position, fear of disfavor

With riches, fear of hostile people

With honor, fear of humiliation

With power, fear of enemies

With beauty, fear of old age

With scholarship, fear of challengers

With virtue, fear of traducers

With the identification with body, fear of death

Everything in this world is done with fear

Renunciation alone makes one fearless.

 **Don't Forget**

Renunciation doesn't just mean to renounce things, but to renounce your attachment to things.

Moving beyond desires and attachments

When you're dealing with desires, nothing is ever enough. Haven't you noticed that when you finally get something you've been wanting, you almost immediately begin to want something else? Desires are like hair that keeps growing no matter how many times you cut it. Desires, attachments, and sense pleasures can bring many troubles:

- **Desires and attachments keep your mind and heart occupied with things that won't last.** When making life choices, you may have to choose between momentary pleasures and eternal, spiritual happiness. Remember that eternal happiness also includes happiness in each moment – making eternal happiness the extra-special, super-deluxe, all-in-one deal.

- **Sense pleasures may bring temporary happiness, but can also block your deeper, long-term happiness.** Indulging your senses too much lowers your will power and limits your enjoyments to the outer surface of life. For example, scratching an itchy scab may bring some immediate pleasant sensations, but can also keep the wound from healing and even open your skin to infections. In the same way, indulging in too many sense pleasures can create various spiritual, mental, and physical problems and can keep you from experiencing the much more exquisite and long-lasting joys of spiritual happiness.

- **Worldly pleasures usually cause pain somewhere down the line.** Perhaps you lose what you once had or become bored after the initial excitement wears off. For example, you may be attached to somebody and feel really great when you're with the person, but when she's gone, those happy feelings may turn to sadness or loneliness. Or you may be thrilled to have someone respond in kind to your desire to get to know each other, only to become bored or irritated once the person has been around for a while.

Don't Forget

Rather than relying on other people or objects to make you happy, your best spiritual course to long-term happiness is to find the source of happiness within yourself. Then you can create a great life that includes all the people and things you like and love, but without having the kinds of attachments and desires that bring pain when the external situations change — as most external situations eventually do.

With non-attachment, you can let something go when you're done with it. This approach of letting go applies not only to worldly attachments, but also to spiritual ones. Suppose that you pick up a book at random and find words that give exactly the guidance you need to address the challenges before you – as though the words in this book are flowing to you directly from the lips of the beneficent universe itself.

When you have non-attachment, you can fully receive and appreciate a divine message without feeling obligated to spend the next 20 years reading the same book over and over again, regardless of whether it continues to have the same profound effect on you. Attachment makes you focus your energy on the outer form that has carried and delivered a blessing, rather than on the blessing itself. With non-attachment, the grace energy of the universe can guide you in the most efficient and powerful way in every moment, as you move more gently and freely with the flow of life.

Entering a vision of equality

Everybody is unique. Compare not yourself with anybody else lest you spoil God's curriculum.
                    — Baal Shem Tov

One of the most important spiritual qualities to attain is the state of equality consciousness. With *equality consciousness,* you see the universal creative force behind, within, and expressing as each form, rather than only seeing the outer details of the form.

With equality consciousness, you see the spiritual power that exists equally in everything even as you relate appropriately to all the necessary perceptions, judgments, actions, and decisions of life.

- Equality consciousness helps you let go of binding desires and enter a place of inner freedom.

- Equality consciousness brings peacefulness of mind.

- Equality consciousness allows you to make better long-term decisions based on a bigger picture view of universal spirit.

- Equality consciousness inspires you to be excellent even when nobody is watching.

Having equality consciousness is like being a jeweler who is purchasing gold. To the jeweler, gold is gold, regardless of its outer form. He weighs whatever pieces people bring to sell and pays them according to the weight of gold. The gold may be in the form of beautiful jewelry, a religious statue, or a lumpy brick, but none of those external details matters to the jeweler. His only interest is in the carats and weight of gold.

Seeing with equal vision is like being a jeweler of spirit. What matters most are not the details of outer forms, but the divine nature that exists within those forms. Equality consciousness helps you see people's worth beyond the usual determining factors, such as how much money or worldly stature they've achieved. Instead, your vision shifts from worldly matters to the great spiritual value that exists within each human heart.

With equality consciousness, you know that the servant is as valuable as the king, and the secretary is as valuable as the CEO. In fact, one thing I learned while working for various television and film studios in Hollywood is the immense power of a benevolent secretary to help get you that desired meeting, or the power of a friendly cleaning crew member to let you into the studio when you've lost your key.

With equality consciousness, you break free from the common materialistic focus and find as much appreciation for inner peace, a child's laugh, or a beautiful sunset as some would experience from getting a promotion, getting married, or winning an award.

Just think: If you could feel as much joy from taking a breath of fresh air in the morning as you would experience from achieving a worldly goal that has taken years of effort, then you get to experience happiness, joy, and contentment much more often than if you withhold and save your happiness and appreciation for only major outer events. Equality consciousness helps you see beyond appearances into the spiritual value of everything. With equality consciousness, you know that in spirit everyone is equally important – not just in terms of what they can do for you, but inherently so.

With equality consciousness, you still see all the different qualities of people and forms. You can distinguish their features, and even feel preferences for certain qualities over others. Yet, you also know that – just as all objects are made up of the same protons, neutrons, and electrons – everything is also made up of one Supreme Spirit. Each contributor to this dance of universal creation has a role to play and a melody to add, whether they're kind or not, beautiful or not, and accomplished or not.

Be Careful

Equality consciousness doesn't mean that you don't see the difference between a hundred-dollar bill and a pile of doggie doo. Rather, even as you pick up the hundred-dollar bill and step around the doggie doo, deep inside, you don't respond with extreme greed or disdain for either.

With equality consciousness, even as you feel that some people are special to you – whether they are family members or friends – you simultaneously know that every living being on this planet is also your brother, sister, and friend.

Some people think that having detachment and renunciation means that they won't get to have fun, be successful, or achieve great wealth. Perhaps this belief exists because many who detach from the common sources of pleasure are able to see more objectively how short-lived these pleasures are and choose to live simpler lives.

Is it possible to live surrounded with worldly pleasures and still stay detached and focused on spirit? Yes, although not very many people can easily achieve this balance. Therefore, some seekers who are firmly committed to spiritual growth above all else may choose to spend more of their time and efforts on what they feel to be more substantial spiritual goals – such as awakening to divine inner wisdom and soaring with sweet freedom in the eternal flow of universal bliss. This bliss is even better than eating chocolate cake, although chocolate cake together with universal bliss can also be a great combination!

From Work to Divine Service

Spiritual Wisdom

What is Divine Service that is done with joy and goodness of heart? This is song.

      – Talmud

Divine service is striving to do what the universe guides you to do, with good intentions and freedom from attachment to the results. Divine service is a magical willingness that helps you receive guidance on how you may be helpful to a person, a place, an event, or humanity. Divine service is doing what needs to be done because the need has come before you and you're in a position to do it.

You may serve by establishing or supporting charities that serve various societal needs. Or you may serve by giving smiles and kind words as you walk through your day. Sometimes you may receive pay for your service, and other times you may not receive anything beyond the inner satisfaction of having given freely of your time, energy, and skills to bring more goodness and light to the world.

Once you become more spiritually aware, service is simply what makes sense. Service becomes not so much an effort or burden, but an inner stance in relationship to the world around you. You look for ways to bring greater healing and light to the world. Wherever you are, you can walk into any situation with a gentle willingness to serve.

For example, you sit at a café to enjoy a pastry and notice a single mother next to you who is looking stressed while struggling with her unruly child. You can give a compassionate smile or even have a chat with this new friend to see whether you can say something that would help alleviate her burdens. This is how I tend to walk through the world, and I've found that my inner willingness often brings about meetings and situations where I'm able to give some friendly suggestion or supportive help to a fellow traveler of life.

You can also get to a point where everything you do is done in the spirit of service – including brushing your teeth, feeding yourself with healthier foods than I just ate for lunch (ahem . . .), or walking in nature with a feeling of wanting to enjoy and serve the energy of the environment through your respectful appreciations, peaceful energy, and positive thoughts.

Service also includes efforts you make to sit quietly in prayer or meditation and taking care of your body, mind, and spirit so that you can be a good vehicle for serving in large or small ways from wherever you are in any moment.

Serving without personal motives

One way to shift from work to divine service is to remember and realize the temporary nature of life. The truth is that no matter how much you accomplish, you'll be gone from this world one day.

Here is a penetrating question to contemplate: Would you devote your life to serving God and humanity, knowing the credit for the beneficial results would never be yours and could ultimately go to someone else?

In a sense, all good world leaders make this sacrifice – preparing the way for future abundance they may never receive credit for, at least during their lifetime. Yet they strive to build new benefits for future generations anyway.

The shift from work to divine service comes, in part, from realizing and remembering the temporary nature of life. One sweet day, you'll leave this world. Nobody will remember what you did or who you were, unless you've managed to leave a large enough dent in the world to be remembered for a while. Will you even know or care what people in this world say about you after you're gone? Perhaps so, but probably not.

Mother Teresa was one of the great servants of humanity in the 20th century. She and the sisters of her order cared for the poorest, most forgotten people with love and respect. On her wall, Mother Teresa kept the following advice:

People are unreasonable, illogical, and self-centered. Love them anyway. If you do good, people may accuse you of selfish motives. Do good anyway. If you are successful, you may win false friends and true enemies. Succeed anyway. The good you do today may be forgotten tomorrow. Do good anyway. Honesty and transparency make you vulnerable. Be honest and transparent anyway. What you spend years building may be destroyed overnight. Build anyway. People who really want help may attack you if you help them. Help them anyway. Give the world the best you have and you may get hurt. Give the world your best anyway.

Seeing how service and success work together

Working without requiring material benefits in return may sound strange in this society, where people are used to working very specifically to receive pay, while sometimes filling out time sheets to the nearest 15-minute increment. However, acting with freedom from personal desire can still be compatible with achieving success.

In fact, freeing yourself from expectations of personal rewards can open your mind and spirit into more creativity and inspiration and allow you to make initially unpaid efforts that may pay off handsomely in the future.

Here is one of those strange spiritual laws: sometimes you get more when you're less attached. Just think of times in your own life when you may have wanted something very badly, and what you wanted came to you only after you gave up your intense desire and moved into a receptive state of allowing.

Spiritual Wisdom

When an archer is shooting for nothing, he has all his skill. If he shoots for a brass buckle, he is already nervous. If he shoots for a prize of gold, he goes blind or sees two targets — He is out of his mind. His skill has not changed. But the prize divides him. He cares. He thinks more of winning than of shooting — And the need to win drains him of power.

—Chuang Tzu

If you don't have detachment from the fruits of your actions, you won't even be able to meet the very common tests and obstacles along the road to success. For example, you may have to pay your dues somewhere along the line by doing some apprentice or internship work for free to learn certain skills.

Be Careful

Turning your work into divine service doesn't mean that you have to live like a pauper (a lesson I haven't always learned so well!) Even if you're getting paid very well for the work you do, you can still perform your actions as service.

Even if you work in a non-spiritual corporate environment, you can bring a service approach by looking for ways to be helpful to your work environment. You can serve the people around you by bringing a positive attitude, showing a good example, or offering a cheerful greeting. You can make sure that someone who is being forgotten gets the recognition that he or she deserves. You can strive to inspire corporate decisions that are based on integrity and a win-win-win approach where the world also benefits from the company's work.

Wise words about service

Many great spiritual servants have passed through this world. Some are still passing through today. Here are some of their inspired words about divine, selfless service:

- "God can do great things through the man who doesn't care who gets the credit."
  —Robert Schuller

- "Joy can be real only if people look upon their life as a service, and have a definite object in life outside themselves and their personal happiness."
  —Leo Tolstoy

- "Only that which is done not for fame nor name, nor for appreciation or thanks of those for whom it is done, is life's service. "
  —Hazrat Inayat Khan

- "The test of real service of God is that it leaves behind it the feeling of humility."
  —Baal Shem Tov

- "Do your work and perform your duties with all your heart. Try to work selflessly with love. Pour yourself into whatever you do. Then you will feel and experience beauty and love in every field of work."
  —Mata Amritanandamayi

- "All service of God must be performed with gladness and zest, otherwise it is not perfect."
  —the Zohar

- "I slept and dreamt that life was joy. I awoke and saw that life was service. I acted and behold, service was joy. "
  —Rabindranath Tagore

From Forgiveness to Gratitude

I have learned silence from the talkative, tolerance from the intolerant and kindness from the unkind.

—Kahlil Gibran

Somewhere along your journey through life, people will betray your trust in them. Someone will break his word or even break your heart, and you may end up feeling resentment for the pain caused by their harmful actions.

The problem with feeling resentment is, well, that you're feeling resentment. Who wants to walk around feeling resentment all the time? Or any of the time?

Plus, after you awaken to a more expanded, more spiritual view of life, you come to realize that there is no good reason to be angry or resentful toward anyone, at least not on a long-term basis, because you know that

- Everybody does the best they can with whatever they have to work with. You may think that someone could or should be doing better than they are, but each soul is going through an array of seen and unseen life lessons that can create bad habits, wrong understandings, and materialistic obsessions. These negative qualities can distort a person's ability to make good decisions.

- Everyone is an expression of universal spirit; therefore whatever they do is somehow part of the perfect universal plan — even if its plan is to tick you off! Just entertaining this point of view will help to make your spiritual journey happier and smoother. When someone is being really irritating, you can chuckle to yourself or even shake your finger at God saying, "You divine trickster. What a strange form you took to ruffle my feathers this time."

- Resentment dampens the light of your own happiness. Resentment and anger also cause a lot of other potential problems, such as drawing to yourself more opportunities to feel more resentment and anger. As Chapter 15 explains, your thoughts are very powerful in drawing to you more of whatever you focus on.

Making efforts to forgive is a great spiritual practice, but pretending that you've forgiven when you haven't really done so can keep you from processing your thoughts and feelings properly so that you can eventually grow into true spiritual forgiveness. As with other challenging experiences, your angers or resentments must be acknowledged so that they can be brought forth from the shadows of hidden thoughts and into the light of divine spiritual awareness.

Forgiving someone's bad actions also doesn't mean that you should ignore or hide what they've done. Even with a forgiving heart, you can still take steps to keep yourself and others from being harmed by the person's actions in the future. The key is to respond without burning in the flames of anger, resentment, and hatred.

Spiritual Wisdom

Words from forgiving folks

"In spite of everything, I still believe that people are really good at heart."
—Anne Frank

"We must develop and maintain the capacity to forgive. He who is devoid of the power to forgive is devoid of the power to love."
—Rev. Dr. Martin Luther King, Jr.

"If we could read the secret history of our enemies, we should find in each man's life sorrow and suffering enough to disarm all hostility."
—Henry Wadsworth Longfellow

"You must forgive those who transgress against you before you can look to forgiveness from God."
—Talmud

"Love in the making sees faults, but forgives them. Love in its grand fulfillment never sees any faults; hence it has nothing to forgive."
—Papa Ramdas

"To err is human; to forgive, divine."
—Alexander Pope

Moving beyond forgiveness

Many therapists, books, and tapes are available to help you forgive your parents, siblings, friends, enemies, boss, spouse, children, and, of course, yourself. However, spirituality ratchets the forgiveness paradigm up a notch or two.

I call this section "Moving beyond forgiveness" because forgiving another person means that you're still judging him or her, and possibly harboring some hidden resentment inside yourself. Also, judging another person can leave yourself open for judgment in return. The Lord's Prayer teaches the importance of forgiving by asking God to *"Forgive us our trespasses as we forgive those who trespass against us,"* a statement that is also in harmony with theories about karma (see Chapter 15). As you forgive, so you are forgiven.

True forgiveness is to rise into a bigger view of universal oneness, and to have faith that whatever happens in your life is a part of the big-picture experience of joys and sorrows that you're meant to experience as a human being living on planet Earth at this time.

True forgiveness is so powerful that one Indian scripture declares that someone who is truly forgiving cannot be burned by fire or drowned by water, and that even wild beasts become docile before a truly forgiving person!

Maintaining an attitude of gratitude

Spiritual Wisdom

When you arise in the morning, think of what a precious privilege it is to be alive — to breathe, to think, to enjoy, to love.

—Marcus Aurelius

You have a choice, no matter who you are or what your life is like. You can either be grateful for whatever you have, or you can be ungrateful. I suggest that making an effort to be more consciously grateful for whatever large or small blessings have come into your life is a good idea. Gratitude is the magic formula, not only for forgiveness, but also for happiness and peacefulness, along with worldly and spiritual success.

When you're grateful, you're likely to be in a better mood, and when you're in a better mood, you're likely to be kinder and friendlier with people, generating more friendliness in return. Being in a good mood automatically makes your life better and helps you work, play, and love better.

Having a bigger-picture spiritual view of life gives you many more opportunities to feel gratitude. Everything is a gift from God and divine spirit, and the more grateful you are, the more opportunities you'll likely have to experience even more gratitude. The world inherently draws to you people and experiences that reflect your thoughts and feelings; therefore, having gratitude can reflect back to you in wonderful ways.

Eventually you may achieve a state of mind that maintains a base level feeling of gratitude at all times and in all circumstances. True gratitude is ultimately independent of the specific details of your life. A true attitude of gratitude is an unconditional appreciation for everything, all at once.

Spirituality in Action

Thank you, God!

Here's a contemplation that can help you feel more gratitude for everything in your life:

1. **Take a few moments to contemplate something you're especially grateful for in your life.** Allow your feelings of gratitude to come forth, while remembering all the details about whomever or whatever you're feeling grateful for.

2. **Now, remove the outer circumstances from your mind and focus your attention on just on the feeling of gratitude that remains.**

3. **Allow that essence of gratitude to expand throughout everything in your life.**

Be grateful for life itself, without limiting your gratitude to anything in particular.

From Greed to Divine Abundance

Spiritual Wisdom

Who is rich? The one who appreciates what he has.

      —Talmud

I've enjoyed the comforts and pleasures of life as much as anyone else — well, maybe not quite as much as some, having spent ten years living a monastic life in an Indian-based ashram. But then I had a chance to try out the other side, when I moved from the ashram to Hollywood. Within a few years, I went from living a very simple life to generating a six-figure income and hanging out with actors, directors, and other folks "in the biz."

A few years later, another shift came when I was recovering from some health issues, beginning a new career as author, and focusing on spiritual and charitable works, while once again living a simple and austere life.

One thing I've learned from these materialistic ups and downs is that the amount of happiness experienced from acquiring things is relative to what you have at the time. On one particular day in the ashram, I remember experiencing great happiness from buying a new toothbrush. I returned from the store and happily showed my acquisition to a visiting acquaintance, who said, "Now I know this yoga really works if you can be so happy about a toothbrush!"

In fact, it has become clear to me that contrary to what all those commercials say, the relationship between external accoutrements and inner happiness is sketchy at best. I know many who have gone to great lengths to satiate all their desires, yet who seem less deeply fulfilled than those who have less.

Isn't it true that gourmet food on a full stomach doesn't taste nearly as good as even the simplest fare when you're exceptionally hungry? The understanding that no quality can exist without its opposite helps to bring a sense of comfort to even the most troublesome times. Without darkness, there is no light; without sorrow, no joy; without hunger, no satiation.

Can you really have it all?

One common saying today is that "You can have it all!" Well, the harmonious combination of spiritual abundance and material abundance is not quite as simple as it sounds. Is it good to enjoy life? Yes! However, what does it really mean to enjoy life? Can you really have material abundance along with spiritual abundance? Are most materially rich people equally wealthy in love, joy, happiness, and spiritual wisdom? Why did so many saints and sages choose to live simple lives when they could have just used the secret law of attraction to live in luxury?

These questions are especially important to consider in today's world, with so many enticing things to enjoy, and where money, relationships, and career aren't considered so much as options, but goals and requirements in their own right. Here are two contrasting takes on this topic, both from a spiritual point of view:

- **No, you can't have it all.** For centuries, monastics of every tradition have concluded that keeping themselves away from the temptations of worldly pleasures was necessary to keep their attention focused on their spiritual or religious efforts. I personally spent a decade in a monastic-style ashram and very much enjoyed the experience of leaving the media-laden, commercial world in favor of a spiritually focused, simple (but nevertheless exciting and challenging) life. I didn't read newspapers, rarely watched television, and went to only one or two movies during these ten monastic years. I wasn't interested in money, relationships, or climbs up a corporate ladder.

  Yet, although I didn't have a chance to enjoy what many would call the good things in life, inside I was receiving precious spiritual treasures. My inner being was empowered and uplifted by my focus on scriptures, prayers, devotion, and enthusiastic service.

- **Yes, you can have it all.** Some modern-day preachers attract huge masses of followers by giving the enticing message that God — yes, God Himself — wants *you* to be rich! Even some ancient scriptures suggest that you can have material and spiritual abundance at the same time. One of the philosophies Swami Muktananda introduced to the spiritual mix of the late 20th century was a spiritual philosophical tradition called Kashmir Shaivism, which I cover in more detail in Chapter 14. This ancient and fairly obscure philosophy is one of the most complete, wide, and all-encompassing views of the nature of reality that I've come across.

One of the main teachings of Kashmir Shaivism philosophy is that this entire world and everything in it is made of divine consciousness. According to this view, anything can be a porthole for experiencing the divine, if you have the right kind of awareness.

Many philosophical schools and spiritual teachers from India set divisions between worldly life and spiritual life; however, Muktananda traveled the world, telling everyone to "attain God" right in the midst of their lives. While giving spiritual teachings and practices such as meditation and chanting, Muktananda explained that you don't have to leave your families, your jobs, or your homes to attain spiritual realization, because this entire universe and everything in it is a play of divine consciousness. He would tell us to enjoy and witness the play of our lives. He'd encourage us to be filled with joy and ecstasy, and through spiritual disciplines and blessings, to see the supreme consciousness that exists in and as everything. He'd tell us not to despise or run away from this world, and explained that with a shift of spiritual awareness, you can attain God right where you are. Muktananda said, "Change your understanding. Change the prescription of your glasses. Know that you are a part of God."

Clearly, this teaching suggests that you really can have it all. However, the key is to elevate your vision and understanding to a level from which you're free from the traps of this world while still enjoying the world.

Finding true generosity

One afternoon, a wealthy man was riding in the back of his limousine when he saw a small group of poor people who were so hungry that they were eating grass from the roadside. The wealthy man ordered his driver to stop and stepped out to find out more about their situation. He asked one of the men, "Why are you eating grass?"

"We don't have money for food," the poor man replied.

"Well, you can come with me to my house," replied the wealthy man.

"But sir, I've got a wife and three kids here, and my brother's family also."

"Bring them along!" insisted the wealthy man.

They all excitedly climbed into the limousine, and while being driven to the wealthy man's house, the poor fellow gratefully said, "Sir, you are too kind. Thank you for taking all of us with you."

The wealthy man replied, "Glad to do it. You'll love my place. The grass is almost two feet tall."

This humorous analogy demonstrates the way some people behave when they think they're giving. Just as a child may give only the Halloween candy that she doesn't want to her little brother, so some people who seem to be giving are in fact giving what they want to get rid of, or giving with strings attached, or to make an outer show of generosity, or to create a situation that will ultimately benefit themselves. Not everyone understands the spiritual practice of true generosity, where you strive to give the right thing to the right person at the right time, and in the right way.

Living in pursuit of lasting fulfillment

Spiritual Wisdom

Anyone who thinks money will make them happy, doesn't have money.
—David Geffen

This world would look very different if we were able to simply remove the entire element and effects of greed from its fabric. Just imagine the effects of a greedless society:

- Everyone would have enough.

- People would be healthier, because food manufacturers would make products with more nutritious and better-quality ingredients.

- Nobody would spend millions of dollars to try and get you addicted to harmful substances.

- Politicians and world leaders would make decisions only with the purest intentions to make life better for all.

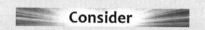 **Consider**

Dealing with the fluctuations of material life

Here is a simple recipe for staying content and steady during the financial ups and downs of life:

- If you have less money, lower your wants.

- If you have more money, use what you have to benefit yourself and others.

From Relationships to Divine Love

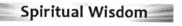 **Spiritual Wisdom**

Though I speak with the tongues of men and of angels, but have not love, I have become sounding brass or a clanging cymbal. And though I have the gift of prophecy, and understand all mysteries and all knowledge, and though I have all faith, so that I could remove mountains, but have not love, I am nothing.

—1 Corinthians 13-1-2

All you need is love

The topic of love pervades most music, books, and television and movie scripts. Love is the essence of your spirit; therefore, finding ways to release and reveal your love can also help you to experience and express your spirit. Here are some wise words about love:

- One word frees us from all the weight and pain of the world; that word is Love.

    —Sophocles

- Love consists in this, that two solitudes protect and touch and greet each other.

    —Rainer Maria Rilke

- In love the paradox occurs that two beings become one and yet remain two.

    —Erich Fromm

- Love gives naught but itself and takes naught but from itself. Love possesses not, nor would it be possessed; for love is sufficient unto love.

    —Kahlil Gibran

- Love takes up where knowledge leaves off.

    —Saint Thomas Aquinas

- At the touch of love everyone becomes a poet.

    —Plato

Along with the inherent blessings of experiencing love, good relationships can bring great opportunities for spiritual, mental, and emotional growth. Human beings are naturally drawn to relate with other people. It is through relationships with others that we grow and discover more about the world and ourselves. Jesus has said that he is present whenever two or more are gathered in his name, indicating the importance and power inherent in joining with other souls during your journey through life.

Mutual affection soothes the heart, while intelligent conversations spark new vistas of thought. The support you feel and receive from loved ones gives you the strength to move forward courageously in whatever you're inspired to do. Even when some aspects of your relationships may be rubbing you the wrong way, a spiritual focus can help you to see the blessings beneath the irritations, and the lush growth budding beneath the outer storms.

Love, relationships, and potential potholes

My wife and I were happy for 20 years. Then we met.
          —Rodney Dangerfield

Okay, seriously folks: Any corporation with a failure rate as high as today's divorce rate — right around 50 percent in the United States — would have to reexamine its internal structures and would probably go out of business. This high percentage of marital breakups is an indicator that things may be changing and evolving in human-relationship land.

Most people want to find a soul mate who will love, understand, relate, respect, and live with them happily ever after. However, few people are fortunate enough to find a true soul mate in this life. Even so, many still want to have some companionship along their paths, and so they settle for relationships that seem to be compatible and loving in the moment, but which may change into being not so compatible or loving in the future.

Due to cultural traditions, a couple may feel obliged to sign on the dotted line of vows that don't necessarily carry the full depth of their souls' conviction, such as promising to stay together "in sickness and in health, until death do us part," when these vows may not reflect their true feelings and intentions. Even if both parties are fortunate enough to stay alive and healthy, today's focus on individual growth may bring some to seek their future growth in different directions from their partners. Therefore, honesty, respect, and communication are paramount in any relationship. Don't just repeat vows you don't really mean. Either rewrite your vows or contemplate deeply to make a true commitment to keep them.

Even with all the shifts and changes that are inevitable with two intertwined lives, you can keep your relationship vibrant, strong, and ever-deepening. With mutual respect and flexibility, you and your partner can allow and support each other in following your dreams and aspirations while maintaining your connection of love and commitment. The key to keeping your vows without selling out your greater dreams is to understand and appreciate the preciousness of life and of each soul's journey in this world. Without respect for each other's growing and changing interests and inspirations, a previously promising relationship can end up crumbling into resentment, dishonesty, and anger.

Maintain good communications with your loved one about what you really commit to and how you plan to keep growing individually and together. Everyone has different beliefs and expectations when it comes to the "rules of relationships." Discuss yours with your partner so that you can both make real vows that you can honor and keep while you are together, and also if the time ever comes that you move and grow into separate directions.

A not too far-fetched scenario

A husband and wife are having dinner at a very fine restaurant, when a gorgeous young woman comes over to their table, gives the husband a big kiss on the lips, says she'll see him later, and walks away.

The wife glares at her husband and asks, "Who was that?"

"Oh," replies the husband, "she's my mistress."

"Well, that's the last straw," says the wife. "I've had enough! I want a divorce."

"I can understand that," replies her husband, "but remember, if we get a divorce it will mean no more shopping trips to Paris, no more wintering in Barbados, no more summers in Tuscany, no more Lexus in the garage, and no more yacht club. But the decision is yours."

Just then, a mutual friend enters the restaurant with a beautiful young woman on his arm.

"Who's that woman with Jim?" asks the wife.

"That's his mistress," says her husband.

"Ours is prettier," she replies.

Although this scenario is meant to be a humorous commentary on why some relationships stay together, every person can look at their own lives and situations to find ways that they may be selling out what is really important — in the case of this story, true love — for lesser comforts and materialistic benefits.

I would like to give a disclaimer here and say that having lived with a monastic focus during most of my life, I haven't had a lot of opportunities to personally explore too many relationships, although I have experienced my share of spiritual devotional love. So while I do my best to present helpful information about the topics of marriage and romantic relationships from a spiritual point of view, if you look very closely, you may find just a teeny-tiny bit of bias on my behalf toward opting for the single life.

Marriage is a great institution, but I'm not ready for an institution.

—Mae West

Avoiding mediocre relationships

Sometimes people want to have a relationship so badly that they'll settle for a mediocre one. My parents did this and went through many years of unhappiness with one another before finally going their separate ways (and for you Freuds out there, yes, seeing and hearing their plentiful arguments probably did help inspire me to go for a monastic-style relationship with the divine).

Making insincere long-term commitments to a mediocre relationship just to please others or fulfill an expectation or desire can possibly hold you back on your greater spiritual journey, because:

- Mediocre relationships can keep you from growing past the level where you and your companion meet intellectually, emotionally, and spiritually. As Henry David Thoreau said, "The man who goes alone can start today; but he who travels with another must wait till that other is ready." If you and your partner have a deep soul level connection, then you'll be able to give each other the space to grow individually as you also continue to grow together.

- Your companion may not support your spiritual efforts. Some spouses may even feel jealous if you start paying more attention to God or spirit than to them.

- Relationships can consume a lot of precious time and energy. A good relationship or marriage can give greater value to your time and efforts, but a mediocre one may leave you in the end feeling the burden of unfulfilled dreams and wasted years of useless activities and meaningless arguments and banter.

- You can't really be too spontaneous and carefree when someone else is depending on you to always be exactly who and how you have always been. While steadiness is a great quality to develop, at some point you may be spiritually guided to make some dramatic changes in how you approach and relate to life.

Don't Forget

You need to be your own guide as to whether having a close relationship or marriage is best for you.

Adding spirituality to your relationships with devotional love

Devotional love is like a magical elixir that soothes and sweetens your heart and soul. Devotional love brings many good qualities, including contentment, gratitude, enthusiasm, service, humility, sacrifice, and a willingness to grow. Devotional love keeps you focused more on divine and great qualities than on limited circumstances. Devotional love brings touches of spirituality into all of your relationships, as it helps you to see the best in yourself and your loved ones. Here are three equations to consider regarding the importance of devotional and worldly love:

- Devotional love plus worldly love = great.
- Devotional love without worldly love = still great.
- Worldly love without devotional love = not so great.

Spiritual tips for making romance work

Consider

If you want to spiritualize your romantic relationship, approach your relationship with spiritual awareness. See God in your companion, as you love and worship each other in your hearts and souls. Give each other space to grow, and be supportive of each other's greatest dreams and aspirations.

People today are much more individualized and self-focused than their forefathers were. Carbon-copy, cookie-cutter families of the 20th century are no longer the norm. The media explosion and a lot of cultural shifts in recent decades have created some very self-focused generations who are not necessarily prepared for the sacrifices necessary to maintain a long-term monogamous marriage.

As conscious spiritually focused beings, you and your partner need to communicate enough to know what your true feelings, hopes, and commitments are. Regardless of whether you have a legal piece of paper or not, you need to explore and create a powerful, supportive relationship that works for both partners and has room for expansion and a commitment to continued positive communications and mutual respect regardless of where life's twists and turns may lead.

Contemplation and self-inquiry can help you stop replaying the same scenarios over and over again in the ongoing situations of your life. Have you noticed how certain relationship patterns can keep arising with different people until you figure out what inside yourself is creating or allowing those events to arise? For example, you may be very generous with others and feel betrayed when they don't reciprocate as you think they should. The spiritual guidance from this kind of situation may be to stop giving more than you're comfortable giving or to keep giving enthusiastically but without having so many expectations about what should be given in return. This lesson can help you to give more freely and experience less disappointment in the future.

By staying centered in your soul connection through spiritual practice and awareness, you and your partner can help one another step-by-step, healing old wounds and exploring new realizations as you move alone and together toward the eternal, absolute oneness of pure spirit. Anchored in higher understanding and purity of feeling, you grow together with love, care, and the highest mutual respect.

Understanding the power of company

Keep away from people who try to belittle your ambitions. Small people always do that, but the really great make you feel that you too can become great.

—Mark Twain

Are there people in your life — whether family, friends, coworkers, or other groups of associates — where you come into their company feeling great but walk away feeling disempowered, upset, or angry? These emotions may be signs that either these associates aren't beneficial to you, or that they're triggering personal issues you need to clear up, or both.

Be Careful

Paying attention to the power of company is not intended to make you avoid all uncomfortable or challenging situations. Sometimes the people who challenge you are the ones who help you grow.

Here are some questions you can ask to contemplate the beneficial or harmful nature of the company you choose to keep:

- **Ask yourself whether the people around you are the right people for you to spend a lot of time with.**

  Do they respect and support you and your positive ambitions?

  Would they be happy or jealous to see you achieve your dreams?

  Are these the kind of people you want to be like?

  Are you hanging out with an uplifting crowd, or are their lowered expectations for themselves keeping you down?

- **When you're with people that upset you, examine the tension or anxiety that is coming up inside. Ask yourself:**

  What emotional buttons are being pushed?

  Where do your anxious feelings come from? Can you remember feeling a similar reaction to the same or other people in your life? Don't forget to look all the way back to childhood, especially if it is your family that is pushing your buttons, as only family can.

  How much of your distress is coming from the other person's behavior, and how much is from your projections on their behavior? Usually, experiences tend to be a mixture of the two.

  What's really bothering you about the situation? Is it something you can just discuss openly and honestly with the person? Is the outer tension a reflection of an inner struggle you may be having with your own conflicting desires and beliefs?

  Is the tension you're feeling a sign that you shouldn't be spending time with the person or group, or that you need to adjust some element in the relationship?

If your friends or family are judging some aspect of your life and their fault-finding is upsetting you, look to see whether some part of you may hold the same judgments about yourself. You may be feeling upset because someone is speaking an uncomfortable truth. Also, if you find certain problematic circumstances arising over and over again in your relationships, you can contemplate how these problems may be coming from something that you need to shift or resolve within yourself.

Because it may not always be possible to avoid difficult people – especially when dealing with family and work situations – you need to ultimately become clear and strong enough to withstand any outer situation that may arise.

As you continue on your spiritual journey, you may even begin to sense that some challenging people and events are appearing in your life for an important and potentially beneficial purpose. For example, these challenging people may be coming to strengthen your resolve and inspire you to contemplate and be moved to express, explain, and demonstrate your beliefs and convictions in an even more tangible form than you have before.

Spiritual Wisdom

The Indian sage Sri Ramakrishna explained the importance of company in different phases of your spiritual journey with this analogy:

"A young plant should be always protected by a fence from the mischief of goats and cows and little urchins. But when once it becomes a big tree, a flock of goats or a herd of cows may find shelter under its spreading boughs, and fill their stomachs with its leaves. So when you have but little faith within you, you should protect it from the evil influences of bad company and worldliness. But when once you grow strong in faith, no worldliness or evil inclination will dare approach your holy presence; and many who are wicked will become godly through your holy contact."

Finding love inside yourself

Some people get upset when a relationship ends, leaving them alone and lonely. However, what is more important than finding someone else to fill your loneliness is to develop a genuine, loving relationship with yourself. Truly, the ache of loneliness is deepest for those who are lonely for a relationship with themselves.

Wise words about solitude

Many great thinkers have found solitude to be the best company. Here are some of their well-expressed odes to the greatness of solitude:

"The more powerful and original a mind, the more it will incline towards the religion of solitude."

—Aldous Huxley

"The greatest saints avoided the company of men as much as possible, and chose to live with God in secret."

—Thomas à Kempis

"The happiest of all lives is a busy solitude."

—Voltaire

"Many teachers praise love as the highest of virtues; I, however, place solitude higher than love."

—Meister Eckhart

"The man who makes everything that leads to happiness depend upon himself, and not upon other men, has adopted the very best plan for living happily."

—Plato

"A man can be himself only so long as he is alone, and if he does not love solitude, he will not love freedom, for it is only when he is alone that he is really free."

—Arthur Schopenhauer

"Settle yourself in solitude, and you will come upon God in yourself."
—Teresa of Avila

Spending time alone gives you the space to peel back mental concepts and ideas that cover your spiritual essence. Therefore, whether you're in or out of a relationship, you may want to consider spending some time alone to:

- **Get to know yourself.** Find out what you like to do. Pay attention to your thoughts. Look through your old memories and contemplate where you've been and why you're here. Contemplating these questions is not like coming up with the right answers for a test, but more of a continual process of growing into greater self-knowledge. Look within and remember who you really are.

- **Let go of misconceptions about yourself.** Solitude gives you the precious space to sort through what you really feel and believe, and to slough off old, outdated, and unproductive ideas about yourself. When you're alone, see whether any critical thoughts about yourself come up. If they do, take some time to contemplate where those words may have come from and whether they can be addressed or released. Consider that anything but pure love and respect for yourself is a veil that has been placed over your pure soul sometime during your journey.

- **Be your own best friend.** Enjoy doing things with yourself. You can have an intriguing, creative, and powerful relationship with yourself—hopefully without too much fighting, because this is one marriage you can't end by getting a divorce!

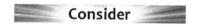 **Consider**

The ultimate goal is to become so strong in your solitude that you're able to pierce through and find your communion with the divine in each moment, no matter where you are or whom you're with.

Chapter 12

Turning Troubles into Triumphs

Topics in this Chapter:

* *   Finding blessings in challenges
* *   Softening suffering with spiritual awareness
* *   Growing from adversity

Difficult times are inevitable in everyone's life. Unwanted events and uncomfortable times bring with them the potential for making not-so-good choices, such as responding with extreme sadness, anxiety, or anger. During these traumatic times, choosing powerful spiritual efforts and thoughts over destructive ones is an especially good idea.

Along with seeking to create circumstances that bring greater happiness and avoid unnecessary suffering, you can also use spiritual wisdom and awareness to enjoy and benefit from all of your experiences — whether they are pleasant or unpleasant.

When troubles come up in your life, along with looking for ways to alleviate the problems, you can also seek to grow spiritually and personally by contemplating how these problems may have come to be. Sometimes things just seem to happen without any obvious cause on your part, but other times, you may be able to consider whether something you've done, either through actions or thoughts, commission or omission, may have contributed to attracting this obstacle to you. (See Chapter 15 for more on the laws of attraction and karma.)

Consider

Contemplating the possible underlying causes of problems can give you the tools to avoid creating, supporting, or giving space for these problems to arise again in the future.

Along with contemplating the possible causes of your troubles, you can also look for ways to encourage positive results. Ask yourself, "What can I learn from this situation?" or, "What strengths can I gain by persevering through this obstacle?" As your self-knowledge increases through addressing and contemplating these kinds of questions, your troubles start to become triumphs.

Seeing Troubles with a Positive Eye

Seeing life with a positive vision brings good energy and a healthy outlook to any experience. You can actually train yourself to look at everything that comes and goes from your life with the glasses of optimism. A touch of surrender and detachment also comes in handy when you're looking to stay calm and contented in times of struggles and strife. And don't forget to bring that all-important sense of humor!

Spiritual Wisdom

Life is like photography. You use the negative to develop.

—Swami Beyondananda

The key to cultivating a positive vision is to trust in an ultimate universal goodness. This one shift of belief filters down through all the different areas of your life, including the way you experience and respond to problems. With trust, you can stay positive and focused on appreciating and growing from whatever blessings or challenges come before you.

Looking at trials and tribulations with a positive eye isn't meant to create more troubles or deny you happiness. Au contraire! With a positive view, even troubles can bring happiness as they inspire you to improve yourself. Sometimes challenges act as tools that can pry you loose from a smaller worldview and push you — running and screaming, if need be — into precious new realms of spiritual awareness.

Anyone who wants to accomplish something great, whether in worldly or spiritual life, must sacrifice certain immediate wishes and comforts. Whether you seek to be an Olympian athlete, an effective parent, an honors student, a successful businessperson, a great entertainer, or a divine spiritual being, any great accomplishment requires a sacrifice of time, attention, effort, and energy. Some achievements also bring discomforts, such as the muscle pain that can come while practicing and perfecting a physical sport or the lack of personal time that can come with being an involved parent. When you know that your pain is leading to a greater benefit, these challenges become easier to bear.

Don't Forget

The road to success in any endeavor is to choose what is beneficial in the long run over what may be pleasant in the moment.

Seeing troubles with a positive eye doesn't mean that you never experience suffering. Rather, even in the midst of suffering, you can simultaneously enter a place that's free from suffering — an awareness that reaches beyond the level of your body and the physical world into the realm of spirituality.

Spiritual Wisdom

When a true spiritual aspirant gets difficulties in life, he may feel sad for one moment, but he will definitely be happy in the next moment.

—Swami Vivekananda

Rising above suffering

Rising above suffering doesn't mean to ignore or numb yourself from all pain, but rather to appreciate and respect every inner and outer experience that comes as part of the glorious dance of your life, whether pleasant or painful.

With a spiritual approach, when you're experiencing one pain or another, you feel the suffering, sadness, unhappiness, or other emotions that arise. However, at the same time, you're remembering spirit. You're remembering beneficial guidance. You're remembering that a new door will open to let in the sunlight of happiness once again. You sit with the pain for a short time and then come out of the darkness to walk on with hope in your heart and a trust in the divine presence that walks with you.

Consider

When you grow spiritually to the point where you are watching your life as a divine play, then you experience all the events, lessons, challenges, and growth as part of this divine play. You are in the events of your life while also watching as what the Indian scriptures call *sakshi bhava*, or *witness consciousness.* You are in the world, but not of it, suffering yet not suffering.

Experiences of pain and suffering depend on the individual threshold of the person who is experiencing them. For one person, small inconveniences can cause more distress than major disasters do for another. I've watched an actress friend get more upset about a bad hair-tinting job than do others who are dealing with devastating tragedies.

Challenges affect you according to your understanding, beliefs, and state of mind, along with the arms of divine grace that come to carry you above the hottest sands and deserts of life.

When those inevitable difficult moments come — such as when you've lost someone or something precious to you, or if you don't achieve a goal you've been working toward, or when your mind, body, or spirit are in a state of pain or suffering — you can see such times with some objectivity. Even while taking intelligent steps to alleviate the suffering, you can remember that you are spirit having a physical experience, a child of the eternal who is currently enrolled in this "school for the soul" called life (see Chapter 4).

Don't Forget

With a spiritual perspective, even if you have some agitations here and there, you can still be aware of the part of you that's free from agitation. T.S. Eliot called this place "the still point of the turning world." It's the eye of the storm, the peaceful inner cave of your heart that remains positive and peaceful even in the midst of a full and eventful life. From that positive, peaceful place, you know that after every storm comes a chance to awaken into a new golden sky with colorful rainbows that will delight your heart, nourish your soul, and rouse your spirit.

Something to talk about

A new priest came to town, and during his first confessional, an elderly woman came to confess her sins.

"Father, I have sinned. Fifty-three years ago, I committed adultery." The woman went on to describe various details about the event.

The priest was moved to hear that after so much time, this woman was finally confessing her sin. He gave her some penance to do and left the church feeling especially buoyant and cheerful. After all, his purpose in joining the priesthood was to relieve people of their burdens and sins.

The next week, the same elderly woman came for confession. Once again, she confessed the same adultery sin from so many years ago. The priest wondered whether her advanced age had made her forget that she'd already confessed the same sin a week earlier, or maybe she was feeling so guilty about her adulterous affair that she felt a need to confess it again.

Three more Sundays came, and each week, this woman arrived to confess the same transgression of adultery from 53 years ago, always in great detail. The priest finally decided to speak up and told the woman, "You've already confessed this same sin several times, and I assure you that through the grace of Our Father, your sin has been forgiven. There is no need to keep confessing it every week."

The woman responded, "I know, but I like to talk about it."

Like this woman, many people enjoy talking about not only their salacious sins, but also their terrible troubles. Some people practically become tabloid shows about themselves — sharing every detail of each dramatic challenge over and over with various friends.

Spiritual Wisdom

The more you move towards the goal, all sorrow will cease. Even if there is sorrow, you will become impervious to it. It will not touch you. There will be an inner strength created within you where even sorrow will not have a meaning for you. You will smile even at misfortune and suffering.

—Chidananda

Finding blessings from tragedy

The struggle of life is one of our greatest blessings. It makes us patient, sensitive, and Godlike. It teaches us that although the world is full of suffering, it is also full of the overcoming of it.

—Helen Keller

Sometimes tragedies actually bring out the best in people. Have you noticed how people get together and help one another so much more easily when they're in the midst of a disaster? Tragedies can bring together neighbors who had previously hardly even bothered to say hello to one another.

Tragedies and disasters have a way of shaking off many layers of illusion-based distractions to reveal a deeper awareness of the shared flame of humanity. Natural and manmade disasters, such as floods, tornados, hurricanes, terrorist bombings, and earthquakes, all bring (along with images of devastation) equally powerful portrayals of human beings helping and even heroically saving others.

Here are some ways that suffering can uplift your spirit:

- Suffering inspires humility, vulnerability, and openness.

- Suffering teaches compassion and kindness.

- Suffering brings greater appreciation and gratitude for all you have.

- Suffering guides you to contemplate and reconsider your thoughts and actions.

- Suffering encourages renunciation — an important quality for spiritual growth.

- Suffering inspires you to pray and ask for divine grace.

Many people have awakened to religion, spirituality, and the presence of God for the first time after going through traumatic events. In fact, suffering can be one of the most potent forces for spiritual transformation and awakening. I know that may not be exactly what you wanted to hear!

Understanding the benefits that can come from suffering shouldn't make you start courting difficulties or becoming a martyr who looks for more suffering to grow from. Nor should you just suffer on and on without making efforts to heal the problems in your life. In fact, with spiritual awareness, you can remove unnecessary discomforts not only through outer efforts, but also by combining the power of your mind with spiritual practices, good actions, and higher intentions.

Spiritual Wisdom

Wise words about the trials of life

Great teachers from many traditions have pointed out how valuable life's trials can be for one who is seeking to grow from them. Here are a few of their views on this topic:

"Tragedy is like a strong acid — it dissolves away all but the very gold of truth."
> —D.H. Lawrence

"Sorrow makes a man think of God."
> —Ramana Maharshi

"Suffering is not an evil, it is the consequence and nearly always the remedy of evil."
> —Eliphas Levi

"The soul that is without suffering does not feel the need of knowing the ultimate cause of the universe."
> —Anandamayi Ma

"Love your suffering. Do not resist it, do not flee from it. Give yourself to it. It is only your aversion that hurts, nothing else."
> —Hermann Hesse

"Never to suffer would have been never to have been blessed."
> —Edgar Allan Poe

Recognizing That There Are No Mistakes

A water bearer in Nepal had two large pots that he would carry to the river to fill with water every day. Each water pot hung on the end of a pole, which balanced across his shoulders. One of the pots was perfect and always delivered a full measure of water at the end of the long walk from the river to the water bearer's house. The other one had a crack and would arrive only half-full.

One day, the leaking pot spoke to the water bearer, saying, "I feel that I should apologize to you."

"Why?" asked the gentle man.

The leaky pot explained, "During these past two years, I have only been able to deliver half my load because this crack in my side causes the water to leak out all the way back to the house. Because of my flaw, you do all this work without receiving the full value from your efforts."

The water bearer felt compassion for the old cracked pot and told it, "As we return to my house, I want you to notice the beautiful flowers along the path."

Indeed, as they went up the hill, the faulty pot took notice of the beautiful wild flowers on one side of the path. When they arrived at his house, the man asked the leaky pot, "Did you notice that there were flowers only on your side of the path, but not on the other pot's side? That's because I've always known your flaw and put it to good use. I planted flower seeds on your side of the path, and every day as we walk back from the river, you water them. For two years I've been able to enjoy these beautiful flowers. Without your being just the way you are, there would have been so much less beauty in my life. Thank you, my friend."

Consider

Sometimes making a mistake ends up being the perfect thing for your spiritual evolution. In some cases, you may have to make a big mistake before you can truly grow and become free from whatever incorrect ideas had been motivating many other mistaken thoughts and actions.

When you make mistakes or lose yourself in anger, fear, or whatever contracted emotions push you out of your equanimity and self-control, there is always a new opportunity for growth. It may hurt oh so bad! You may not want to make the shift to see the lessons behind a painful event. Sometimes it is easier to complain, blame someone, or put yourself down than to do the real work of respectful self-examination.

Yet, the opportunity is there, waiting for you to make the leap — waiting for you to see your weakness and make internal (and, if need be, external) changes. What's important in any situation is your own growth. How can you learn humility, detachment, love, and faith? How can you use this breakdown to open up into another great breakthrough?

It's Not Punishment, but Guidance

Q: How do we experience painful circumstances without becoming embittered by them?

A: By seeing them as lessons and not as retribution. Trust life, my friends. However far afield life seems to take you, this trip is necessary. You have come to transverse a wide terrain of experience in order to verify where truth lies and where your distortion is in that terrain. You will then be able to return to your home center, your soul self, refreshed and wiser.

—Emmanuel (as channeled by Pat Rodegast)

Here's an analogy for one way to look at what may appear to be punishments from God or the universe. Imagine that you have a little dog that you really love, but your beloved pooch frequently chews up your socks. You aren't really angry with your sweet pup, and you even may think it's cute how he looks up at you with a guilty face and pieces of shredded sock in his paws. Nevertheless, you have to feign anger enough to communicate to your pup that he shouldn't chew up any more socks.

Still, even while you're yelling "No!" or giving the pup a gentle swat on the nose, you are still loving him and wishing you could be cuddling instead of training him. But you know that if you kept smiling and petting your little friend, he wouldn't understand that his behavior needed to change. If you don't let your pup know that what he's doing is wrong, then you may end up with a closet filled with shredded socks and a grown dog who has moved on to chewing bigger and more expensive things.

If the puppy gets your message right away and changes his incorrect behavior after just a tiny chastisement, then everyone can go back to sweetness and cuddling very quickly. However, if the little dog doesn't get the message and continues to chew up your socks, then you have to continue to be forceful in punishing and training him.

In the same way, when you seek to be in harmony with the universe by paying attention to the many avenues of divine guidance that are available inside and out, then you are more likely to do what is right and less likely to "chew up any socks." When you do more of what is right and less of what is harmful, you draw to yourself fewer negative results and less chastisement from a universe that is not so much punishing as guiding you to be your best.

Trust is the key

When you ride one of those space blaster, thriller, rollercoaster rides, it's your trust that transforms what could have been an extremely scary and traumatic experience into fun. Try going on the same rollercoaster ride after being told that ten significant bolts have been removed from its structure.

In the same way, trusting God and the eternal perfection behind this visible universe makes the ups and downs of your life-ride less scary and more fun.

Transforming Challenge into Ecstasy

Spiritual Wisdom

The heart, like the grape, is prone to delivering its harvest in the same moment it appears to be crushed.

—Roger Housden

Some ancient philosophies from India describe intense emotions, such as great joy and paralyzing fear, as potent opportunities to break free from the world of illusion and move into a higher awareness.

One scripture called the *Spanda Karikas* explains that during experiences of vehement anger, surprise, and fear, your mind automatically stops. These moments are some of the best times to focus your attention inside yourself with the intention of gaining entrance into the background consciousness behind your thoughts. This practice of vigilance in the midst of emotional challenge can help you grasp the ecstatic experience of supreme reality that exists behind all the illusions of worldly life.

One example given in this scripture is of someone who is running for his life from an elephant — a more likely event in ancient India than it is in modern societies! Picture this person, though. An elephant is running after him. The fellow is running for his life, and while that's happening, he remembers the greater vision of universal reality and shifts into a spiritual awareness beyond the running, beyond the fear, and beyond thought. He becomes identified with the witness who is dreaming the dream of his life.

Weathering the storms

With spiritual eyes, everything is a gift from God — even those terrible moments of deep inner suffering when you wish you didn't exist. Such times may be blessing you by clearing out your soul and washing you clean with tears of grief to prepare a proper space for more divine spirit to come into your life.

Imagine that you've spent your life living out in a field, dealing with occasional fluctuations of elements. One day, a big, terrible hurricane comes through, forcing you to seek shelter to save your life.

While running, you find a small, abandoned hut that you had never noticed, and you go inside the hut to stay safe from the storm. The great news is that after the storm ends, you'll still have that newly discovered hut to live in!

This, too, shall pass

One day King Solomon decided to humble his most trusted minister, Benaiah ben Yehoyada. He said to the minister, "Benaiah, there is a certain ring that I want you to bring to me. I wish to wear it for the holiday of Sukkot, so you have six months to find it."

"If it exists anywhere on earth, your majesty," replied Benaiah, "I will find it and bring it to you. But what makes the ring you seek so special?"

"I want a ring that has magic powers," answered the king. "If a happy man looks at it, he becomes sad, and if a sad man looks at it, he becomes happy." King Solomon knew that no such ring existed in the world, but he wanted to give his minister a little taste of humility.

Spring passed and then summer, and still Benaiah was unable to find such a ring anywhere, though he searched high and low throughout the land. On the night before Sukkot, Benaiah decided to take a walk in one of the poorest quarters of Jerusalem. There, he passed by an old merchant who had begun to set out the day's wares on a shabby carpet. "Have you by any chance heard of a magic ring that makes the happy wearer forget his joy and the broken-hearted wearer forget his sorrows?" asked Benaiah.

He watched the old merchant take a plain gold ring from his carpet and engrave something on it. When Benaiah read the words on the ring, his face broke out in a wide smile.

That night, the entire city welcomed in the holiday of Sukkot with great festivity. "Well, my friend," asked King Solomon, "have you found what I sent you after?" All the ministers laughed and Solomon himself smiled.

To everyone's surprise, Benaiah held up a small gold ring and declared, "Here it is, your majesty! This ring will make a happy man sad and a sad man happy."

As soon as Solomon read the inscription, the smile vanished from his face. The merchant had inscribed three Hebrew letters on the gold band: gimel, zayin, yud, which began the words "*Gam zeh ya'avor*" — "This, too, shall pass."

At that moment, Solomon realized that all his fabulous wealth and tremendous power were fleeting, and that one day he and all he owned would be nothing but dust.

King Solomon's quest to humble Benaiah had taught both Benaiah and Solomon an important and humbling lesson: Everything in this world is temporary. Whatever is happening in life — whether easy or hard, happy or sad, pleasant or unpleasant — shall pass. Good times will pass, and troubling times will pass. Remembering this truth during the good times helps to keep you focused on deeper aspects of life; and remembering that all things shall pass during difficult times gives you the hope and strength to persevere and turn your troubles into triumphs.

Chapter 13

Finding the Deep Calling of Your Soul

Topics in this Chapter:

*   Living a creative, fulfilling life
*   Finding and empowering your vision
*   Sharing what you know

Some spiritual traditions suggest that even before you were born on this earth, the divine creator put deep into your heart the knowledge of what you're supposed to do in your life, including what you're meant to give and receive from this world.

From a spiritual perspective, it doesn't matter if your deep calling is to be big or small, famous or publicly unknown, loved or feared, a leader or a follower, or any combination of these and more. What matters most is to find the avenues of experience and expression that are right for your soul's journey in this world at this time. The challenge is to find your soul's deep calling beneath all the layers of outer experiences and expectations that have been piled upon you throughout your life — from friends, family, schools, television, music, writings, movies, and more.

 **Consider**

Spiritual wisdom and practices help you clear away the cobwebs of mediocre, unenthusiastic living so that you can experience joyful, passionate inspiration and discover and fulfill why you are here. Taking time to pay attention to your soul's deep calling is a good use of that time!

Discovering Your Dharma

What are you here to do? What is your job in life? The Sanskrit word *dharma* can be helpful in contemplating the deep calling of your soul.

Dharma doesn't have an exact English translation, but it can be paraphrased as "righteous living". Dharma is the way you are meant to live — in general as a human being, and also as an individual with a unique set of lessons to learn, experiences to have, and gifts to give. In a way, your dharma is also your mission in life.

When you have a sense of what your mission is, you make better choices about what to do and not do during your time in this world as you. When you live in accordance with your greater destiny, you are naturally guided to do what is right in both large and small situations.

All human beings share certain big-picture dharmas, such as to take care of this planet and one another, while discovering, expressing, and honoring the divine nature of life. Some spiritual sages say that the ultimate dharma is to live so that you go to Heaven or to follow practices that will bring spiritual enlightenment or liberation from this illusory world of limited experience (see Chapters 14 and 17).

Along with common group dharmas that should be followed by all human beings, each person also has his or her own individual set of dharmas. For example, someone may have the personal dharma of always being as honest as possible, regardless of the possible repercussions. Another person may feel deep inside that it is her responsibility to help when she sees someone who is in need, regardless of whether others would expect her to take responsibility in those circumstances.

Consider

Sometimes people find their dharma through challenges or tragedies. For example, many celebrities and others who have experienced certain illnesses come to sense that helping to find cures for these illnesses would fulfill their mission by helping to heal their loved ones, themselves, and the greater good of humankind. Their dedication to a good cause gives meaning to their suffering and helps remove the suffering of others, which is a great dharma for anyone to follow.

Discovering your righteous path of living

Spiritual Wisdom

A musician must make music, an artist must paint, a poet must write, if he is to be ultimately at peace with himself. What one can be, one must be.

-- *Abraham Maslow*

Your dharma is what fulfils you. It's what floats your boat, buoys your spirit, and opens your heart. Following your dharma may not always be comfortable or easy, but it brings a sense of underlying serenity and rightness that stays strong behind even difficult or challenging times.

When you're following your dharma:

- Even if obstacles arise, they don't overwhelm you.

- You feel yourself flowing with time rather than resisting its flow. You are neither pining for the past nor waiting anxiously for the future.

- You have a sense of fitting comfortably into yourself and your life as if you are sitting in a seat that fits perfectly.

- You trust that the challenges and temptations that come your way are helping you grow and giving you an opportunity to strengthen your commitment to following your dharma.

Spirituality in Action

Leaving a footprint

Take a moment to contemplate your life and your eventual death. Think of what it will be like to leave this place called earth and these life circumstances called you and your life. What meaning has your life held? What have you received and given to this world during your stay? Others may have their own views about who you are and what you've done, but what are *your* views about yourself and your own life?

Think of all the lessons you've learned, all the people you've known, and all the outer objects and expressions you'll have to leave behind when your time here is through. Think of all your personal qualities that will be silenced from this world when you are gone.

Now imagine that you want to leave a footprint behind in this world — something that expresses who you are and where you've been. Maybe you'd like to leave a letter behind to your children or loved ones, or maybe a statement to the whole world. Some choose to leave a creative legacy through scrapbooking, painting, or writing poems.

The truth is that you are inevitably leaving a footprint behind on this world. The key here is to choose some of what it will be. Parents automatically leave a legacy to the world through the children they've raised. Just in living a good life, you may be leaving legacies through all the people you touch with kindness and wisdom. If you're a comedian, you may leave a legacy in all the audiences who find laughter in the future while remembering your humorous observations. Those in service professions, such as nurses, teachers, and police officers, also leave their legacy through all the people they've helped.

Finding your calling

A sense of deep fulfillment arises within you when you're following your calling and giving to this world in a way that is in harmony with your nature and destiny. Once you stop resisting what comes to you, you'll be a smoother canvas upon which the divine creative spirit can paint a new and beautiful landscape — the landscape of your great, fulfilled life.

Here are some more tips for finding the deep calling of your soul:

- **Pay attention to your thoughts and feelings about what you should be doing above the opinions and expectations of others.** Do listen to positive suggestions from trusted friends and family with an open mind and heart, but remember that your life is *your* life and *your* responsibility!

- **Make friends with your inner knower.** Some call this inner knower the subconscious mind or the superconscious mind, while others call it the inner Self, or the divine seat within a human being. As you go through your day making decisions about what to do, where to go, what to buy, and how to respond to immediate situations, feel the presence of your inner knower. Understand that this inner knower is your friend and give it your friendship in return.

- **Do what your love.** Let go of your focus on the worldly benefits you may be receiving from a particular job or career and contemplate whether you'd still want to do that thing. Sometimes you can't really change jobs on a whim, but at least you can put your mental energy and intention into doing work that fulfils your calling as much as possible. One way I measure this quality in my own works is to strive to do for pay only what I would gladly do for free. (Of course, with my background of monastic service, working for free is not as shocking an idea as it may be for many people.) Even when projects come up that don't seem to fit my personal bill but are necessary for *paying* bills, I do my best to approach the unavoidable work with a positive feeling, trusting that there is some reason for me to be in that job that may contribute to fulfilling my calling now or in the future. With this faith, I do whatever I can to harmonize with the situation and make the work interesting or fun.

- **Remember death.** When people forget death, they don't feel pressured to seek and follow their dharma. They don't treasure each moment or feel the need to find out how to make the very best use of the time they have in their life. They sell out today thinking there will always be tomorrow. Then in their last moments, these forgetful folks often have regrets over what they could or should have done — and it isn't usually a regret that they didn't accumulate more stuff!

Being guided from within

Once you sense your heart's calling, that connection becomes a guiding light for everything you do:

- With an awareness of your heart's calling, you can measure actions and decisions by the yardstick of your life's mission and eliminate as many incongruous efforts and experiences as possible. For example, you may be a member of certain groups and clubs, but find that these memberships are taking your time and energy away from things that really tug at your heartstrings. Once you sense and understand your heart's calling, you're better able to rearrange your commitments to focus on what is most in harmony with your greater destiny.

- Focusing on your heart's calling will also help you experience and approach life with a greater spiritual respect and vision. When you have the confidence of knowing your heart's calling, you're able to give yourself fully to whatever you do. If your heart's calling is to pick up trash in a community park, you do it cheerfully instead of grumbling about all the inconsiderate schlubs who left their garbage on the ground.

- Focusing on your heart's calling reflects in the world around you and brings more opportunities for you to live in harmony with your great intention. (You can find out more about how your thoughts affect the world in Chapter 15) When your intentions are clear, the world naturally brings what will help you to act and live in harmony with those intentions. When you're focused on your heart's calling, you may find that the right things, people, pets, homes, and jobs come into your life quite spontaneously.

Seek and find your heart's calling, whether it is to bring a beautiful child into the world, to help create better social systems, to give people joy through your cooking, singing, dancing, loving, speaking, praying, or to follow any one of countless possible avenues of expression. If your heart's calling leads you to several different avenues or to one and then another, stay open and trusting, while also using common sense to make good decisions that are both intelligent and inspired.

Following your bliss

Bliss is different from usual sense-based pleasures. With bliss, you feel a sense of perfection exactly as you are and where you are. With bliss, you are not anxious to change or fix things. Even if you do make changes from the state of bliss, you do so joyfully, enjoying the perfection of what was and what will be as you act with blissful inner freedom.

My personal calling

I've clarified a number of heart's callings during my life. One of my most significant guiding principles came to me at a time when I was physically ill in the mid-1990s and was preparing for the possibility of leaving this world. I'd quit both of my jobs as associate producer and editor of the childrens' television shows *X-Men* and the *Mighty Morphin' Power Rangers* while experiencing several challenging physical ailments all at once.

I was actually feeling at peace with the possibility of leaving this world, having already lived a life filled with many unexpected blessings. But then a surprisingly clear inner message came booming into my meditation like the voice of God in the Ten Commandments movie when He told Moses to take off his shoes because he was on hallowed ground. It seems that the vulnerable surrender I'd been experiencing may have opened me up to receive a clear message of guidance.

The booming voice of God said, "First you have to share what you've learned." With this dictate, I moved into a birds-eye view of my life and saw the eclectic nature of my journey — from exploring psychology intensely as a child, to studying neuroscience and film-video in university, to spending a decade of deep spiritual immersion while researching, producing, and editing hundreds of powerful videos about spirituality and meditation, and then to my years of Hollywood work, editing and producing entertaining television shows with many talented and colorful folks.

"First you have to share what you've learned." That is exactly what I've been doing since receiving this guidance and vision of my calling. As I've learned more, I've shared more. Did the message come from God Himself, or was it a subconscious expression of a hidden aspiration? Ultimately, this question didn't matter, because once the instruction and vision of my life came before me, I recognized that sharing what I've learned is indeed part of my calling, my dharma, and my mission in life.

Look for touches of bliss in your life. Discover what supports your experience of bliss and see how you can increase those elements. If playing with animals gives you that special bliss, then consider how you can increase your interaction with more animals. Consider studying to enter the veterinary profession, adopt some homeless pets, or volunteer at an animal rescue house. Learn how to train animals, set up a bird feeder, or bring peanuts along when you walk in nature so that you can feed the squirrels. The light of bliss helps to guide you in choosing how to spend the precious wealth of your time here on earth as you.

Being an Artist of Life

Every child is an artist. The problem is how to remain an artist once we grow up.

— Pablo Picasso

Being an artist of life means to express with your full palette of colors and your vibrant creative spark in even the small moments of life. Sometimes you may be painting a happy face, and sometimes you'll be expressing sad tears. Sometimes you are dancing a joyful dance, and sometimes you may be singing a song of loss.

Being an artist of life doesn't mean that you have to become big and famous. Creativity comes in many forms, and from a spiritual perspective, small creative expressions can be as meaningful and valuable as larger ones.

Some express their creativity in cooking, gardening, music, dance, event planning, home design, crafts, business decisions, or journal writing. One of the most creative "jobs" is to be a good parent who comes up with educational and fun projects for your children.

Creativity and spirituality are great friends. Both require qualities such as self-respect, one-pointed focus, openness to inner guidance, and a willingness to express your truth.

Sharing your abundance

One beautiful form of creativity comes when you feel that you've received so much in life — so many experiences, so much wisdom, and so many blessings — that you must express and share what you've received and learned with others.

When creative expression, gratitude, and service-mindedness come together, your joyful inspiration can overflow the boundaries of ordinary life. Maybe you offer creative service to your place of worship, or you start a blog to share some aspect of your life with the world, or maybe you're a great cook and you offer your skills to a service-oriented volunteer group that brings food to those in need.

When you share the abundance that the universe has given to you, your act of giving back helps to create a beautiful dance of giving, receiving, expressing, and sharing of the abundance of life with the delicious energy of creative service.

Finding your own style

Finding, accepting, and enjoying your own personal style is a great achievement and a wonderful blessing. Spiritual wisdom allows you to step into a higher vision of your life as an expression of divine universal creative spirit.

From this higher viewpoint, you can look at yourself with a bit more objectivity. You can even look at your faults and mistakes without feeling too much ego discomfort. You can be like a comedian who appreciates and uses even his faults to get big laughs.

Knowing your inherent greatness increases your self-respect and also sets a foundation for exploring, refining, and weeding out any aspects of your expression that are not in harmony with your greater self.

Spirituality in Action

See how it feels for you to say and think these words: "I am great just as I am." Say the phrase aloud and then repeat the words mentally as you breathe in, and again as you breathe out. Here are some possible reasons why you may not be fully appreciating and expressing your own style:

- **You may think that your style is boring.** However, thinking that you're boring doesn't mean you really are boring. I used to think I was totally boring during my years of monastic life, where the people around me seemed to have a lot more dramas and opinions than I did. Even now, on a day-to-day level, my life is generally quiet and not so outwardly exciting. But looking from a larger perspective, my life has been pretty creative and interesting. Sometimes you may think you are boring when you're really percolating into a more fragrant cup of you. Your creative spark may be growing silently under a simple surface just as colorful flower seeds germinate quietly under a blanket of white snow.

- **You may think that your style isn't good enough.** Maybe you don't think you're clever enough or considerate enough. Maybe you're not a good listener or a caring son, daughter, mother, father, sister, brother, worker, or friend. Even if you find these kinds of shortcomings in yourself, you can still accept and love yourself while also taking steps to improve your personal style. Take a respectful inventory of your style. See which of your personality traits are natural, which have been created by imitating other people, which have come from the environments and cultures around you, and which aspects of your style and personality are serving you well versus creating obstacles to your greater good.

You are the artist of your life. Choose your colors. Choose your topics. Choose your modes of expression. If you don't want to have so many dark colors in your life-painting, then stop mixing so many dark colors and start opening up tubes of brighter yellows, oranges, and reds.

Spirituality in Action

Words from some who found their style

Here are some quotes by free-spirited creative folks who understood the value of following the beat of their own inspired drum:

> "When I die and appear before the heavenly court, I will not be asked, 'Why were you not Moses?' I will be asked, 'Why were you not Zusya?'"
> —Rabbi Zusya

> "The greatest thing in the world is to know how to be oneself."
> —Michel de Montaigne

> "Loyalty to petrified opinion never yet broke a chain or freed a human soul."
> —Mark Twain

> "Not to be bound by rules, but to be creating one's own rules—this is the kind of life which Zen is trying to have us live."
> —D. T. Suzuki

> "Be who you are and say what you feel, because those who mind don't matter and those who matter don't mind."
> —Dr. Seuss

Once you've done your best to change unwanted behaviors and personality traits, then make who you are work for you. If you have a cantankerous style and find other people getting offended by your comments, see whether you can add humor to make your expressions less offensive and more entertaining. You could even consider becoming a shock jock, or an opinionated blog writer or news host.

How many people must have said to Picasso, "Why can't you just paint a face that looks like a damn face?" However, Picasso stayed true to his own style, and that unique style is what has kept his name and works alive, unlike the works of so many other artists that have been covered by the sands of time.

Sharing the treasures of your journey through writing

Spiritual Wisdom

True education begins only when a man turns from all external aids to the Infinity within and becomes as it were a natural source of original knowledge.
— Swami Ramtirtha

The most basic tenet of nearly every great philosophical system is to "know thyself." Knowing yourself is not a narcissistic luxury, but what life demands from everyone.

Every person reaches from the heavens to earth, and perhaps beyond (see Chapters 3 and 14). However, most people are too busy focusing on their immediate, outer lives to take time to unfold all the wisdom that can be gained by unpacking and seeing more deeply into each event, moment, feeling, and experience.

Don't Forget

Life is truly more wondrous than fiction, which is one reason reality shows have become so popular in modern television.

Appreciating your story

Consider how interested people have been in every detail of the lives of famous and infamous celebrities and this month's scandal or heartwarming tale du jour? Well, that is how interested you should be in your *own* life!

Every life is an amazing story, no matter how boring the outer circumstances may seem compared to others. The processes you've already experienced while growing from childhood on inherently carry countless profound stories and lessons. Your job is to dig for the gems in everything that comes and has previously come your way.

One way to approach your untapped terrain of inner knowledge is to use the process of writing to dive deeply into events that have unfolded and continue to unfold in your own life. Whether outwardly exciting or ordinary, you can discover lessons and insights hidden within each twist and turn on your path, by writing about them with an intention to gain greater insight and appreciation.

Contemplative writing:

- **Teaches you to respect the intricate beauty of your life, while extracting its juicy lessons.** Instead of only living on the surface of daily events, you take time to honor the deeper lessons, patterns, and colors inherent in the details of every moment by giving form to them in words.

- **Opens a way for you to drink deeply from the fresh spring of inner wisdom, insight, and expression.** Taking time to write about past experiences and insights you've had keeps your higher level awareness freshly invoked in your mind as you approach the current events and thoughts of your daily life.

- **Teaches you to give yourself the respect and reverence that every human being deserves.** Contemplative writing is a way of asserting that your inner wisdom is so grand and that your life is so precious and valuable that your thoughts and experiences deserve to be explored and expressed as a novel, poem, journal, or autobiography.

- **Gives you a chance to explore and organize your memories, feelings, and beliefs into a more objective view of everything you encounter.** Contemplative writing shows you how to notice patterns of events and guides you to give structure to your thoughts and experiences so that you can see the world with a bigger-picture view.

- **Enriches your life by helping you pay more attention to life.** When it comes to life, quality is definitely more important than quantity. Paying attention to life gives you a much greater experience of life.

Ultimately, it doesn't matter whether you plan to publish your words, although sharing what you've learned — opening yourself to the extent where you're willing to share personal thoughts with complete strangers — can also be a powerful experience.

In addition, if you have done the inner work to contemplate your experiences, others can also benefit from the fruits of your contemplations. One thing I've learned is that even with very different cultures and upbringings, people share similar ranges of experiences.

If you're able to pierce through to the essence of an experience that you're writing about, others will also be able to relate to your story and apply the healings and understandings you've achieved to their own lives.

Consider

Some people prefer to set strict disciplined schedules for their writing — for example, they plan to write a certain number of pages every morning or evening — while others prefer to write only when they feel moved to express something. As with every practice, you have to know your own nature and decide what approach works best for you.

The purpose of contemplative writing is not only to share your thoughts with others, but also to teach you to look at things with a more conscious eye and to contemplate, clarify, and empower your beliefs using the tool of words.

Regardless of whether it's your calling to make what you write available to others, it is still in your best interest to take advantage of the power of words to explore and heal your body, mind, and spirit.

Don't Forget

Your beliefs create your reality. Uplift your beliefs and you uplift the world!

Part Four:

Connecting with this Conscious Universe

Chapter 14

The Individual Nature of Universal Creation

Topics in this Chapter:

* Seeing life with a spiritual worldview
* Exploring the nature of universal creation
* Understanding where you fit into the bigger picture

In this chapter, I introduce you to one way of looking at the world with spiritual eyes. Many of the ideas in these pages come from an ancient spiritual science called *Kashmir Shaivism*, along with other traditions.

The beginning of this chapter is a little more technical than other chapters in this book; it describes a theory of universal creation that can be helpful in expanding your awareness into new vistas of possibility, with an inclusive view of the universe that makes logical sense and has a scientific flavor.

 **Consider**

As you move forward on your spiritual journey, check out religious and philosophical ideas that resonate with your understanding and interests and bring those ideas and theories together with your own stream of inner wisdom to build an intelligent, individual, personal view of life that continues to grow and evolve.

The Spiritual Science of Universal Creation

I'm astounded by people who want to "know" the universe when it's hard enough to find your way around Chinatown.

—Woody Allen

When you're talking about universal creation, you have to move into a bigger picture view that goes beyond just one planet, one time frame, and one physical dimension. The theory of universal creation I introduce to you here offers a big picture view of the universe that has a place for just about anything you can possibly think of.

Whether you're talking about Christian ideas of heaven and hell, Tibetan descriptions of different realms of existence, new age messages from the "other side," or various worlds of gods described by the cultures of Greece, Egypt, and India, all these different realms can coexist within the theory of universal creation that I share with you in this chapter.

Different ways to view life

Each religious tradition has its own ideas about the nature of life. Different people and traditions see life differently, whether as a game, as a series of challenges, as an opportunity to grow, or as a divine play. Some believe that life is made of suffering, while others say it is of the nature of supreme bliss.

Seen from a more universal perspective, these views are neither right nor wrong, but merely different faces of the ultimately unknowable nature of life.

One common analogy used to describe how seemingly opposing theories can fit together within an unknowable bigger picture is the story of six blind men who came upon an elephant.

The first man touched the elephant's leg and announced, "The elephant is a pillar." The second man touched the tail and disputed the first, saying, "Oh, no, it is like a rope." The third touched the trunk of the elephant and said, "It is like a thick branch of a tree." The fourth touched the elephant's ear and said, "It is like a big hand fan." The fifth blind man touched the belly of the elephant and declared, "It is like a huge wall." And the sixth man touched the tusk of the elephant and said, "It is a solid pipe."

Different philosophical approaches to the nature of the universe are like the different interpretations of these six blind men. All these blind men are both right and wrong, with each giving a different piece of the puzzle of what an elephant really is. Each viewpoint is valuable to consider and contemplate, but you wouldn't want to limit your understanding of the elephant or the universe to any one definition or close the door to other possibilities.

Instead of trying to memorize the specific details covered in this section, let the words enter your awareness gently, without straining or feeling frustrated if you don't fully understand the stages of creation being described. This kind of teaching is not meant to be memorized as you would study for a test, or to be used to build a rigid belief system. Theories of universal creation should be used to bathe your mind in higher-concept spiritual philosophies that have the potential to transform your outlook and uplift your life.

The map in Figure 14-1 is based on the philosophy of Kashmir Shaivism, which is said to have developed around 900 A.D. in the state of Kashmir, which is in the northwestern corner of India. This chart shows how divine universal Consciousness becomes all the levels of creation, down to the physical world and your experience of it.

Now, even though Figure 14-1 may look like a sequential process that moves from supreme consciousness at the top to the physical universe at the bottom, the truth is that the whole chart is happening all at once. Universal Consciousness is always there — pure, eternal, and unaffected by the creation that is described as being projected like a big multidimensional movie upon its screen. And just as a movie screen is unaffected by the nature of the movie being projected on it, so the screen of pure consciousness remains unaffected by all the universal creations that play upon its screen.

Don't worry if you don't fully understand how this process of universal creation works. Sages from many traditions have spent decades of intense spiritual practices to catch even a glimpse of a higher universal view of creation. Just to come upon elevated spiritual teachings shows that you've already achieved a certain resonance with higher truth and are ready to open up to its gifts in a new way.

Is Figure 14-1 a perfectly accurate and all-inclusive map of reality? No, of course not. Is there such a thing as an all-inclusive map of reality? No way. If a map were all inclusive, it would not be a map, but the thing itself. Is this graph of universal creation a set of ideas that can open many doors to understanding how the entire universe – including you – can be divine? Yes indeed!

The following sections describe each stage of creation as numbered on the chart. Again, these stages are both sequential and eternal: They take place in order and are also happening all at once. The goal of spiritual efforts in the context of this philosophy is to move your awareness from the bottom rungs of this ladder of universal creation — representing the physical world and sensory experience — up to the higher realms of spiritual realization and universal freedom.

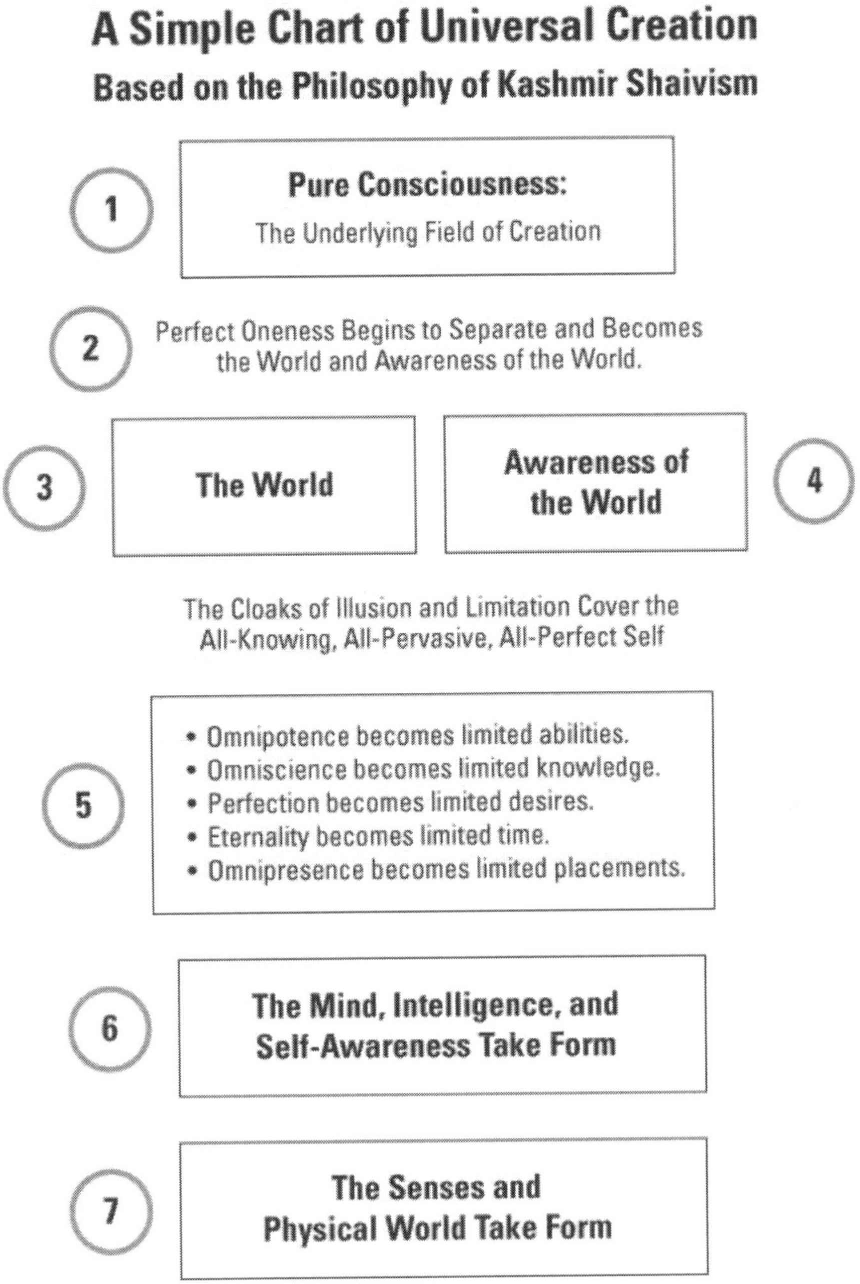

A Simple Chart of Universal Creation
Based on the Philosophy of Kashmir Shaivism

1 — **Pure Consciousness:** The Underlying Field of Creation

2 — Perfect Oneness Begins to Separate and Becomes the World and Awareness of the World.

3 — **The World**

Awareness of the World — **4**

The Cloaks of Illusion and Limitation Cover the All-Knowing, All-Pervasive, All-Perfect Self

5 —
- Omnipotence becomes limited abilities.
- Omniscience becomes limited knowledge.
- Perfection becomes limited desires.
- Eternality becomes limited time.
- Omnipresence becomes limited placements.

6 — **The Mind, Intelligence, and Self-Awareness Take Form**

7 — **The Senses and Physical World Take Form**

Figure 14-1: A map of the stages of universal creation.

Stage 1

In stage 1, pure Consciousness exists as the underlying field of all creation. Universal creation begins with a blank slate of *pure Consciousness* – existence without content, potential without expression. This indefinable source of all creation is like the space within a tiny seed that contains the energetic potential of a huge tree, complete with branches and leaves.

Even after it becomes the physical universe, this Consciousness remains pure and eternal. Jesus expressed his identification with the eternal nature by saying, "Before Abraham was, *I Am.*"

Stage 2

In stage 2 of creation, the separation from oneness begins. The move to creation begins with an initial energy pulsation, a subtle throb of and a hint of creation to be. You could think of this stage as being like the initial process that takes place in a cell that will one day become a living animal or human being. This stage is like the moment when the spark of creation is struck in a cell, before it begins to multiply.

In stage 1, you have the cell of pure Consciousness. Once this creative spark enters that cell in stage 2, it divides into two cells, which are represented in this chart by stages number 3 and 4.

Stage 3

During stage 3, a glimmer of the world begins to take subtle form. You can think of this stage as being similar to the state of your computer right after you push the button to turn it on. None of your individual folders or icons are visible or available on the screen, but the computer's processor is starting to access the information, and is humming with the promise of your upcoming computer experience.

Stage 4

In stage 4 of this chart of universal creation (see Figure 14-1), awareness begins to take form. The experience of this stage of universal creation is similar to the experience you may have just before waking up, as your awareness prepares to move from the darkness of deep sleep into the colorful world of your bed and beyond.

When you're about to awaken from a good night's sleep, a vibration of your upcoming wakefulness starts to pulsate through the still field of your sleeping, unconscious mind. You begin to grasp a subtle remembrance of a world outside yourself, without feeling any separation between yourself and the world. You're in a peaceful state of awareness that is free from the complications, expectations, and judgments of ego-based thoughts and desires. The scheduling, thinking mind is not yet in place to diffuse your peaceful awareness into the upcoming responsibilities and concerns of the day.

At this point, you're still one with pure creative Consciousness and free from any sense of limitation. You're completely powerful, with nothing holding you back in any way. You sense a world that exists outside of yourself, yet at the same time you know that you're completely one with everything.

Stage 5

Once creation gets to stage 5, *maya* enters the picture, and that's when everything hits the fan. The Sanskrit term *maya* is often translated as "illusion," which is the closest English translation for this deeply metaphysical word. Maya comes from the root verb *ma*, which means "to measure, limit, and give form," and is sometimes translated as "that which measures." The idea is that the measurings of time and space are the basis of maya.

With maya in the picture, time and space are now measured and therefore limited. Within the previously all-pervasive and eternal universal Consciousness, five cloaks of limitation come into the picture and reduce universal freedom to limited experience.

Until this stage, universal Consciousness is unlimited, pure, and perfect within itself — eternal, omniscient, omnipresent, omnipotent, and perfectly contented. Now, with the forgetfulness that comes from the power of illusion, the dream of this world begins. Universal Consciousness becomes covered with the five cloaks, which translate into Sanskrit as *pancha* (five) *kanchukas* (cloaks), or *pancha-kanchukas*. (I always like to share the fun-sounding Sanskrit terms with you.) And these kanchukas do pack a punch! The five powers that become limited by these five cloaks are omnipotence, omniscience, perfection, eternality, and omnipresence. These cloaks act like veils that cover and limit the full powers of supreme Consciousness.

Once the cloaks are in place, supreme Consciousness can do certain things but not others, can know some things but not others, can be in some places but not others, is satisfied with some things but not others, and can exist in one time but not others. When your true nature as universal Consciousness is covered by these five cloaks of illusion:

- **Omnipotence (universal authorship) becomes limited abilities.** Your previous ability to do anything and everything turns into limited action, where you can do some things but not others.

- **Omniscience (universal knowledge) turns into limited knowledge.** Your omniscience of being aware of everything at once becomes limited knowledge, where you know some things and don't know others.

  Before this stage of creation, you were all-knowing, but now you have to study to learn things. Without this cloak, there would be no need for schools or universities, because the awareness that is everyone would already know everything.

- **Perfection (universal satisfaction) turns into limited desires.** Supreme Consciousness has no need for the roller coaster of fulfilled and unfulfilled desires. It experiences perfect satisfaction and contentment within itself. However, once this cloak of limited satisfaction comes into place, the universal experience of perfect contentment is compromised by desires, fears, fulfilled and unfulfilled hopes, attachments, aversions, and expectations.

- **Eternality becomes limited time.** Before this stage, supreme Consciousness experienced everything all at once as an eternal awareness and presence, but now it is limited by time constraints of past, present, and future. This limitation of time brings a whole slew of problems.

  When your true nature as eternal Consciousness becomes bound by the illusion of time, you begin to hope for something in the future or worry about things that happened in the past. You become locked into an idea of yourself as a separate being in time. From within this limited experience of sequential time, you can't see things objectively or from a bigger picture perspective, but only in bits and pieces and in time-based succession. With this cloak, you feel that you belong only to this time, that you didn't exist before, and that you won't exist in the future.

- **Omnipresence becomes limited placement.** Before this cloak, you were completely free and all-pervasive. You existed everywhere all at once. Now, you have to travel to go somewhere, and you know how much of a hassle that can be.

One modern analogy for the experience of omnipresence is the world wide Web of the Internet, where everything is existing and available to tap into all from one place – your computer. But once the cloak of limitation is placed over omnipresence, you can only be in one place at a time instead of being everywhere all at once.

This fifth stage of creation is where all-powerful Consciousness becomes trapped in its own dream, so that it appears to be at the mercy of outer forces over which it has no control. This stage sets the stage for the dance of limited world experience to take place.

You may wonder why supreme Consciousness would give up its divine freedom and take on these illusory limitations. The answer may be that only through these cloaks of limitation can the supreme all-knowing Consciousness get to have exciting limited experiences such as being surprised, happy, or disappointed – in and as you and everyone else. Only through forgetting that it is the dreamer of the dream of creation can universal Consciousness experience the play of the world, with all its colorful and exciting twists and turns (not to mention pizza).

My oh maya!

Like an artist, it is the nature of Supreme Consciousness to create. *Maya*, also known as universal illusion, brings the paints with which Consciousness crafts its colorful masterpieces of world creation. But maya also brings some not-so-pleasant side effects along with all the entertainment.

Once maya begins to blossom, universally free Consciousness starts to experience the sense of limitation. All of a sudden, omniscient, omnipresent Consciousness starts to feel, "Oh, I can't do that," or, "I want this, but it's not coming to me," or "I want to know this but it is difficult to understand." Before this level of maya came into manifestation, your awareness knew everything and could do anything without any effort. Now, just look at yourself!

Seriously, look at yourself and your life and see all the creations of maya expressing in and as your life. Learn to watch, explore, and find entertainment in the play of your life.

Stage 6

With the cloaks of illusion and limitation in place, your mind, intellect, and self-awareness take form. In this stage of universal creation, the all-pervasive, infinite, eternal pure Consciousness becomes you, as you know yourself to be. Shrouded by illusion and forgetting its own nature, the limited individual experiences a world of duality through the mind's faculties of self-awareness, mental comprehension, and intelligence:

- **Self-awareness:** In this stage, the self-conscious ego takes birth, which is not the sense of "I" as the highest "I Am" consciousness, but rather the ego's "I am this but not that" awareness of being a separate, limited individual who thinks of everything in terms of: me, me, me, me, and me.

- **Mental comprehension:** Along with this limited "I" consciousness comes a thinking, perceiving mind, which is also called the "lower mind." This thinking mind builds worlds of experience from the internal and apparently external materials of images, concepts, and words.

- **Intelligence:** Mixed in with this mental bundle at stage 6 is the superior mind, or intellect. In Sanskrit, this higher intelligence is called *buddhi*, which is related to the name of the spiritual figure Buddha, who is said to have achieved the great unfoldment of this superior mind.

The buddhi brings forth intuitive perceptions and intelligent understandings that penetrate deeply into the nature of things. This superior intellect can become the doorway for the lower, limited person to re-enter the higher realms of experience.

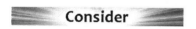 **Consider**

Calming your mind and ego by reading potent spiritual philosophies and doing practices such as meditation and inward reflection can help to strengthen and polish your higher intelligence.

Stage 7

Once your mind, intellect, and ego are in place, the senses and physical world take form. On the bottom rung of this creation ladder are the physical senses (smelling, tasting, seeing, feeling by touch, and hearing), the physical universe, which is composed of elements such as earth, air, fire, water, and ether, and all the actions each person expresses into the physical world.

Tadaa! Perfectly free universal Consciousness now takes the form of all the strange and amazing creations in this world.

Waking up from the illusions of maya

You can think of the experience of awakening from maya as being like the experience of awakening from a dream where you were running from a gang of criminals. Upon awakening, you realize that the whole storyline and experience was an illusion. The criminals didn't exist, nor was anyone really chasing you.

Nevertheless, the experience wasn't completely unreal. Certainly, your fear and pounding heart were real. This is where a subtle distinction comes regarding the unique nature of maya versus the common use of the word illusion. Illusion is generally used to refer to something that doesn't exist but is falsely portrayed as existing. Maya, on the other hand, is existent and non-existent at the same time.

The experience you had while running for your life in the dream was real while the dream was occurring; therefore, the maya of this dream can't be called non-existent. Yet, through the sobriety of wakefulness, you can see that the dream was an illusory world.

The only problem is that there is no objective experiment you can run to prove that the waking state you're experiencing right now is any more real than last night's dream — which probably also felt completely real at the time. If you *are* in a dream right now, I hope the alarm doesn't go off until you finish this chapter!

Don't Forget

Even though the chart in Figure 14-1 appears to show a sequential transformation of consciousness moving down the chart over time, the whole multi-leveled process is also happening all at once.

It isn't so much that pure Consciousness stops being pure Consciousness when the world takes form. Rather, even as pure Consciousness descends into the lower stages of having personal experiences in a physical reality, it never moves from its highest state of pure being.

A popular Indian prayer says, "That highest Consciousness is perfect; and this creation is perfect. Perfection arises from perfection. Even if you take some of the perfect from perfection, still it remains as completely perfect."

Imagine moving your personal consciousness up the chart in Figure 14-1, walking back up the ladder of creation from the physical world and senses, through the mental conditions, beyond illusory limitations, and into the great freedom of your true nature as universal Consciousness. Imagine being an enlightened person who can live in the entire map of creation all at once, being aware of all the levels of consciousness at the same time.

What is the world made of?

This universe isn't just some kind of inconsequential, random spark that has blasted through a big black hole somewhere beyond the space/time continuum. I mean, it may be that, but it is also much more than that. In all of its reality and unreality, its confusion and confidence, its love and hate, creation and destruction, this universe is magnificent and unfathomable — more brilliant than can be beheld or understood by mere senses or mind.

One view echoed in many spiritual and scientific traditions is that the entire universe is, as Buckminster Fuller described, "Energy radiantly manifest at relative rates of regarded speed." This description means that all the things you see, hear, feel, taste, smell, know, and touch are nothing but different energy vibrations.

According to science, these vibrations are imported through our sense organs and transformed by a complex electrochemical cocktail of brain functions, including cognition and memory, along with a touch of unquantifiable personal consciousness, to create what is basically a mirage of subjective experience that represents an apparent outer world. Neuroscience says that we aren't so much perceiving as creating what we experience.

This scientific theory fits in well with ancient spiritual assertions that this world is maya – a kind of waking-state dream that continues to manifest itself merrily, merrily (and sometimes not so merrily or gently!) down the ever-flowing stream of worldly life.

Scientists have discovered that what you see as visual images of different colors are not inherently those colors but rather different amplitudes of light wavelengths impinging on little receptors called rods and cones in your eyes and translated into the subjective experience of red, blue, and other colors by your brain.

Even solid objects can be considered as solidified vibrations — frequencies so deep and dense that they take form as tangible objects. Just think of what happens when someone (not you, I'm sure!) blasts his or her music so loud that the whole room or car shakes. The sound vibrations take on physical forms that are strong enough to move objects around. If you take these vibrations a few notches deeper down the energy vibration spectrum to the point where your ears can no longer translate those particular waves as sound, voilà! You've got yourself a solid object.

Merging science and spirituality

Two decades ago, while studying neuroscience at the University of Michigan, I had an earth-shattering encounter with eastern spirituality. Engaged in an internal struggle between the two vastly different worldviews of western science and eastern spirituality, I brought the problem to my spiritual teacher, confessing that I was having trouble merging science and spirituality. He very matter-of-factly replied, "You don't have to merge them because they are   already one."

It sounded so simple, yet at the time, I had no idea what he really meant. However, many years later, when I was steeped in the concentrated spiritual practices of a monastic life, the edges of my tendency toward black-and-white thinking began to soften. This softening eventually opened an appreciation for the oneness — not only of science and spirituality, but of everything. In deep inner contemplation, I would enter a state of mind within which the ancient spiritual scriptures and modern science could be seen as rays of the same one sun of supreme Consciousness.

How this world is like a movie

Consider an actor who plays a scary bad guy in a horror film. When you watch this awful, evil man on the screen, you're having an experience that is similar to the kind of illusion called maya.

While watching the movie, you're afraid of this man. You may even hate him. You want bad things to happen to him, because he is such a bad guy.

Yet, at the same time, you know that he's really an actor who is probably a very nice fellow with lots of money who goes to Hollywood parties and such. Certainly, you don't really hope a bomb will explode in his face, nor do you want him to die so that his poor victims — who are probably also feeling quite fine in their own Hollywood homes — will be freed from his scripted wretchedness.

Spirituality in Action

Think of someone in your life who has played the "bad guy" for you. Now imagine that the same universal Consciousness has created both this bad guy and you, and is playing both roles, perhaps to give Itself a bit of challenge to experience and work with.

While immersed in watching a movie, you can see how easy it is to even voluntarily allow yourself to fall for objects that seem to exist, but don't really. In the case of this movie, you may despise the evil character being portrayed by the actor, even while knowing deep down that if you saw him on the street, you would probably want to ask him for an autograph.

This scenario is similar to what life feels like when you start to see beyond the illusions of life. It doesn't mean that nothing will ever surprise, disturb, or scare you, nor does it mean that you won't see what appear to be negative events or people. However, with a more enlightened perspective, you know that all the joys and sorrows, colors and textures, and ups and downs of life are not quite, totally, ultimately real.

With a vision of Universal Creation, you experience the situations of your life and enjoy the plot twists. You know that a divine actor is playing every part in this movie of life. Behind every personal interaction, you can sense divinity winking at divinity through all the players involved.

Consider

Watching your life as you may watch a movie is a state of awareness that some ancient scriptures called *witness consciousness*. Witness consciousness doesn't mean that you just space out and disengage from the world, but rather that you watch the play as a witness even while you enthusiastically perform your role in the play.

Just as universal Consciousness is both watching and creating this universe, so you are also watching and creating your universe, your personal expression, and your role in this play. Sometimes you're watching a comedy, sometimes a romance, and other times it may even be a horror story. Yet, your deepest inner state remains constant throughout all the stories.

Don't Forget

In this reality show of your life, don't forget to smile for the "camera"!

Rising above illusions

Some religious and spiritual traditions guide you to withdraw from the world and to hide yourself in a cave or go to a mountaintop where you can escape the illusions of life. This approach can help to keep your mind and heart focused on greater matters, however it is not always the most practical approach, nor is it the only way to become free from the bindings of illusion.

You may renounce your home, family, friends, job, clothes, and anything and everything else that you own, however this kind of outer renunciation does not guarantee spiritual liberation or freedom from illusion.

What needs to be renounced is the ego, the self-interest, the petty desires, and sense of ownership. What needs to be renounced are the false ideas about who you are – thinking that all you are is an individual body with a mind that is separate from the universe, from God, and from everyone and everything else. This limited identification is the main illusion that keeps you from entering into higher spiritual awareness.

If you have a luxurious mansion with several expensive cars, closets full of clothes, and all the fortune anyone could want, and you remove your attachment and identification from all these achievements and objects, knowing that they are just flickers on the screen of supreme universal Consciousness – then you are able to rise above illusion even while enjoying all the benefits and blessings of an abundant life in this world.

Why God created the world

Okay, I'll admit it. I thought it would be fun to make a sidebar called "Why God created the world." Nevertheless, one reason proposed by spiritual sages is that God separates from His own eternal oneness and becomes you so that He (or, if you prefer, It or She) can love Himself, experience Himself, and create amazing worlds within Himself.

That one divine light not only appears to become separate from its own profoundly perfect self, but it also creates all these different forms, like you and me, so there are many others to love – or in some cases, to learn to love!

Or maybe, like this sidebar, He creates it all just for fun.

Spirituality in Action

The following exercise can help you to rise above the illusions of your own life-movie by giving you a way to practice controlling your levels of absorption in the illusions of a theatrical movie.

1.   **Go to a movie theater and watch a movie — with friends or alone.** Intense dramas are especially good for this exercise, but any movie will do.

2.   **Let yourself settle in as the movie begins.** Enjoy your popcorn or soda as you would on any movie occasion. Watch the opening credits and the set-up scenes.

3.   **Ten minutes into the movie, close your eyes and gently pull your conscious awareness away from the story you've been watching.** Take the reins of your mind into your conscious control. Instead of just letting go into wherever the movie has been guiding your mind, use the power of your will to become consciously aware of who and where you really are.

4.   **Take a moment to remember whatever events have just happened in the past hour or so — how you arrived at the theater, any interactions you may have had with your friends or other people, and so on.** The idea behind this part of the exercise is to reaffirm who you are in the nonmovie reality, even while the movie is playing.

5.   **Now open your eyes and let your awareness go back to the movie.** Sorry if you missed an important clue for the surprise ending, but it's worth the sacrifice to know how to do this!

6.   **Let yourself become fully absorbed in the movie for 30 or so more minutes.** A particularly dramatic moment during this part of the film is the best time to go to Step 7.

7.   **Right in the middle of a dramatic moment, pull your attention away from the movie again, but this time, look around the theater.** See the forms of people sitting in the audience. Listen to the crunching and sipping sounds and people shuffling their feet around. Smell the air in the theater. Take a sip of your drink and let all your senses take root in the reality that you're sitting there in the movie theater. You can do this for a few minutes or however long you'd like.

8.   **Go back to watching the movie with the goal of enjoying it fully, but at the same time, consciously remembering throughout the rest of the movie that you're sitting in a theater watching a movie.** To do this step, you have to access two different mental viewpoints at the same time. You may find yourself bouncing back and forth from awareness of the movie to awareness of sitting in the theater, which is fine. You're exercising your mental muscles of staying in witness consciousness during dramatic events.

9. **When you leave the movie theater, you can take this exercise to the next level.** Remember the feeling of having the two co-existing viewpoints, and apply that sensation to the events that unfold around you. Talk with your friends and enjoy your dinner, but keep a simultaneous awareness that you are a seat of divine conscious awareness watching the movie of your life as it unfolds. Even if you don't fully believe or understand that this is what you are, it's still fine to do as an exercise.

Life is but a dream

Spiritual Wisdom

Wake up! At least now, wake up, o foolish one. Consider this whole creation as a mere dream. This world is like a flower in bloom; as you watch it, it wilts right before your eyes. So, why are you attached to it?

—Brahmananda

One way to describe the nature of this world is to use the metaphor of a dream. When you're dreaming, you experience all these objects and events. You have perceived histories with the people in your dream and may go through conflicts, communications, responsibilities, and phases of good and bad fortune. In the dream state, your unconscious mind can create any scenario and characters it desires.

What are your dreams made of? What are the people in your dreams made of? Who are they really? What are the situations and obstacles in your dreams made of? Every one of them is made of nothing but your own consciousness.

Think about it – you pick something up in a dream, and feel that it's solid and separate from you, but it's neither solid nor separate from you. It's your own consciousness manifesting as the illusion of that object and all the other objects in your dream.

If a spiritual person came up to you in your dream and said, "We're all one!" your dream persona may think the person is a little strange or "out there." But the person would be absolutely right. Everything in your dream is created from the same creative consciousness of your so-called "unconscious mind."

This dream metaphor is similar to what some of the world's most profound philosophies say this entire universe is. You are one with the creator of the whole thing, but you disguise yourself and cover the truth. Then you get to experience your life as real and existing outside of yourself. It's exciting because you never know what will happen next!

Don't Forget

Above all the goals and concerns you may have within your waking-state-dream, the foremost goal from a spiritual perspective is to know that you're dreaming and to WAKE UP!!!

Interpreting your life-dream

You walk out of the door one day, and every person you meet is smiling at you with beaming looks of love. A puppy runs over to greet you. Every traffic light seems perfectly timed to turn green just when you want it to. An unexpected gift comes in the mail, and that song you love comes on the radio. Have you ever had days like this?

Then there are those other kinds of days, where everything seems to go wrong — from big things to little things, right down to the bad-hair day and lost car keys. Sometimes you may even think that a big meeting was held for everyone you know, where they were all given instructions on how to make your life difficult!

One way to apply a higher perspective viewpoint to your life is to realize that, just as in your dreams, your waking state is also filled with a rich tapestry of symbolism. Without a spiritual view, the world can appear to be quite drab and meaningless. However, after you begin to appreciate the profound symbolic nature of your waking state dream, even difficulties or boring times can become fascinating and educational. Everywhere you look are lessons, omens, patterns, and synchronicities to discover.

Shifting into a Higher Perspective

Shifting into a higher perspective means living with a "universe is Consciousness" attitude. This shift means that you know it's all God even when it doesn't all *feel* like God.

This shift doesn't mean that you have to follow a certain set of behaviors. Being in a higher perspective doesn't mean that you never feel sad or weep, but that when you weep, you weep fully; and when you're done weeping, you stop.

When you live in a "universe is Consciousness" perspective, you're not trapped by the past or afraid of the future. You have equal respect for everyone and everything. You know that everyone who comes before you is a manifestation of Consciousness – even telemarketers (although it is fine to cut conversations short with certain forms of supreme Consciousness!)

Swami Lakshman Joo, one of the great teachers of Kashmir Shaivism, said, "You can recognize Lord Shiva through the universe, not by abandoning it, but by observing and experiencing God Consciousness in the very activity of the world."

Does the world really exist?

Philosophers through the ages have considered this question: Does the world really exist, or does it not really exist? According to some spiritual philosophies, the answer is both. The world exists, and it doesn't exist. One scripture uses the analogy of a reflection in a mirror to describe what the manifested world is like.

You have a mirror that is showing an entire city in its reflection, but without there being any actual form of the city in front of the mirror. There's just the reflection. So the question is – does that city exist? Well, it does exist, because the reflection is there. But does the city exist independent of the mirror? No. Can the contents of the image of the city change the mirror at all? No. Does the mirror care if the things being reflected in it are beautiful or ugly? Probably not.

This is where the idea of equality consciousness comes in (see Chapter 11), where you see this whole universe as a reflection in the perfectly pure Consciousness that exists before, during, and after all creation. That mirror of Consciousness is your true nature, and upon the face of that mirror plays the whole saga of this world and your life. To the pure, elevated part of yourself that is Supreme Consciousness, it doesn't matter if you have pleasant or unpleasant experiences. These events and experiences are merely reflections playing upon the pure mirror of your soul.

First cause versus second cause

What if you slept? And what if in your sleep, you dreamed? And what if in your dream you went to heaven and there plucked a strange and beautiful flower? And what if when you awoke, you had the flower in your hand? Ah! What then?

—Samuel Taylor Coleridge

A vase that sits on a table in your dream is made of your very own consciousness. It may take on the appearance of glass, metal, or clay, but the first-cause "substance" of which the vase in your dream is made is consciousness. You could call the other perceived qualities of the vase second-cause.

If you drop a glass vase in your dream, it is likely that the vase will appear to shatter and equally possible that you may cut your dream-finger while picking up the glass fragments. Aha! Physical evidence that the experience is real, right?

Here are observations of the first and second causes in this dream experience:

- **Second-cause:** The shape, color, and sharpness of the glass shards are *second-cause qualities* of the vase.

- **First-cause:** Your own creative consciousness is the *first cause* behind the dream vase as well as your bleeding dream finger. According to the ancient spiritual sages, a higher-level form of the same first-cause consciousness that creates your dreams has also created your waking state and the so-called real world.

Universal first-cause is the mother of this whole creation. First-cause can change anything, create new worlds, and answer any prayer. (See Chapter 15 for more on how this first-cause power manifests in your life.)

With an awareness of the divine nature of this world, you can look at everything as an opportunity to interact with the Divine. Look for God in all the right places, which is everywhere. Touch God, feel God, taste God inside and out. See God in nature, in trees, in birds and other animals, in the sun and the rain, and in the moon and stars that shine at night. See divine Consciousness manifesting in and as your loved ones, your not-so-loved ones, and of course yourself.

Spiritual Wisdom

Jesus said, "I am the light that is over all things. I am all: from me all came forth, and to me all attained. Split a piece of wood; I am there. Lift up the stone, and you will find me there." (Gospel of Thomas v.77)

Chapter 15

The Laws of Karma and Attraction

Topics in this Chapter:

* Seeing how your thoughts and actions affect your world
* Appreciating the power of words
* Considering some theories about how karma works

Long before Newton discovered and elucidated the laws of gravity, gravity was nevertheless happening. Things would fall down, and people knew they would fall down, without understanding exactly why. Nevertheless, until the laws of gravity were discovered, observed, expressed, and applied, they couldn't be harnessed for all the great technological advances that were to come, including amazing capabilities such as aerodynamics.

In the same way, exploring, understanding, and applying spiritual laws in your life-journey can help you achieve great and amazing things. This chapter gives you an introduction to the laws of karma and attraction.

The Laws of Karma

Spiritual Wisdom

Cause and effect, means and ends, seed and fruit, cannot be severed; for the effect already blooms in the cause, the end pre-exists in the means, the fruit in the seed.

—Ralph Waldo Emerson

One notable concept from ancient eastern philosophies is the law of *karma*. No English translation does justice to this Sanskrit word, although the statements, "Whatever a man soweth, that shall he also reap" (from Galatians 6:7), the common saying, "What goes around, comes around," Newton's third law of motion, "For every action there is an equal and opposite reaction," and the childhood retort, "I'm rubber, you're are glue. Whatever you say bounces off of me and sticks to you," give some sense of karmic law.

Here's another simple definition of karma: Karma is the currency of your life. With the currency of karmic actions, you purchase and create all your life experiences — good, bad, pleasant, and unpleasant. Karma is the law of cause and effect by which each individual creates his own destiny by his thoughts, words, and deeds.

According to the theory of karma, you have a cupboard filled with karmas: personal karmas, cultural karmas, and karmas that involve the entire human race. The life you experience is a mesh of all your karmas interacting with one another like a big, unique, karmic thumbprint.

 **Consider**

If you want to see what your karma looks like, just open your eyes right now and look around. Every thought you have, every word you say, and every action you perform ripples out into the world around you. These ripples then reflect back to you, although not always in the most obvious ways, and not always right away. For example, someone who performs bad actions may still become materially successful, appearing outwardly to have good karma, but they may have other unseen challenges to go through now or in the future.

If you're in a body, you have karma

Every human being is constantly performing actions. You can't not act. Even in breathing the air, untold worlds of smaller-than-small creatures and microorganisms are destroyed. Every time I water the little garden area in front of my house, it is obvious from all the ant activity that I've created a full-blown disaster for some of these little creatures. I can imagine the ant headlines: "Flooding in the southwest, hundreds killed, thousands injured!"

If even 1 percent of all the rules, commandments, and injunctions listed in the religious texts of every culture are accurate and true, we all have some serious karmic debts on our hands. For example, one rule from ancient yoga philosophy is to refrain from harming any living creature. Some religious sects, such as the Jain religion from India, even go so far as to cover their mouths with cloth to avoid breathing in small insects and to sweep the ground before each step so that their steps won't harm any unseen creatures. What if, by chance, they're right? Can you imagine how many karmas you have created in your life just from breathing and walking?

Karma is a natural law

God does not play dice with the universe.

—Albert Einstein

Basically, if you push something, it moves. Now expand this idea and realize that the entire universe is made up of movements and reactions to movements. Your body was created by the lovemaking movements of your parents and then movements of the sperm burrowing into the egg, zygotes replicating, organs forming, and nutrients being assimilated. Everything that keeps your body alive right now is made up of movements: visible movements, invisible movements, and millions of teeny-tiny electro-chemical movements.

The entire universe consists of spinnings upon spinnings — from galaxies to communities, to electrons circling the nucleus of an atom. Movement is the nature and quality of all creation. So what's keeping it all going?

You can think of the universe as running on the fuel of karma. Have you ever seen those desk ornaments that have a line of silver balls hanging in a row? You pick up the ball on one end and let it go. As it hits the row, a silver ball on the other end flies up into the air. When that ball comes back down and hits the row, the silver ball on the other side again moves up. Once the process is set in motion, you don't have to plug it in, nor do you have to fill it with gas. As Newton's law of action says, every action has an equal and opposite reaction. Thus work the ways of karma.

One good way to grasp the intricacies of karmic law is to watch how karmas manifest inside and around you. Life is a living textbook on the laws of karma. You can

- Observe how life so often creates exactly what you most desire or fear.

- Watch as the most vehement persecutors in any situation seem to inevitably become the persecuted.

- Notice how your own good actions can lighten your heart and create an opening for more goodness to enter your life.

 **Consider**

Even movie scripts and novels generally reflect an intuitive understanding of these laws, as good wins over evil nearly every time — even if only moments before the final credit roll!

You already know these laws

Human beings have been using the laws of karma from their beginning — when an unknown caveman first discovered that placing his hand into a fire created pain and didn't do it again.

Basically, karma is a law of the universe like any other, but not yet fully understood by society at large. So it's sometimes used as a joke, as in "ha, ha, that must have been your karma!" This line would be akin to making a joke after someone falls down, that "ha, ha, that must have been the gravity!" Well?

Karma is like the wind

Beware of spitting into the wind.

—Nietzsche

In visualizing the idea of karma, you can imagine a large, deep lake — the lake of your soul. When the lake is still, you're able to see into its life-filled depths. But on a windy day, with leaves and twigs hitting the water's surface, the lake becomes covered with ripples to the degree that your view into its depths is obscured.

In this metaphor, you can find examples of two kinds of karma:

- **Fresh karmas:** The wind is analogous to the current winds of karma that are being freshly whipped up by your own never-ending thoughts, speech, and actions.

- **Old karmas:** The twigs and leaves on the water's surface would be analogous to old, solidified karmas that aren't so easily discarded — such as karmas relating to your family or cultural traditions. You're more or less stuck with these karmas.

Now, here's the deal. You may not have much control over all those leaves and twiggy old karmas, but you do have a choice of how the winds of the karmas you're creating right now will blow. Even if you have a lot of old karmic debris on your soul lake, if the current winds remain calm, the karmic clutter moves to the perimeter of the lake, leaving the depths visible through the lake's clear surface.

However, if you generate a lot of blustering winds by performing all kinds of noisy, ego-based actions, you're going to have a messy and obstructive surface. With a lot of current karmic winds, even if you only have a small amount of old debris from past actions, your lake's surface will still be obscured by whatever is there, and also by the ripples created on the lake directly by the fresh karmic winds.

Consider

The winds of new karmas become still when you enter into a state of inner peace. You can find inner peace by allowing your thoughts and actions to flow through you unsullied by selfish desires or ego-based motives. When your surface waters are clear, you have a chance to see more clearly what is really at the core of your being — the great light of your spiritual soul.

Spiritual Wisdom

If you help others, you will be helped, perhaps tomorrow, perhaps in one hundred years, but you will be helped. Nature must pay off the debt. . . . It is a mathematical law and all life is mathematics.

—George I. Gurdjieff

So, is the idea to make lots of good karma?

Well, making good karma certainly rates higher than making bad karma, right? At the same time, even the pleasures of this world are said to pale before the universal bliss of regaining one's place as the fountainhead of all creation — living in a state of enlightenment and inner freedom. Therefore, those who are serious about reaching these higher goals are enjoined to give up all karmas, both good and bad.

Be Careful

Giving up all karmas doesn't mean that you shouldn't perform helpful actions or that you get to sit around doing nothing all day. Giving up karmas means to give up your limited ego-based attachments and identifications with your actions.

In fact, it is impossible to live in this world without acting. Just think of the most basic actions that are necessary to maintain life in your body. Every living thing must act. Even so-called inanimate rocks are made of vibrating atomic matter!

> # The basic process of creating good karma
>
> Here's a simple formula for creating blossoms of positive karmas in your life:
>
> 1. **Plant powerful and positive seeds.**
> 2. **Have faith.**
> 3. **Be good.**
> 4. **Wait patiently.**

Good karma, bad karma — stop making karma!

The purpose of clearing up your karmas is

- To uncover the bright, divine spiritual sunlight that had been obscured by clouds of limited self-identification and desire-based actions
- To become free from the bondage of this world
- To live an enlightened, free-spirited life

Don't Forget

The ultimate goal of processing your karmas is to rise back up through the levels of creation (see Chapter 14) to a state of enlightenment, nirvana, Heaven, and pure consciousness. To clear all the illusions from your pristine pure Self, follow spiritual practices and uplift your actions into non-karma-forming ones.

The idea is to uplift all your karmas into higher vibrational energies and to process your old karmas without creating new ones. Here are two ways you can help to clear your karmic waters of impurities:

- **Make a decision and effort to move with the universal Will.** Pay attention to the motivations behind your actions. You may even notice signs from the universe that you've made an error of judgment, or that you are headed in the right direction.

Maybe you think about changing your place of employment, and open a magazine to find an article about another company that is hiring people to do just what you're wanting to do. Or you may come across an article about how unstable that field has become. You think about getting in touch with an old friend, and their business card falls out of your files, or perhaps an old note from the friend that reminds you of why you stopped seeing the person. You may decide to have children and walk by a park where a beautiful laughing child runs up to give you a wildflower, or go into a toy store to see a child driving his mother crazy by screaming at the top of his lungs for a toy.

- **Accept and even relish your karmic lessons.** When challenging situations arise in your life, go through them with a positive attitude. According to the laws of karma, negative experiences can actually be beneficial in the long run if they are clearing up some of the negative karmas from your past actions, thoughts, and words.

    For example, if people are saying untrue, harmful things about you, they may be actually taking on some of your bad karma — through general karmic law and also the law of attraction, which draws to them more of what they are focusing on (More on the law of attraction later in this chapter). You may even find that these gossipers end up with some new struggles while your burdens become lighter. Therefore, when challenges arise in your life, while still making efforts to heal the problems, you can make the most of their karma-clearing potential by accepting and even relishing them with a positive attitude. Look at everything as an opportunity to grow and evolve, and make sure that all those old karmas are burned to a crisp!

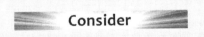 **Consider**

Listening to your karma~o~meter

You know that sinking feeling you get in the pit of your stomach when you say or do some-thing wrong? Give thanks for it! This is your karma-o-meter, letting you know that you may be planting some seeds you don't want in your field!

Cleaning up your karmas

Each man takes care that his neighbor shall not cheat him. But a day comes when he begins to care that he does not cheat his neighbor. Then all goes well — he has changed his market-cart into a chariot of the sun.

—Ralph Waldo Emerson

One way to act without creating karma is to act without any attachment to the good or bad fruits of your actions. Withdraw the importance you place on things of the ephemeral, physical world and begin to deposit your energy toward the eternal, spiritual realm.

Another way to clean up your karmas is through intense devotion and complete surrender to God's will. In the *Bhagavad Gita*, Krishna, a representational form of the universal Lord, says, "Whatever you do, make it an offering to me — the food you eat, the sacrifices you make, the help you give, and even your suffering. In this way, you will be freed from the bondage of karma, and from its results, both pleasant and painful. Then, firm in renunciation and yoga, with your heart free, you will come to me."

According to the theory of karma, you also have to balance your checkbook of action and reaction before you get to graduate from this cycle of *samsara*, this wheel of birth and death, rebirth and redeath, through which you are said to come and go over and over again — until one day your soul becomes free from the noose and bondage of your karmas and rises into greater realms.

Analogies of what clearing karmas is like

Here are some metaphors to help you understand how to become free from the burdensome weight of karmas:

- **Burning karmas is like burning fat.** When you start to burn karma, it's like when you stop eating too many calories so that your energy system has a chance to burn some of your body's old stored fat. When your karma furnace isn't being constantly stuffed with countless actions, and more importantly, constant interpretations of actions (for example, I did this great thing, I shouldn't have said that, and so on), then the karmic furnace has a chance to begin to burn the stored karmas that hold you down just as surely as excess fat does.

- **Cleansing karmas is like washing dishes.** You can wash each dish right after using it, or you can let them pile up a bit and then have an occasional big "dish cleansing" with a full tub of hot suds. However, if you don't know how to clean your dishes (karmas) or don't even know that they're dirty or that they *can* be cleaned, then the dishes pile up in your sink, and eventually all over your entire kitchen.

- **Keeping your karmas clean is like keeping your house clean**. Your house may start out clean, but then it gets messy and you have to clean it again. After guests come for a visit, you may have some extra cleaning to do, just as when "partiers" come into your karmic life. You also have to continually clean here and there, because dust inevitably builds up.

Don't Forget

This analogy isn't just about dishes, but about the karmic residues that accumulate in everyone's life, creating all kinds of unwanted situations.

You can clean your karmic dishes with practices such as contemplation, higher knowledge, meditation, devotion, selfless service, and by letting go of limited desires.

Consider

Just as when you clean your house, cleanliness inspires cleanliness. You can keep your karmic house clean with little cleanings or a massive clean up — or you can live with it being not-so-clean.

Two good signs

Here are two signs that together may indicate that you're acting without creating karma:

1. Your actions bear greater fruit (results).

2. You don't care so much about the fruits anymore.

Ramana Maharshi, a great sage from India, has said, "If the fruits of action do not affect the person, he is free from action."

Picture your accumulated karmas as being like a spider web, with you in the center. The people and things in your life all have threads going to and from them like the web of a spider. Part of your job is to cut the harmful threads while strengthening your connection with good, powerful threads and the divine source energy behind the whole web.

Spirituality in Action

Here is an inner process that can help clear your web of karmas from within, without your having to take any actions outwardly:

1. Think of a person who creates obstacles in your life. It can be someone you are currently involved with or someone from your past. It can be someone you're not speaking to or someone you love. Or both! Bring up all the feelings you have toward this person and evoke memories of things they may have said or done that hurt or upset you.

2. Cut the subtle, unhealthy, karmic threads going from you to that person, using your mind and intention. Depending on your preference and circumstances, you can even shout, inside or outwardly, "Cut the karmas!" Take back your energy like tendrils coming back into yourself. "I take back my energy! I cut these karmas!"

Improving your karmas through mindfulness

Mindfulness means being completely focused on the present moment. Whatever you're doing, you do it while being fully present right here and right now. If you're planning what to do tomorrow or next year, that's okay, too. Just make your plans consciously and in the present moment.

Consider

Being focused on the present moment is a kind of meditative state. The ripples and thoughts of your mind calm down and create an opening for you to see more clearly into the waters of spirit. With this focus and openness, you open the door to receiving and experiencing "new and improved" karmas.

Two more ways to clear karmas

Here are two more paths you can take to clean up old, unwanted karmas:

- You can clean up old bad actions by balancing them with new good ones. If you've caused some harmful actions to someone, you can make efforts to balance that harmful action out by doing something helpful to that person or to another person. In fact, looking for ways to be helpful in general is a great idea because your kind actions may balance out negative karmas you didn't even know existed!

- You can clear old bad actions with a deep process captured by the Catholic sacrament of confession — by humbling yourself at the feet of the Lord and asking for forgiveness, redemption, and grace. A more eastern approach to this method would be to use spiritual practices to raise your awareness into a higher consciousness view of universal creation, from which you can look upon yourself and your actions with compassion and forgiveness (while still committing to behave better in the future.)

Here's a formula for bringing more positive karmas to all your actions:

1. **Before you do something, stop and feel the energies of the moment.** Become focused on the present moment as you approach the threshold of beginning an action.

2. **Invoke positive energies in yourself and the action.** You can add your own touches to this practice, such as speaking a devotional phrase or using a ritual to solidify your positive intention.

3. **Become so completely focused in the present moment that your limited sense of individuality disappears.** According to spiritual vision, the experience of yourself as a limited being has its roots in the past and future. In the present moment, there can be no roots, because the present moment is pure freedom, pure clarity, pure light, and pure spirit. Being completely present allows your actions to flow from a greater place than your usual levels of self-effort (not that there's anything wrong with a good dose of self-effort!)

4. **When you've completed the action, pause again and feel good about the action you've done.** Faith and gratitude can bless your action even after you've completed the action, because grace and spirit exist beyond time.

Examples of karma in action

Here are some examples Buddhist scriptures use to explain the way actions can manifest as karmic circumstances in your current or future lives:

To be free from want in food is the result of your providing food to the poor in your previous life.

To be miserly and unwilling to help the needy gives rise to future starvation and clothlessness.

To have ample housing is a reward for donating food to monasteries in your past life.

To abstain from eating meat and to pray constantly to Buddha will assure that you'll be born a very intelligent child in your next incarnation.

To have good parents is a reward for your respecting and helping those who were lonely and desolate in your past life.

Being short-lived is the result of your committing too many killings in your previous life.

To distort truths habitually will cause you to suffer blindness in your next life.

To be pretty and handsome is the reward for your respecting and offering flowers to Buddha's altar in the past.

To have committed evil with your hands in your past life is the cause for you having disabled hands now.

To be struck by lightning or burned by fire will be the punishment for dishonest trade dealings.

To build temples and public shelters will give you future prosperity and happiness.

One way to stay centered in divine grace and positive actions is to offer every action to the divine. When you understand that the divine exists in everything, large and small, you respect every moment as equally significant and precious. Then, cleaning your house, watering your garden, washing your clothes, filling your car's tank, and feeding your children or pets can become just as spiritually potent a ritual as bowing before an altar, lighting a candle flame, or closing your eyes and praying.

The Law of Attraction

The basic idea of the *law of attraction* is that your thoughts determine your experience. You attract what you think about, whether you want it or not.

Like karma, the law of attraction is not about blame or guilt — it's just a simple reaction, a law of the universe that applies to everyone equally, regardless of whether you are a saint or a sinner. What you focus your attention on tends to increase. Of course, this law is just one of many coexisting universal laws, so I encourage you to keep your mind from settling into a simplistic view of any one universal law without taking into account the unavoidable potential for exceptions and conflicting views.

The law of attraction is based, in part, on the idea that the universe is made up of vibrations being drawn to other vibrations that are most like themselves — in the same way that plucking a string on one violin will cause a string on a nearby violin tuned to the same note to also vibrate.

This *metaphysical* (more than physical) philosophy says that your power of thought affects the outer world in ways that go beyond the physical realm, and that you have the power to effect changes in your outer world not just through strenuous outer efforts, but also by shifting how you think.

For example, if you are wanting to lose weight or relieve yourself of your financial debts, the law of attraction would suggest that you not focus too much on the problems at hand — in these cases on the larger sizes and unpaid bills — but that you spend time visualizing what you would like your life to look like. This way, you're feeding the details of that vision with your thought energy, and if you do it right — so the testimonials say — you end up with the very house you visualized or the car you cut out from a magazine and pasted above your desk. Or even better, on spiritual levels you become happier, healthier, and more spiritually attuned, peaceful, and beneficial to the world.

What is better than a parlor game kind of approach to metaphysics is to learn the useful principles from these manifestation theorists — such as the idea of focusing your attention on what is good — and to combine these principles with solid spiritual information, wisdom, virtues, and practices to really uplift your whole life in ways you may have never imagined. Don't just vision for an expensive new car, vision for a great, spiritually vibrant, divinely inspired life! Two main steps help you benefit from these metaphysical laws:

1. **Discover what the universal laws of attraction are.** Getting to know metaphysical laws is an interactive and ongoing process of personal evolution and exploration into new vistas of understanding. You can't simply learn metaphysical laws by only reading books or taking courses, because universal laws are like life itself — big, flexible, and endless in their expressions.

   Along with reading and hearing information about metaphysical laws, pay attention to how these laws manifest in your life. See whether you can find examples of when you've personally experienced these laws so that you can explore those events and develop a more personal and intuitive sense of how metaphysical laws work in action.

2. **Apply the universal laws to your life.** This step sounds easy, right? After you discover a metaphysical rule or universal law, all you have to do is follow it. Yet how many people apply all the physical laws they already know in their own lives? People know, for example, how much money they earn, but what do they do anyway? Overspend. They have studied nutrition and health enough to know the laws of proper digestion, but then they go out and eat huge, greasy meals anyway.

Spirituality in Action

Experiment with trying out different universal laws in your own life situations. For example, you may decide to stop thinking negative thoughts for a certain amount of time or to follow more austere rules of integrity, honesty, and faith. See if shifting to more positive thoughts and actions bring positive shifts to your outer life as well as your inner experience.

Your living is determined not so much by what life brings to you as by the attitude you bring to life; not so much by what happens to you as by the way your mind looks at what happens.

—John Homer Miller

Checking out some laws

Okay, these laws of attraction are not as neat and well-documented as government laws. Wouldn't things be easier if you could just read a list of clearly coded laws explaining exactly what kinds of punishments or benefits you'd receive for following each one? But, alas, all you have are the breadcrumbs that have been left by those who have explored these laws. Here are a few of these laws for you to contemplate, consider, and explore. Let these aphorisms unfold in your own deep wise soul:

- Everything comes from the universe and is delivered to you through people, circumstances and events by the law of attraction.
- Be careful how you think. Your life is shaped by your thoughts.
- All that we are is the result of what we have thought.
- Whether you think you can or can't, either way you are right.
- Life is a mirror of your consistent thoughts.
- What you resist persists.
- Follow your bliss and the universe will open doors for you where there were only walls.
- It is done unto you as you believe
- Imagination is everything.

Applying the laws

The best way to apply these laws of attraction is to keep them in mind as you act, think, and express yourself into the world. Notice how you think about things and experiment with ways to create more positive with your words, thoughts, and actions. Also understand the power of the company you keep. Do your best to keep your mind focused on people, places, and things that are in harmony with your greater goals.

To share a personal example of how I apply this law of attraction theory in my life, I personally choose not to watch some of the popular shows that take place in hospitals, because I don't want to draw more hospital experiences into my life. Some of the law of attraction teachers also suggest staying away from people who are undesirable in one way or another — whether sick, poor, or fat — so that you won't take on their qualities. This teaching suggests that someone who works with people who have been harmed or violated in one way or another may be inviting similar experiences into their own life.

Be Careful

However, this somewhat heartless approach of avoiding anyone who is not perfectly free from flaws may actually end up attracting more of what you don't want, because avoidance of things can also attract them to you. It is the energy of your mental focus that makes certain events or things manifest more powerfully. Who would really want to live in a world where people are so selfish that they don't help others out of fears of getting some kind of "karmic cooties" from them? Taking a simplistic or selfish approach to universal laws can create these kinds of strange interpretations that are less likely to come about when the metaphysical laws are allowed to express naturally as part of your spiritual maturation (See Chapter 16 for more on why it's not always good to fool Mother Nature).

Consider

Therefore, along with paying attention to what you are creating with your mind, thoughts, and words, and along with being careful about the company you keep, you want to also follow the law of allowing. Don't put too much thought, attachment, or avoidance toward anything that you don't wish to increase in your life. Keep your attention focused on higher spiritual matters even while in the midst of so-called "bad company." Your higher focus will not only protect you from the potential ill effects of their company, but will also help you to be good company for them (which equals more good karma for everyone concerned!)

The Universe likes to say, "Yes"

One metaphysical law is that whatever you focus your attention on gains more power in your life. If you have a bad habit and think day and night about how awful it is that you have the habit and how you wish it would go away, you may find the habit becoming stronger instead of following your wishes.

This is because the universe is a conscious field of spiritual awareness that likes to say "yes." It's like a doting grandmother that only wants to please, but doesn't always get things right according to your preferences.

The universe says "yes" to whatever you focus on. Even if you're saying "no," the universe is nevertheless saying "yes." For example, if you're saying to yourself, "Don't eat chocolate, don't eat chocolate," the universe is editing out your "don't" and replacing it with "yes!" Because of this universal tendency to say "yes," it is less beneficial to focus on a habit you want to get rid of than to focus on the positive thoughts and freedom you'll feel after the habit is gone.

You are a co-creator

There cannot be a crisis next week. My schedule is already full.

—Henry Kissinger

According to the law of attraction, you are ultimately the cause of every event and experience of your life. Whether this principle is in fact always so, nobody can really know or prove. Still, you clearly have many lines of input into the circumstances of your life — from the power of your intentions and efforts to your attitude and frame of mind, along with the metaphysical connections and communications between you and your world.

Be the player

Here is a contemplation that can help you understand your own power: For a moment, think of the entire universe as an interactive video game, in which one person is playing on one screen. All the characters are animated and moved by the same person, the player — you!

In this metaphor, the player has a choice of whether to identify with the characters in the game or to remember himself as the player who is expressing through those characters. Perhaps during particularly intense moments of the game, the player may forget himself and become completely identified with the different characters in the game. He may become upset if he misses a target in the game or is "shot at" by "other players." He may forget that he is the one who specifically set the parameters of those enemy warships. He is the one who chose the difficulty levels before pushing the start button!

A player who gets absorbed in the video game may not even notice that he's getting tired while sitting there. He doesn't think about what he is going to have for dinner after he finishes the game. He loses awareness of himself as himself and becomes completely identified with the false characters in an illusory game-world.

This scenario, according to some spiritual philosophies, is what has happened to all of us. We are really the player of this game of life, but we have so identified with the characters and small battles that we've forgotten our true nature and our profound personal power.

The philosophical model in Chapter 14 gives one way to understand how your thoughts communicate with the great universal Creator, how your vision connects with the divine vision, and how your dream resonates within the divine dream.

Your mind is like a contracted form of the universal mind — like a chunk of ice floating in the ocean. Your mind is the universal mind's "Mini Me."

Understanding your position as a co-creator allows you to use your power to bless and uplift your life and the entire world. Right now, settle into this awareness of your power as a co-creator and pray for a blanket of protection and grace over you and your loved ones, over your city, your country, over the world, and throughout the solar system, galaxies, the entire visible universe, and the entire invisible universe.

Untangling the web of desires

Spiritual Wisdom

Let people hold on to these: Manifest plainness, embrace simplicity, reduce selfishness, have few desires.
—Tao Te Ching

The web of desires is made up of all the strands of information and misinformation that have been built around you since the day you took birth into this world. It is this web of multifaceted desires that drives you into so many different directions. Here is a technique that can help you look at and uplift everything in your life:

1. **First you accept that on some level, you're creating everything in your life.** If you don't fully understand or believe that you are a co-creator, you can still use this technique as a contemplation exercise and pretend that you are ultimately responsible for everything in your life.

2. **Next figure out why you're creating certain things that you don't want to have in your life.** For example, if you have problems with your boss, co-workers, family, and friends, you can look at what subtle perks may be coming from those conflicts. Why would you have created a particular hostile situation? Maybe you like the drama, or maybe having other people look at you in a negative light helps keep you humble or feeds some dark corner of your own shadow beliefs about yourself or others. In this step, you consider and contemplate what the possible reasons might be for creating certain seemingly unwanted things in your life.

3. **Once you've accepted your seat as co-creator and have considered what may be motivating you to create certain things in your life, then you accept everything in your life with nonresistance and a sense of gratitude.** This combination of acceptance and gratitude breeds the very powerful state of contentment.

4. **Now, from a position of contentment, authorship, and empowerment, you decide what changes should be made in your life.** If some useful benefit is coming from an unwanted situation, find ways to derive the same kind of benefit from positive, wanted situations.

Spirituality in Action

Giving your stamp of approval

Here's a contemplation you can use the next time you're about to send an important letter or e-mail, maybe to someone you love or to a potential employer:

1. **As you're about to put the letter into the mailbox or hit the Send button, stop for a moment.**

2. **Pause and align yourself with the present moment awareness.**

3. **Dip into the grace of the present moment and from there, bless your letter or e-mail.**

4. **Then put your message into the mailbox or hit the Send button with a feeling of confidence and trust.** If you have a favorite phrase, blessing, or mantra, you can repeat it as you hit the send button.

5. **After the e-mail or letter has gone its blessed way, pause again and turn your attention inside yourself.** Savor the flavor of the moment. Can you taste it? Does it taste like success and blessings?

6. **Offer your gratitude to spirit, along with your own version of "God's will be done."**

This practice can turn an ordinary moment into a power moment and your ordinary awareness into the state of mindful grace!

Ask for the whole cosmos!

As we express life, we fulfill God's law of abundance, but we do this only as we realize that there is good enough to go around — only as we know that all God's gifts are given as freely and fully as the air and the sun.
—Ernest Holmes

One powerful practice is to imagine that you could create anything at all in your life and see what you choose. Sometimes you may think that you want something, but if you really had the chance to create a desired object or circumstance — along with all the attending necessities for maintaining it — you may very well choose what you have now rather than the greener looking pastures over the fence of your previous desires. Taking time to contemplate what you really want in life is a great practice for self-discovery and self-empowerment.

Many people don't even know what their hopes and dreams are, beyond the basic necessities of each day. Taking a few moments to contemplate and even write down your dreams and goals — from your highest aspirations to your most basic requirements — can be an excellent use of a few minutes of your time.

Don't Forget

Remember that many of your desires and goals may be based on societal and culture-based ideas that may or may not be in harmony with the highest will of God or your heart's deepest aspirations.

Appreciating the Power of Words

Spiritual Wisdom

In the beginning was the Word, and the Word was with God, and the Word was God.
—St. John 1:1

Your entire thought structure is bound together with the threads of language, and these word-based thoughts create the world you experience. Therefore, understanding the nature and power of words isn't only an artistic endeavor, but a personally and spiritually beneficial one as well.

The ability to use words well can uplift all the elements in your life — from your state of mind to your relationships to your career, to winning your case in traffic court. An improved relationship with language also brings improved personal and spiritual growth. According to success coaches, for example, the process of clarifying your desires by writing them down as definitive goals can work wonders in helping you to fulfill your dreams and aspirations.

How life is like an improvisational play

Have you ever seen an improvisational comedy team in action? A group of actors gathers on stage, and the audience calls out words that will decide the nature of their play, such as where they are, who they are, and what they're doing. Well, you can say that life is also like an improvisational play. We are the actors on stage, and we are also the audience calling out the circumstances that determine the details of the play.

Now imagine that some of the people in the audience don't even know that the words they're calling out will have anything to do with the plot unfolding on stage. They're just randomly saying words like "donut shop!" and the next thing you know, the drama is unfolding in the context of a donut shop. The audience member may not even notice the correlation or may feel surprised, thinking, "Hey, what a coincidence. I was just thinking about a donut shop!"

Empowering your affirmations

I'm good enough, I'm smart enough, and gosh darn it, people like me.

—Stuart Smalley (played by pre-senator Al Franken on *Saturday Night Live*)

Affirmations are statements you make to yourself — declarations of what you wish to be. Affirmations have been used for many centuries, such as in the form of mantras or prayers, mainly because they tend to work. Of course, it is important that you present your affirmations with the right words. Just saying, "I want to have a million dollars" isn't necessarily going to mean you'll wake up tomorrow morning with a whole new bank account, although far be it from me to say it couldn't happen.

Positive affirmations allow you to consciously activate and elevate principles such as love, selfless service, creative expression, truth, generosity, prosperity, faith, surrender, and divine guidance in your life.

Even if you learn about affirmations from spiritual teachers or texts, you should eventually be able to create your own personalized affirmations as you go through life. Your own guiding force knows the specific combination of what you need within your specific circumstances, and affirmations can help you to open up to its guidance.

Before stepping into an event, you may want to say an affirmation or prayer that the event will be positive, successful, and wonderful. You can even affirm a positive experience from going to the grocery store, blessing the event so that you'll meet whatever people will be mutually beneficial to meet.

Several elements affect the potency of your affirmations:

- Your affirmations should be carefully composed.

- Be sure your affirmations are positive and focused on a vision of what you desire instead of on what you want to get rid of. Remember that whatever you think about, you empower.

- The best way to speak an affirmation is to declare your vision to already be true. "My life is filled with divine grace" or "I see that divine grace fills my life" are better affirmations than saying, "I *want* my life to be filled with divine grace." With the last version, you may actually be empowering your *wanting* of divine grace rather than affirming its presence.

- Your affirmations should be spoken with one-pointed intention and faith.

- If you just toss out one desire here and another there, forgetting about earlier requests as you continually make new affirmations and resolutions, you're doing two things:

- Dissipating your power by fragmenting the rays of your attention in conflicting directions.

- Planting too many seeds without enough consistent focus of energy to nourish any one intention so that it can grow and fully blossom.

- Your affirmations should be in harmony with universal laws.

- If your desires and declarations are contrary to the universal laws, they won't be truly sincere. You may think you want the declarations to come true, but if your deep inner being knows these desires aren't in harmony with the highest universal good — which is also your highest good — then you won't have the full force and confidence of your whole self behind the affirmation.

- For example, you may be in a relationship that's not really good for you, but your codependent nature causes you to nevertheless want the person to love you and stay with you. You may repeat affirmations that this person and you are becoming closer. However, if deep inside you know that it really isn't the best relationship for either of you, and that your desire of strengthening the connection is really coming from fear or codependency, your affirmations may not have a strong impact on the outer events.

 **Don't Forget**

Faith is the heart of all affirmations. As Jesus said, "It is done unto you as you believe."

How affirmations affect your mind

Affirmations work when your super-powerful subconscious mind hears your words and programs your experience and behavior to reflect and give life to them. Your subconscious mind is so powerful that some of the magic ascribed throughout history to wizards, psychics, gods, and goddesses can be explained as powers of the subconscious mind.

Affirmations also work on a mundane level. Believing that you're destined to be wealthy inspires you to act with a greater assurance and to make decisions based on a sense of empowerment and security rather than fear or neediness. Approaching life with positive and confident qualities would tend to bring about more favorable and prosperous circumstances.

If you affirm that you will succeed in getting a particular job and convince yourself that this job is already yours, then you'll walk into the interview free from the baggage of doubt, fear, and needy desire, none of which are good friends to take with you into a job interview. If you can walk into the room feeling secure and steady, you'll be much more likely to make a good impression and get the job.

If you're saying to the interviewer, "I know I'm the right person for this job because I have all the right qualifications," but your body language and subliminal speech are saying, "I know you probably don't want me," this inner doubt would likely hamper your efforts.

The interviewer may not necessarily think, "Hey, he says he is qualified, but subconsciously he is communicating what a loser he thinks he is." However, her subconscious mind may read your subtle signals and decide that you're not the right person for the job — perhaps inspiring the interviewer's mind to come up with an unrelated excuse to justify her subconsciously guided decision.

If, on the other hand, you walk into a job interview after using affirmations to set yourself in the certainty that you're absolutely qualified and that the job is already yours, this confidence would do much to bring your subconscious communications in harmony with your outer presentation.

Affirmations are more than just repeated phrases; they're contemplations, visualizations, and emotion-based vehicles that can open and access the magical power of your own imagination. Even beyond the outer words you use, what you think, feel, and desire in your heart is what most determines your life. If you're repeating, "I'm a winner, I'm a winner," and what your subconscious mind sees is someone who thinks they're a loser saying they're a winner, then these robot-style affirmation repetitions won't help you move significantly closer to being a winner.

How affirmations transform the world

Affirmations not only affect your thoughts, actions, and attitudes, but they also affect the world in metaphysical ways. As Chapter 14 explains, you're not ultimately separate from the world around you. Everyone and everything in this world is made from the same divine universal Consciousness and is living, as it were, in the Mind of God. Your thoughts are also expressions of that universal Consciousness and are therefore more powerful than you would probably like to think they are!

This truly is a magical world, and the more you can open to the possibility of this magic, the more you're able to experience it. You don't have to learn all kinds of incantations at Harry Potter's Hogwarts School for the Magical Arts to affect the external world. Just understand that whatever words you speak with a strong focus and intention do have an effect on the world around you.

Spirituality in Action

New Year's resolutions have long been a way to tap into the power of affirmations to create new, more positive karmas. Can you remember the resolutions you've made in years gone by? Consider writing them down so that you can read and remember your goals as you move forward into new phases and new goals.

Grasping the power of your thoughts and words requires that you accept a new level of responsibility, just as you've had to do while growing through various stages of personal growth and development throughout your life. If you go around saying that this or that makes you sick, well, what do you think the outcome of those words may be? If you sing songs about failure and heartbreak over and over with a recording by your favorite singer, guess what kind of words you're expressing into the universe for your recipe of life experience? And I hope I'll never again hear a mother yell to her playing child negative affirmations like, "I know you're going to crack your head open!"

Be Careful

Many an affirmation is said in jest! Remember that everything and anything you say can be an affirmation, especially as your spiritual power becomes stronger and more powerful.

The Universe is always listening

Most people aren't aware of all that they're asking for through their thoughts and actions. The best way to find out what you've been asking for is to look at everything around you — all the circumstances of your life. If you don't like what you see around you, it means one or more of the following:

- You're asking for the wrong things.
- You're asking for too many conflicting things.
- You're asking in the wrong way.
- You're asking without enough spiritual power to back up your goals.

Don't forget that there's more going on than in life you can possibly comprehend, so sometimes you may just have to surrender to some circumstances you don't like, trusting that the "universe knows best."

Be Careful

Certain possible pitfalls may arise when you get good at using affirmations.

- One problem with gaining more control over having your desires fulfilled is that many of your desires are certainly — if not for the wrong things — coming from a limited perspective (see Chapter 16).

- Another possible obstacle comes when you have a specific idea of how you want your goal to come about. You may not realize that a reshuffling of other elements in your life would be necessary to make your wish or desire come true. For example, you may repeat affirmations for a specific change in your career, without realizing that this goal will bring shifts and changes in other areas of your life, such as your relationships or living conditions.

Don't Forget

Affirmations don't have to be for specific worldly acquirements! You can affirm your connection with the divine, your commitment to remembering your own greatness, or your beautiful creative spirit. Affirmations plus surrender to God's will are an excellent combination for creating more great experiences in your life.

Chapter 16

When Thy Will Be Done Becomes My Will Be Done

Topics in this Chapter:

* *   Using spiritual principles in the right way
* *   Defining your greater goals
* *   Trusting divine spirit to do what is best

It's not difficult to see that most people in today's world are more interested in increasing their material possessions than in achieving spiritual greatness. Even religious people often have a difficult time focusing, for example, on Jesus' teaching to *"Seek ye first the Kingdom of Heaven, and all things will be added unto you,"* or Buddha's declaration that one of the main causes of suffering is desire. Most people today find it difficult to take the leap of faith required to move beyond materialistic obsessions. Such is the nature of living in an overly commercialized society.

In response to some of the current spiritual fads that guide you to focus your attention on achieving materialistic goals, I offer this chapter. Here, I give tools and suggestions that will help you to sort through some of these fads, so that you can make intelligent and powerful decisions on your spiritual journey.

Spirituality and Worldly Desires

Some of today's spiritual teachers give presentations that appeal to people's desires to get more and better stuff — whether good stuff, such as happiness, creativity, and positive relationships, or the usual stuff, such as a more expensive car, house, or watch. Certain modern-day "prophets" are even willing to bend the highest spiritual and religious teachings to get more profits.

Some metaphysical prosperity teachers take valid belief systems — such as the idea that that whatever you focus on expands — and turn these spiritual principles into infomercials that focus on triggering and gratifying people's lower desires.

I've even received email solicitations from "spiritual" companies and teachers who are offering courses on how to bypass customers' conscious minds through hypnotic techniques to make them want to buy your wares on subconscious levels, even if they don't really need or want your products consciously. For spiritual people to use metaphysical or hypnotic techniques to fool people into buying things is, as they say, all kind of wrong.

Today's prosperity teachers may guide people to use spiritual principles to satisfy material desires with different positive or negative intentions.

Some teachers may teach prosperity for positive reasons, assuming that once you fulfill your worldly desires, you'll be in a better position to seek the "higher Kingdom." After all, if you're hungry and worried about how to feed your children or pay this month's electricity bill, these concerns may keep you too preoccupied to give you the freedom to focus on spiritual matters.

Although conversely, times of need can also encourage you to stay even more focused on connecting and conversing with God in a very raw and real way through prayer and paying attention to your thoughts and actions. For someone who understands metaphysical laws, living on the edge can be somewhat like being in a spiritual marathon or on probation for a job – you may become extra vigilant about your thoughts and actions when there is no visible security net below to catch you if you were to fall over that edge (although of course the big divine universal safety net is always there).

An Indian sage named Sai Baba of Shirdi was famous for giving blessings that helped improve people's outer lives, although his deeper purpose was to guide people to spiritual liberation. When asked about his methods, Sai Baba of Shirdi said, "I give people what they want so they'll want what I have to give."

Others who teach people how to use spiritual principles for material desires may mostly be "seeking first" the best approach for ensuring their own mass-marketing financial success.

Don't Forget

Regardless of what anyone else's approach is, you are responsible for your own spiritual journey. Just because people you know may be jumping up and down over the latest fad doesn't mean you have to jump with them. Respect that everyone is in a different place on their spiritual journey, requiring different kinds of teachings and incentives to entice them to grow.

You are the one who can keep your spiritual approach free from lower pulls such as greed and jealousy. You are the one who can discern the difference between useful empowerment techniques and methods that are designed to hook your mind and your wallet.

You are the one who can cut through the rinds of materialism to get to the delicious fruit of authentic spirituality.

After you have read all the books and heard all the lectures, you must still be the judge of what is for you. Only if something within you says, "This is truth - this is for me" does it become a part of your experience..

—Peace Pilgrim

Clarifying what spirituality is by describing what it's not

Here are some clarifications about what spirituality is not that may help you to understand what spirituality is:

- Spirituality is *not* about trying to bend the universe to conform to your desires.

- Rather than striving to bend the universe to conform to your desires, spirituality guides you to be in tune with the great universal Will, which always moves toward the greatest good.

- Spiritual principles are *not* just tools for getting the universe to give you want you want.

- Spiritual principles are better used as tools for preparing yourself to receive and give to the universe the best of what you're here to give and receive.

- Spirituality is *not* about reducing God to a nice daddy who gives you what you want so that you can say, "I wanted a car, and He gave me a car!"

If you ignore something, does it go away?

Some new age teachers tell you that pretending something isn't there makes it go away. I used to have a cat who thought that if she couldn't see me, I couldn't see her. After all, she was only a cat. But you're not a cat; you're a human being with human intelligence and knowledge.

Yes, from the highest philosophical views, it is true that our beliefs create and limit the scope of our reality. This is why spiritual study can be so helpful in expanding our belief systems as well as the world as it manifests around us. And yes, what we focus on tends to expand so that, for example, if you want to get rid of a habit, you are better off focusing on positive results that would come from releasing the habit than to direct too much attention toward the habit itself.

Still, if you know that something exists and are just putting some positive frosting on top by pretending it is not there, you may be ignoring useful signs and information that would help you to make better decisions in your life. For example, choosing to ignore potentially uncomfortable aspects of your thinking or behavior may end up creating an environment of denial that allows those negative aspects to seep more deeply into your life, as they tiptoe by your closed eyes like harmful viruses sneaking past your immune system.

Using manifestation techniques

Of course, adding more positive images and affirmations to your thoughts is great; however you don't want to slip into thinking that you're going to use metaphysical principles to "put one over" on your destiny or to sneakily overturn God's will. Without a deeper understanding of the relationship between the individual soul and the universal soul, your use of metaphysical and spiritual laws of manifestation could be but a step away from cheap parlor tricks that may amaze your friends, but also reduce you to being somewhat of a *karmic* thief.

Be Careful

Here's the thing about metaphysical manifestation techniques: If you already have spiritual maturity, then these techniques and theories offer some interesting ideas and useful tips. However, if you don't have spiritual maturity, then focusing too much on certain manifestation techniques can make you more greedy, materialistic, or uncaring.

The Indian scriptures say that through the practices of yoga — which lead toward union with the divine — a person's thoughts can be controlled to produce a state of concentration that naturally gives powers that are meant to be used for the person's ultimate enlightenment. Supernatural powers come naturally as a person follows yoga paths that lead to their evolution of consciousness. My guru used to say that these supernatural powers, called *riddhis* and *siddhis*, "sweep the doorstep" of a yogi. He doesn't have to grab them. All he has to do is uplift his own consciousness into greater spiritual realms, and these powers come naturally, along with the spiritual maturity to use them properly.

Jesus gave another example of how true spiritual practices bring supernatural powers when he said, "*Truly I say to you, if you have faith the size of a mustard seed, you will say to this mountain, 'Move from here to there,' and it will move; and nothing will be impossible to you.*" Of course, once someone has attained this level of faith, they also have faith that the mountain is where it is for a reason!

Be Careful

Most yoga scriptures and gurus add big warning flashes about not getting stuck in supernatural powers. Many look at metaphysical manipulations as a low-class form of spirituality. These metaphysical powers can become obstacles to your attainment of higher realms, because they tempt you to be distracted by outer pleasures and keep you from reaching the precious gems of divine self-knowledge that exist in the inner sanctum of life.

Without knowing what to want, you could put forth a lot of effort, use all sorts of metaphysical techniques, and go down all kinds of roads, just to find a lot of disappointing accomplishments and dead ends.

Spiritual Wisdom

Visit not miracle workers. They are wanderers from the path of truth. Their minds have become entangled in the meshes of psychic powers, which lie in the way of the pilgrim towards Brahman (the absolute universal being), as temptations. Beware of these powers, and desire them not.

—Sri Ramakrishna

Can materialistic prosperity be compatible with spiritual fulfillment? Yes! The key is to keep your spiritual qualities of trust, higher awareness, and surrender strong even as you create an abundant life in this world.

Discovering how to interact with the universe is a very good thing. However, using this precious gift of communication with the universe just to ask for more stuff is like meeting God and asking for a watch, or like receiving priceless jewels and using them to play a game of marbles.

Spiritual Wisdom

It is not wrong to tell the Lord that we want something. But it shows greater faith if we simply say: "Heavenly Father, I know that thou dost anticipate my every need. Sustain me according to Thy will." If a man is eager to own a car, for instance, and prays for it with sufficient intensity, he will receive it. But possession of a car may not be the best thing for him. Sometimes the Lord denies our little prayers because He intends to bestow on us a better gift. Trust more in God. Believe that He who created you will maintain you.

—Paramahamsa Yogananada

It's not nice to fool Mother Nature

Once, a man found a butterfly's cocoon. He saw that a small opening had appeared, and as he watched, the butterfly inside the cocoon struggled on and on, trying to force its body through that little hole. Eventually, the man felt sorry for this poor little butterfly-to-be and used a small pair of scissors to snip through the remaining part of the cocoon.

The butterfly then emerged easily, but with a swollen body and small, shriveled wings. The main waited for the butterfly to enlarge its wings and fly away, but it never happened. The butterfly could only crawl around, because this man had, in his kindness, removed the very obstacle that was intended to strengthen the butterfly's wings and fill them with the fluid they'd need to be ready for flight.

Sometimes struggles are exactly what you need to grow, so an approach that teaches you to avoid all obstacles may be also limiting your potential for spiritual and personal growth. In early 2007, I watched Oprah Winfrey jump up and down on her show in support of the metaphysical manifestation teachings of *The Secret*, but thought it ironic to consider that if Oprah had used metaphysical techniques to avoid all the traumas of her early years, she would certainly not be Oprah as she is today. Oprah herself is an example of how approaching challenges properly can uplift you into untold realms of freedom, blessings, wisdom, grace, service, and greater understanding.

How would you like to watch a movie where everything is harmonious and there are no challenges? You'd probably ask for your money back.

If you use metaphysics to create a boring life movie of constant ease and no challenges for yourself, the universal audience may ask for *their* money back!

Distilling the mysterious secrets of the universe down into personal creation tools is fine if what you're wanting to create is in your best interest. But people don't always want what is in their best interests. They want to fulfill animalistic urges and desires that are being generated by the old, primitive reptilian and mammalian parts of their brains; or they want to accomplish things that a limited society has told them to want. This is one reason why looking beyond current societal fads and into teachings of ancient cultures can give you a bigger picture view and helpful guidance on not only how to create, but more importantly, *what* to create.

The cloak of positive thinking

Positive thinking can bring great positive results to your life. However if you're faking positive thinking or covering things up with a cloak of denial or wishful thinking, you may actually be blocking the positive gifts that would have otherwise come to you. Or you could work hard to tap into your creative power and discover that the ending of your "power to create" story looks like most "three wishes from a genie" stories and has become a metaphysical manifestation disaster.

Seriously, how many wish-granting genie stories have you heard that really have happy endings? Usually the person who has received the wishes is lucky if he still has one wish left that he can use to undo all the damage done by his ill-considered previous wishes.

Are you really ready to drive this thing?

Do you really think you're ready to hold the reins that control this universe if you haven't yet managed to hold back from shouting an angry obscenity to someone who cuts you off in traffic, or if you still wish harm to those you don't like?

The law of attraction is based on a higher spiritual principle that connects your thoughts with the divine universal creative mind, and is best used to attract higher spiritual qualities into your life. The law of attraction is not only about getting, but is also a law of allowing, contentment, gratitude, and satisfaction.

When people learn metaphysical creation techniques without having the spiritual maturity, integrity, honesty, and generosity to use these creation powers properly, then they may very well create problems that will bring themselves and others down. In such cases, ignorance of these manifestation laws can actually be a good thing.

There are only two tragedies in life:
One is not getting what one wants, and the other is getting it.
—Oscar Wilde

Clarifying Your Intentions and Goals

Before using metaphysical principles to achieve your desires, put some time and effort into clarifying your greater intentions and goals. Three efforts that can help prepare you to use metaphysical manifestation principles properly are

- Weeding out any desires that are not in harmony with your greater spiritual goals.

- Asking for spiritual gifts above asking for more expensive material gifts.

- Accepting the inevitable, because even if you're a skilled co-creator or practitioner of the secret laws of attraction, things won't always happen exactly as you've planned — and that's often a good thing!

In the next few sections, I describe these three efforts in a bit more detail.

Weeding your desires

The purpose of weeding your desires is to make sure you want what *you* want, and not just what the commercial world wants you to want. Using metaphysical principles just to create more outer attachments is a misuse of spiritual laws. As Proverbs 16:16 says, *"How much better to get wisdom than gold, to choose understanding rather than silver."*

Therefore, it is worth your while to sort through your desires and weed out ones that are unnecessary or incompatible with your higher spiritual goals.

One way to weed your desires is to imagine that you are in your last moments of life. Your time in this world is about to come to an end, and you're looking back to consider what was most important in your life. Who have you helped? What good have you done? What do you wish you'd spent more time doing?

Everything works for some people

People are always looking for magic fixes — which is why snake oil hustlers have thrived throughout history, whether in the form of preachers soliciting contributions by promising "God's grace" in return, or health proponents pitching the latest liquid wonder for your physical health, or financial success stories of how a book or course gave people the prosperous life of their dreams.

The truth is that you can probably find success stories for nearly any idea you put forth with enough planning and passion. That's because everything works for some people.

Millions of medical studies have shown that the placebo effect — where patients improve based on their belief that a sugar pill is actually helpful medicine — is strong and well in human psyche-land. Sometimes, just thinking that something may be helpful gives those who are ready to improve themselves the nudge they may need to turn around some of the negative factors in their lives.

Asking for the highest

The best things in life aren't things.

—Art Buchwald

What would happen if, instead of only asking God and the universe to improve outer things like relationships, finances, health, or career, you began asking instead to become free?

Jesus' teaching to *"Seek ye first the kingdom of Heaven and all things will be added unto you"* is not just a religious statement, but also a metaphysical law of the universe. Keeping your eyes on the highest prize helps you attract experiences that are clear, uplifting, good, and strong.

Once you rise above the limited levels of illusions, lower emotions, and low self-esteem, blessings come to you more easily — even when you're not actively seeking them. You don't have to grab, but simply receive. You begin to experience a taste of heaven even in the midst of your life on earth.

Here is an example of how to ask for blessings in an open-ended way: I ask for divine grace, ultimate fulfillment, deeper meaning, positive growth, reverence and awe, imminence and transcendence, a blazing life and a glorious death, all in harmony with the Highest Good and filled with unexpected and unfathomable blessings, as I shed layer after layer of illusion, and move into ever new, ancient, exciting and restful waves of life as a divinely inspired human being on this earth and a pure soul beyond this earth. May a benevolent universe fulfill my highest aspirations and release the lower ones in a harmless, appropriate fashion. May everyone in this world and beyond be blessed with everything they deserve in a kindly, forgiving, and loving way.

Empowering your good desires

Once you've uncovered and clarified your greater goals and aspirations, then you can use metaphysical tools to envision and empower those goals. Become aware of how you think and speak about your goals. Imagine how you will feel once you've achieved your aspirations. Some like to create inner or outer visualizations or collages to bring a positive vision of their highest goals into all the layers of their mind.

Always be sure to keep the door open for results that may be greater than what you've chosen to envision and create. Trust that if something doesn't happen according to your desires, it still may be a positive blessing in the long run. The universe has a much bigger canvas upon which to paint your life than you do. Therefore, instead of coming up with a very tight description of what you want, your best bet is to focus on the essence of your greater goals.

Accepting the inevitable

Okay, so sometimes you don't get exactly what you want, no matter how many collages you make or how many times you affirm that you have it. The house mortgage you wanted falls through, your new car gets damaged, the university doesn't accept your application, or your money at hand doesn't add up to the stack of bills on your desk.

Here's another not-so-secret of life: Don't expect things to be what they're not, or you'll be disappointed. Feeling disappointed can also lead to feeling disheartened, which can have even more detrimental effects on your ability to achieve your goals. Therefore, you should always keep the door open for the possibility that the universe could respond to your petitions and affirmations with a clear and concise "No." Just assume that something even better is in the works and do your best to stay light-hearted and positive while enjoying your present moment as it is, warts and all.

An example of accepting the inevitable

Even though the validity of the following story has been disputed by the U.S. Navy, this urban legend so well-demonstrates the importance of accepting the inevitable that I'll share it with you here. These words are said to be from a radio conversation between a U.S. naval ship and Canadian authorities off the coast of Newfoundland:

Americans: "Please divert your course 15 degrees to the North to avoid a collision."

Canadians: "Recommend you divert *your* course 15 degrees to the South to avoid a collision."

Americans: "This is the captain of a U.S. Navy ship. I say again, divert *your* course."

Canadians: "No, I say again, you divert *your* course."

Americans: "This is the aircraft carrier USS Abraham Lincoln, the *second largest ship* in the United States' Atlantic fleet. We are accompanied by three destroyers, three cruisers, and numerous support vessels. I *demand* that you change your course 15 degrees north — that's one-five degrees north — or counter measures *will be undertaken* to ensure the safety of this ship."

Canadians: "This is a lighthouse. Your call."

Even as you make physical and metaphysical efforts to achieve your goals, keep a note of trust and acceptance playing beneath the surface of your awareness. The best way to accept the inevitable is to keep your eyes focused on the highest eternal reality, within which all your temporal desires and goals are not so very important, after all.

The Supreme Surrender

Supreme surrender is like a drop merging into the ocean. The drop surrenders its smallness and becomes one with the great ocean. Supreme surrender is a combination of inner faith and letting go. With supreme surrender, you're not giving up or waving a white flag, nor are you feeling weak or inferior when you truly surrender.

Surrender helps your spiritual journey in many ways, including:

- Surrender helps you remember you that you're here to grow.

- Surrender helps you accept that sometimes you need challenges to grow.

- Surrender helps you understand that spiritual principles are not about making sure everything in your life is always perfectly comfortable and easy, but to help you be in greater harmony with the great divine universal nature so you can achieve your highest potential.

Supreme surrender is a magic salve that allows you to more easily remove the layers of wrong understanding, fear, anger, limited desire, and all those other not-so-goodies that you and I know all too well. In fact, many people think they *are* all those false layers and therefore want to hold on to them that much more tightly. This is where supreme surrender comes in. You release the grasp of your small self and fall into the hand of God.

Spiritual Wisdom

Break the wine glass and fall into the glass blower's breath.
—Jelalud'Din Rumi

The law of allowing

Even better than the law of attraction is the law of allowing.
With the law of allowing:

- You enter into a trusting and harmonious relationship with the universe.

- You enjoy each moment and feel an ever-present sense of contentment.

- You move spontaneously and in the flow with whatever you do.

- You act without attachment and express with freedom.

I said to my soul, be still, and wait without hope

For hope would be hope for the wrong thing; wait without love

For love would be love of the wrong thing; there is yet faith

But the faith and the love and the hope are all in the waiting.

Wait without thought, for you are not ready for thought:

So the darkness shall be the light, and the stillness the dancing.

　　—*T.S. Eliot*

The importance of divine guidance

The best way to move forward in any endeavor is to use your knowledge, determination, and reasoning abilities in combination with the great divine guidance that's available to you. Divine guidance is an especially important part of the positive creation equation because:

- Intelligence alone doesn't guarantee that you're making the right choices in life. There's no way to figure it all out with your mind, because "it all" is way beyond anybody's ability to comprehend. There are times when divine guidance alone can lead you safely even through life's gnarly jungles.

- Earnestness or will power won't guarantee that you're taking the right paths in life. Many people earnestly strive, yet find they have gone the wrong direction. Divine guidance makes good use of your enthusiasm and helps keep your energy focused on positive, uplifting efforts.

- Friends may offer you a helping hand along the way, but where are they really helping you to go? Divine guidance won't steer you in the wrong direction or make you go against your better judgment. Divine guidance won't be jealous of your good fortune. Divine guidance is an expression of your friendship with the creator of this universe.

The sages describe this world as being like a deep ocean that's wide and difficult to cross. They also allude to something on the other side that's well worth the effort — an attainment that is called by terms such as realization, enlightenment, liberation, salvation, and nirvana (see Chapter 17).

Here you are, swimming in the vast waters of worldly life. You want to get there — to that divine state of liberation on the other shore — but there's no map! The way is tumultuous and fraught with distractions and illusions. How are you going to achieve your goal?

You may swim with great fervor, but how do you know you're going the right way? There is no land visible as far as your eyes can see. At times, the sun disappears behind some clouds, and you're not even able to see waters that are right in front of you.

All around you, illusions spring forth, enticing you into thinking that your time could be better spent in stopping to groom some of the sea plants or in going deep into one of many undersea worlds. However, if you fall for these enticements, you won't be able to reach the other side — which was the real goal of your entering this ocean in the first place.

As you swim forward, you have no way to know whether a hand being extended to you is going to help you move toward your goal or take you deeper into the waters of illusion. How can you possibly make it across?

You can cross this ocean of worldliness in only one way. There is only one hand you can trust — the divine hand of God, the great guiding force of grace. After you accept even for the sake of argument that this grace, this God, these angels, this inner soul, or these celestial beings exist and are ready to help you along your way, then your next task is to recognize, receive, and respond to their guidance.

In a way, it doesn't matter whether your image of divine guidance is accurate or not. Divine guidance doesn't care if you think it looks like a man with a beard, a woman with breasts, an elephant-headed boy, a five-headed god, a blue point of light, or a formless presence. What's most important is for you to find some way to relate to graceful guidance so that you can open the door to receiving its blessing.

For example, you don't need to know all the biological and chemical processes that go into creating a stream of water in order to drink from it. However, you do have to have some way of knowing that the water is there and available for you to enjoy. In the same way, you have to discover how divine guidance manifests for you:

- Does your guidance come from within?

- Do you feel that celestial beings are watching over you and whispering hints?

- Is an all-powerful Lord revealing your steps as you walk on your path of life?

- Is this conscious universe teaching you through symbolic hints?

What's most important in receiving guidance is your attitude — your stance of receptivity, humility, trust, and love, along with your pure intentions of serving and bringing greater good to your life and the whole world. These spiritual qualities automatically draw divine guidance to you because the universe likes working with those who are in harmony with its highest good — just like you do!

Consider

Trust your inner voice, and it will speak to you more distinctly.

When you're considering a particular decision, you can use the following contemplation to ask for guidance. As always, feel free to adjust the words to suit your own beliefs and personal nature.

Spirituality in Action

Sit quietly, calm your mind, and ask or state the following:

- God, is there anything you want to tell me?
- Universe, is there any guidance you wish to offer me?
- I am open and receptive to learn.

After repeating these phrases, you may choose to sit quietly and listen for an inner guidance, or open a spiritual book and see what message may be there for you. I've even experienced good results from fortune cookies and the astrology page in *TV Guide!* Truthfully, the universe can speak through anything. Divine messages can come through television shows; via songs on the radio; by walking by and hearing just the right snippet from a nearby conversation; or as a small, still voice in your own heart and soul.

Don't Forget

After you ask for guidance, listen!

Understanding to whom you're surrendering

Spiritual Wisdom

Trust in the LORD with all thy heart, and lean not upon thine own understanding. In all thy ways acknowledge Him, and He will direct thy paths.

—Proverbs 3:5,6

Surrendering to just anybody isn't necessarily going to fulfill all your greatest dreams. In fact, if you surrender to someone who wants to take advantage of your openness, you may lose a great deal. Therefore, surrender must come with discernment and an awareness of who and what you are truly surrendering to.

True surrender is always to God, in whatever form or formlessness you relate to. Remember that God is far beyond any human concept that has or ever will be thought. Therefore, whatever face and name you have placed on this nameless, faceless Lord — surrender to that and let it guide your steps.

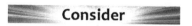 **Consider**

The secret of powerful surrender is to be strong to the world and vulnerable to God.

Bringing strength together with vulnerability

One aspect of surrender is to give up lesser goals for the sake of greater goals — to allow the darkness of your lower desires to dissolve in the light of your higher aspirations.

You surrender the rat-race, accomplishment, proving-yourself, commercialism-based mentality, and rise into a more spiritually mature goal — such as serving God and humanity, unfolding your personal or creative excellence, bringing greater love and comfort into people's lives, or attaining a spiritual state of mind, heart, and soul.

Some forms of surrender may not even sound like surrender. Several times, I've been pushed by challenging circumstances to the point where all I could do was say, "God. You do it." Sometimes I'll say it nicely, like when I realized while writing these words that this chapter is due in a few days. Once or twice, I've even gotten upset with some turn of events and shouted inside myself — "God! You do it!"

I don't think God minds how you say it, as long as you're being sincere and communicating with faith — although it's probably still a good idea to ask nicely!

Welcoming "Thy will be done"

The theme song of surrender is "Thy will be done." This statement can be analyzed from a couple different angles, depending on your understanding of how this universe works.

- **From a duality point of view:** "Thy will be done" is an offering of submission and servitude. There is a little you and a big God, and you agree to do whatever God tells you to do, whether you want to do it or not.

- **From the view of oneness:** The second way to interpret this line involves a deeper, more esoteric meaning. In this case, "Thy will be done" isn't so much an intention to surrender as a declaration of fact and an assertion of the unity of all creation. "Thy will be done" means that even if I try really hard not to do God's will, His will is nevertheless always done, in spite of my intentions. In this view, even your trying hard *not* to do God's will would still be God's will.

Surrendering into a higher understanding of the omnipotence of God's will takes the immense burden of personal responsibility off your shoulders. This unburdening is like someone who has spent his entire life frantically trying to keep his heart beating, who then finds out that it would have kept beating perfectly well even if he had focused his efforts on more important matters.

If you look at those who have achieved great spiritual accomplishments in this world, most had significant hardships to bear. Still, they continued on their journey with a feeling of "Thy will be done."

Saint Frances was a great healer, yet was often ill himself. Saint Paul was despised by orthodox religious authorities who spoke against him and even had him put in prison. Yet Paul played a significant role in spreading Christianity as a world-religion. As Jesus said in Luke 6:26, "Woe to you when all men speak well of you." In this quote, Jesus is acknowledging the often-necessary place of outer hardships in the process of spiritual evolution.

Consider

Therefore, as you grow spiritually, instead of trying to eliminate all discomforts or striving to please all the people who may not understand you or who want to limit your growth, you can look up to the unknowable divine nature and let go, saying, "Thy will be done."

How to be optimistic

To be optimistic, just look for the good in everything. Be like the folks who write those movie ads: A critic will write something like "This movie is a magnificent piece of garbage," and you know that some clever advertiser will have a photo from the movie next to the quote " . . . a magnificent piece . . ." from that critic!

Now, obviously, I'm not suggesting that you be deceptive in any way — with yourself or others. The trick is to see every situation in both a realistic light and a positive light at the same time. Here are some efforts that can help you be a happier person:

1. **Hope for the best.**

2. **Shoot for the best.**

3. **Expect the best.**

4. **Be perfectly content with whatever comes.**

Understanding that everything happens for the best

One of the most helpful understandings you can gain on the spiritual journey is to know that everything always, always, always happens for the best. Not necessarily for the short-term best of getting what you want right now, but for the ultimate, perhaps unknowable, best. This understanding gives you the great blessing of optimism. Because your thoughts are so powerful in creating your experience, optimism is a great and magical force for creating and experiencing a fulfilling life. Optimism is the spoonful of sugar that makes even bitter medicine go down more easily.

Here's a story that may help you to stay optimistic and remember that truly, everything happens for the best:

Once upon a time, there was a king, whose prime minister had a habit of saying, "Everything happens for the best." Whether someone gave him good news or bad news, his response was the same: "Everything happens for the best."

This oft-repeated phrase irritated the king a bit, but not enough to warrant action. However, one day, the king cut his hand on a wineglass that had shattered. It was a rather serious cut that was bleeding profusely and certainly prone to infection in those pre-Neosporin days.

When the prime minister arrived at the King's quarters to prepare for that day's hunting trip, he saw the king's bandaged finger and said, "Well, sire, you know, everything happens for the best."

This statement really made the king angry. His finger was throbbing with pain, and this idiot who was supposed to be a wise prime minister was repeating the same insensitive line. How dare he!

The king decided to teach his prime minister a lesson. He had the guards take him to the dark dungeon of the castle, where the lowliest criminals were kept. Not only would the prime minister have to miss the magnificent hunting trip, but he would also be sitting alone in a cold dark cell from morning until night. "Let's see him say 'Everything happens for the best' to that!" grumbled the king.

Later that same day, the king was hunting in the deep forest, when suddenly his party was overtaken by a large group of local natives who didn't know or care who the king was. As the invaders began to surround them with poisoned arrows drawn, the king's party began to scatter out of fear. "You just can't get good subjects these days," the king thought as his "protectors" abandoned him in their fearful flight. If only the prime minister had been there, he would have surely helped rescue the king — but he was back in the castle, sitting quietly in a dark, stone cell. The kidnappers surrounded the king, bound his hands and feet, and carried him off to their stone temple, intending to offer the king as a religious sacrifice.

The king didn't understand what the group was chanting; however, when they tied him to the stake and began rubbing sticks together to get a spark, he quickly got the picture. The natives began decorating the king with colored dyes as a kind of gift-wrapping for their gods, when they noticed his bandaged finger. One of the men unwrapped the cloth and inspected the cut. Then he yelled out something that made all the preparations stop.

It was considered disrespectful to offer a defective offering to their gods. If they offered this man with the bleeding finger, their gods would be displeased and would hurl wrath upon the land. The kidnappers angrily put down their instruments and released the king by cutting the reeds that were tied around his hands and feet. The king's heart was pounding as he ran as fast as he could away from the tribal village. The royal servants spotted him and carried the king back to the caravan, where he was fed and soothed.

As the king lifted the third leg of turkey to his mouth, he suddenly remembered his prime minister. Oh my. He had said that everything happened for the best, and here it was true. It was the cut on the king's finger that had saved his life. The king felt terrible. He had locked up his friend and confidante in the grungiest dungeon cell. The king put his food down and commanded his men to return their caravan to the castle at once.

The king ran down to the dungeon, and with great remorse, approached the prime minister. The king told him the whole story. "O, prime minister, I was terribly wrong, and you were right. Everything does indeed happen for the best. If not for that cut on my finger, I would be a pile of ashes right now. O prime minister, can you ever forgive me for locking you up in this hellish place for so long?"

The prime minister looked at the king, paused for a moment, and then spoke. "Everything happens for the best."

The king was shocked. "How can you say that? Without good cause, I have locked you up in this awful, rat-infested cell. If you had been with me on the hunt, you surely would not have abandoned me as the others did. I wouldn't have had to go through that whole ordeal!"

"Yes, my king," the prime minister agreed, "I would surely have stayed by your side. But remember, I do not have a cut. I would have been the perfect sacrifice!"

Depending on Spirit

Spiritual Wisdom

Take no thought for your life, what ye shall eat, or what ye shall drink; nor yet for your body, what ye shall put on. Is not life more than meat, and the body more than raiment? Behold the fowls of the air; for they sow not, neither do they reap, nor gather into barns; yet your heavenly Father feedeth them. Are ye not much better than they?

—Matthew 6:25-26

In life, people become dependent on so many things. You may be dependent on family members, on a lover, on your children, on your employer, or on friends. And if you've been dependent on anyone for any length of time, you've likely discovered that none of these people are always, ultimately, consistently dependable. People are people, and people have flaws. People have self-interests and their own opinions about what's right — which may conflict with yours.

Consider

Not everyone will do what you think you would do in a particular situation, and perhaps even you wouldn't do what you'd think you would do when confronted with certain circumstances. You can't depend on your job, you can't depend on your house, and as I learned during the 1994 Los Angeles earthquake, you can't even depend on the earth to remain stable.

Everything changes over time. Your best friend can become an enemy and vice versa. Your children who love and depend on you may grow up and complain about what you didn't give them. Husbands and wives can lose the spark of love and cheat on one another when just a few short years earlier they were committing their entire lives to one another. What can you depend on in this topsy-turvy world?

I've come to the conclusion that the only thing you can depend on is God, and that if you can really, truly depend on God, He will bring a steadiness to your life and a protection that can't be found in any other dependence. The thing about God, in whatever form you may choose to think of — Him, Her, It, and so on — is that you're taking refuge in something so unbelievably pure that it can't be properly represented in the world of mental images and labeling systems. God is like a divine fire, and everything you put into that fire becomes pure.

My personal experience of sorting through goals

Here I'll share with you how I first understood the importance of keeping your intentions clear as you acquire more spiritual power on your spiritual journey. During my college years, I had my own version of a spiritual awakening, which may have been sparked by my long-standing interest in hypnosis and the unconscious mind. I would sit quietly and turn my attention within for hours each day, exploring the amazing terrain inside my own mind and soul in a practice I called "exploring my unconscious":

At one point, I tapped into an awareness of the amazing power each person has to create anything he wishes in life. This realization was pivotal for me, because I had to transition from feeling at the mercy of forces beyond my control to a new plateau of personal responsibility. It was no longer acceptable for me to toss wishes out here and there, hoping some would stick to the karmic wall. I had to ponder deeply what I wanted from life. Here is an excerpt from my memoir that describes this transition to a new level of personal and spiritual responsibility:

I began to notice how having a particular attitude would not only color my sub-conscious expectations and affect my outward demeanor in the world, but seemed to somehow get underneath the very fabric of life, creating undeniable modifications in the world around me.

Although it would be many years before I'd encounter a philosophy that would explain this sense of personal potency, I nevertheless began to appreciate my own channel of input into the heretofore-random waves of life. I had discovered my own power of co-creation.

This was the time to decide what I really wanted. The doors of possibility opened wide. Should I become beautiful? Famous? Wealthy? Brilliant? Respected? Loved? I sorted through all the potential desires that came up, and one by one tossed them to the side. In an objective light of real possibility, each of these potential desires crumbled into insignificance. They were based on goals that had been injected into me by contemporary society; they were not my own. What did I really want from life?

I wanted to do whatever was right, based on a big picture I could never see. I wanted to be whatever I was meant to be and to be happy with whatever my destiny brought. How could I ask for specifics when I was embroiled in cultural illusions? How could I ever know what was really important in life?

After casting aside a long list of potential goals, I realized that all I really wanted was to be content. No matter what porridge of experience was placed before me, I wanted it to taste good. I wanted sweet times to taste good, and I wanted sour times to taste good as well. I wanted to move with the natural flow of life, instead of asking that my shortsighted desires be fulfilled. I wanted my desires and actions to align with whatever was meant to be. I wanted to be in tune with the universe. Clearly, the all-pervasive intelligence that guides the atoms and galaxies to move with such perfection could choose the best path for my life. My best course of action was to get out of the way of its flow, and to be happy with whatever unfolded. Unknowingly, I had tapped into the secret of surrender as a path to happiness.

Consider

Can spiritual power help you to get rich? Sure. Can it make a person you love fall in love with you? Quite possibly. Nevertheless, unless you've first made the transition described earlier in this section — the surrender to knowing you don't know and to being open to inner and universal guidance — you may end up making wrong wishes and bad choices based on ignorance or greed that actually set you back in your soul's journey, bringing future pain. Therefore, keeping your intentions pure during the process of spiritual evolution is of the highest importance.

Indeed, you can live a magical life of blessings and fulfillment while staying open and receptive to the divine Will. By surrendering your small desires into a bigger trust in a benevolent universe, you open yourself to greater fields of experience than you may have ever imagined to ask for.

Chapter 17

Liberation, Enlightenment, and the Cosmic Joke

Topics in this Chapter:

* Reaching the goal of spirituality
* Drinking a fresh cup of grace every day
* Laughing with life

Okay, so you've come to accept that you and the world arise from a divine source. You follow spiritual practices and principles and use your resulting spiritual powers only for good. Well then, what's next?

Dessert! The crown jewel of spirituality! The big cherry on top – enlightenment, nirvana, fanaa, moksha, God-realization, oneness, bodhisattva, the pearly gates, satori, self-realization, the kingdom of God, liberation!

Zen masters often speak of enlightenment as being like a moon that shines brightly in the dark sky. Teachings about enlightenment are like fingers that point up toward the moon. What is important is to look at what exists where the finger is pointing. However, many people prefer to look at easy, tangible things and end up staring relentlessly at the pointing fingers instead of at the moon.

In this chapter, I share ideas that can help point your attention toward the elusive state of enlightenment.

What Enlightenment Is Like

With enlightenment, you move beyond mere relaxation techniques or positive thinking. Enlightenment is a complete shift of perception, in which you flow with absolute inner freedom in an awareness that reaches deeply into the unseen realms. With the blessing of enlightenment:

* You have no more fear, no more greed, and no more aggression.
* Your love becomes unconditional and untainted by mundane expectations.

- You're able to let things happen naturally rather than trying to force them to happen.

- Every action you perform springs forth from the flow of universal energy through and as you.

To experience enlightenment, you have to be willing and able to let go of who you thought you were so that you can paradoxically become that which you have always really been.

Giving up all you think you are is a big sacrifice to make. But remember that if you don't do it now, Father Time will come and do it for you one day. Therefore, the Sufi sages gave the command to "Die before you die!" Die to your small self before the small self dies. Loosen your identification with the leaf and remember that you are the great tree. Then, when that particular leaf turns brown and falls to the ground, dissolving particle by particle into the elements of the earth, you will still be here in all your grand and divine glory.

Spiritual Wisdom

People ask 'What do you get by realizing God?' You get eternal peace and bliss. You are in a state of bliss in all conditions and circumstances because it comes from the source of your being. The fountain of joy will open in you and you will be flooded with it. In that state of happiness you work in the world, and that will be for the good of all.
—*Papa Ramdas*

You know how big the whole physical universe is, with endless blankets of stars, galaxies, and unfathomable distances and warps of time and space? Surely, you've seen the Hubble telescope images, and on clear nights have looked up to see planets and stars sparkling across the dark sky.

Well, enlightenment is like going through all the day-to-day events of your life—including brushing your teeth, feeding your pet, working at the office, taking a walk, and buying groceries – while remaining constantly and completely aware that you are a speck within this huge blanket of massive universe. Imagine walking through your day being equally as aware of the universe filled with stars as you are when you look into the nighttime sky. Except with spiritual enlightenment, you're not only aware of the immensity of the physical universe, but of its spiritual breadth as well.

With an enlightened perspective, you know that you are a speck of nothingness in the grand scheme of things and you also know that you are greater than you've ever imagined.

What Enlightenment isn't

Along with "finger-points" toward what enlightenment is, here I share a few "thumbs down" about what it isn't:

- Enlightenment is not about stuffing more and more information into your head.

- Enlightenment is not about feeling superior and going around pronouncing judgments about who is or isn't enlightened.

- Enlightenment is not about changing external appearances or looking more spiritual, but is a shift of awareness that may or may not be visible to others.

- Enlightenment doesn't mean that a person will only act in nice or pre-approved ways. Even an enlightened person can appear to act like a jerk sometimes!

- Enlightenment isn't something that you pay a certain amount of money to acquire during a course that ends with you walking away with a certificate of enlightenment. Enlightenment is not that cheap (even though it's technically free)!

Spiritual Wisdom

Keep two truths in your pocket and take them out according to the need of the moment. Let one be "For my sake the world was created." And the other: "I am dust and ashes."

— Rabbi Simcha Bunam

Here are some more descriptions that point toward what enlightenment is like:

- **Being enlightened is like being an actor in a play and knowing that all the scenes are just dramas for entertainment.** Even if you get angry or pleased with someone, you remember that you're really the actor, who is free from anger and is just playing his role. Those who remember that they are actors in this universal play get to smile at one another from behind the scenery even if outwardly they appear to be at odds.

- **Enlightenment is to be comfortable with paradoxes and seemingly opposing viewpoints.** Psychologist Abraham Maslow described *self-actualization* as a state that resolves dichotomies, where, "Opposites are seen to be unities and the whole dichotomous way of thinking is recognized to be immature." Maslow continues by saying, "For self-actualizing people, there is a strong tendency for selfishness and unselfishness to fuse into a higher subordinate unity. Work tends to be the same as play; vocation and avocation become the same thing. When duty is pleasant and pleasure is fulfillment of duty, then they lose their separateness and oppositeness. The highest maturity is discovered to include a childlike quality. The inner-outer split between self and all else gets fuzzy and much less sharp, and they are seen to be permeable to each other at the highest level of personality development."

- **With enlightenment, you see both the perfection and imperfection of the universe at the same time.** You realize that everything is perfectly complete even when there is still much to be done. You feel the perfection of everything even while you enthusiastically act to make improvements.

- Being enlightened is like someone in a dream who starts saying to other people, "I really do believe that this is all a dream." Even if you don't go around saying it to other people, you know in your heart that everything that takes place in life is like a dream in the mind of universal Consciousness.

- **With enlightenment, you're not afraid of all the turmoil going on in the world, nor are you too obsessed with it.** Even as you take steps to help improve the world, your vision stays focused on the spiritual realm of universal creation that is bigger than all the concerns of this physical world. You remember that many sides and points of view can coexist, depending on how you choose to look at a situation.

- **When you're enlightened, you may notice yourself becoming a conduit of grace.** Synchronicities may occur more often around you, and the spiritual presence of your company may inspire people around you to go through various transformations that bring them to a better place of awareness. Of course, keep in mind that grace doesn't always look like grace at the beginning. Sometimes grace comes in the form of revealing a problem so it can be resolved.

- In the state of enlightenment, you are fully present in your life and also fully ready to leave this world when the time comes. You enjoy life while remaining detached from it. You don't get trapped by things. You live with a sense of allowing, acceptance, and inner freedom.

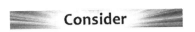

Two conditions come together on a successful quest for enlightenment: You have to want it, and you mustn't want it too much.

Living the goal

Enlightenment is like the feeling you have when you're standing in the middle of an awe-inspiring scene of magnificent nature – when you're at the precipice of the Grand Canyon, or at the foot of Niagara Falls, or walking through the amazing beauty of Machu Picchu. But when you're enlightened, you have this feeling even when you're sitting in your home, walking down the street, shopping for groceries, or doing your job. Even if the external situations you're in are not exactly beautiful or awe-inspiring, you still have a sense of the inherent awe and beauty that comes from seeing the world through enlightened eyes.

A popular Zen saying says, "Before enlightenment, I chopped wood and carried water; after enlightenment, I chopped wood and carried water." After enlightenment, your outer life may look just as it did before you were enlightened, with the same usual daily tasks to do. However, when you're living the goal, your inner state is free and expansive. Your mind is quiet and serene. Your heart is peaceful and warm, and your attitude is good!

When you live your life with an enlightened perspective, your enlightenment automatically helps the world, even if you don't speak about it. When you live in an awareness beyond limited ego, your positive vibrations and thoughts become amplified and extend throughout the world. In this way, many unknown monks and sages uphold the positive energy of this world through their enlightened meditations.

You become yourself but more so

Spiritual Wisdom

It doesn't interest me what you do for a living. I want to know what you ache for, and if you dare to dream of meeting your heart's longing.

— Oriah Mountain Dreamer

One of the biggest myths of spirituality is the idea that you have to become something or someone very different from who you are — as though you'll come out of the other side of enlightenment acting emotionless or robot-like. Many people make the mistake of assuming that becoming self-realized means they won't have any personality characteristics — or certainly not the ones they have now.

Maybe you have the idea that achieving inner peace means that you must act very serious, without ever becoming excited, or that you'd have some other limited behaviors. However, when you see the great saints, they're not limited at all. They're free. Many of them laugh and joke around. They're spontaneous and can even appear to get angry.

Don't Forget

Self-realized beings still have personality traits, but with one big difference. They know they are divine, and they know that you are divine. This awareness is the key to spiritual self-recognition.

The point of spiritual growth is not to become something other than what you are. Rather, it is a shift of awareness through which you begin to know and express more of who you really are.

Be Careful

Be yourself, but not your obnoxious self!

With their elevated awareness, even when self-realized beings trip and fall, they know that the universal play is tripping and falling in its own ecstasy. Even when they're physically sick, it's the universe experiencing illness through them. Enlightened ones don't limit themselves to judging each event as to how wonderful or horrible it was. They know that you can play the horrible-wonderful game your whole life, and never move beyond the endless cycles of fulfilled and unfulfilled expectations and desires.

Enlightened beings see everything that comes to them as a play of divine Consciousness, as an expression of their destiny, and as one more opportunity to leap up and rejoice in the awareness of their higher Self.

Again, the ideas in this chapter are some general pointings toward the collections of awareness that fall into the category of "enlightenment." Some enlightened ones may have very different experiences of enlightenment.

How will you know?

How will you know when you're enlightened? Some enlightened masters would tell you: "You already are enlightened, but your mind doesn't know it."

That's what all of the spiritual practices and principles in this book are for — to move you beyond a limited view of yourself so you can remember and realize your true nature.

In a way, enlightenment exists within each of us all the time. The trick is to remove the clouds of false thoughts that block the sunlight of supreme reality — the light of Consciousness — and to thereby become enlightened.

A seeker asked the spiritual teacher Poonjaji, "How can I tell if I'm enlightened or not?"

Poonjaji answered, "Open your eyes and look around you. If you still see a world outside and apart from you, you are not enlightened. Why not? The world and the one who sees it are both projections of the mind, and while that mind is there, enlightenment is covered up. When you experience and know directly, without needing the eyes, that the world is an uncaused appearance within your own Self, you will not need to ask whether you are enlightened or not."

Getting enlightened isn't like receiving a degree where everyone who has taken certain classes receives the same degree with the same rights and benefits. For example, Hawaiians have many words to represent all the different kinds of rain – from gentle sprinkles to thunderstorms – whereas mainlanders are usually satisfied with calling them all by the same name: "rain." In the same way, the word enlightenment actually represents a wide variety of spiritual states of awareness.

Many people have a taste of enlightenment at least once in their lives. These tastes of enlightenment can take different forms for different people. Sometimes it's a feeling of oneness with everything around them, or a sense that the light shining through a forest is also shining in their heart. Moments of enlightenment can also come when someone who has suffered a great loss feels themselves being pared down to their soul, or when someone has the experience of being in a perfect flow of action, such as during sports or creative art expressions. Some may simply shift into an awareness of the unity of life inside and around themselves.

Many people don't recognize these enlightened moments because they don't have a context to place them in. They may look back at their experience of divine oneness and perfection and say to themselves something like, "Hmmm, that was strange," before going back to life as usual.

Even enlightened masters who are able to hold on to a steady enlightened perspective may still have pockets of growth to unfold – they may make mistakes, go against their own teachings, or do something that modern society thinks isn't appropriate or polite. Let me tell you right now that anyone who thinks that an enlightened person must be perfect in any and every way and that he or she must fit into all of modern society's concepts about how an enlightened or spiritual person should be needs to go back to the fantasy of "Santa Claus Land."

I've heard many former devotees of enlightened masters who see faults in their teacher and decry how they were fooled and how everything they learned was therefore a sham. This kind of approach to the spiritual journey is unenlightened and unintelligent. It is a distraction to get trapped in arguments about who is or is not how enlightened. Focus on your own enlightenment. Learn from whom you can and keep your attention on the state of your own mind, heart, soul, and spiritual connection with Universal Consciousness.

Spiritual Wisdom

Why do you see the speck in your neighbor's eye, but do not notice the log in your own eye?
                        – Luke 6:41

Of course, if you want to learn from an enlightened master, you also want to do some research and keep your wits about you. Also remember that the teachers' words and examples are like those fingers that are pointing toward where you are meant to look. Don't get trapped by their fingernails or the sleeves under those pointing fingers! Don't get swept away by the other people who are also looking at the master's pointing finger. Keep your focus on what the finger is pointing to.

If you find that a particular path or teacher is taking you *away* from enlightenment, then, by all means, bid a fond farewell and move forward courageously and with trust that the divine will guide your steps and unfold your greatest destiny.

Imagine what you'll look like if and when you become an enlightened being. Perhaps you'll end up looking like a guru draped in robes who sits on a throne espousing your wisdom to wide-eyed seekers who are intent on unfurling the meaning in every sentence. Or maybe you'll be a simple person without any outer marks of spiritual attainment other than the light that shines through your eyes and the glowing effects of your words and actions.

Each person's realization is unique and personal, while still being universal. The key is to find your own realization.

It's a shift of awareness

To lead a spiritual life and reach a state of enlightenment, you don't have to leave the world, hide in a cave, or go to a mountaintop, although these options may work for you based on your personal preferences. Just be aware that simply leaving the world doesn't guarantee that you'll spiritually evolve beyond the world.

What is necessary is to renounce your false ideas and identifications with your body, personality, and circumstances. Without these false ideas, you can experience the world in a fresh and clear way and shift more easily into a higher awareness.

One person may see the sun going down and think, "It's time to bring in the animals and pick up the kids." A more spiritually aware person may stop to relish and appreciate the glory of this beautiful, one-of-a-kind sunset that is symbolic of the beauty of divine spirit setting into your soul.

An enlightened person may go through the same events as non-enlightened people, but his awareness has shifted into a higher perspective where he sees the divine in every event, person, and experience.

Don't Forget

The key to enlightenment is to "get it" so that you don't forget it.

Being in the Flow

Surely you've experienced moments of being in the flow. Maybe it happened while you were in the middle of a sports competition, when every movement seemed to be orchestrated by the gods to make you unbeatable. Or perhaps you were playing a musical instrument and suddenly experienced having the most beautiful music play through you. You were doing it and not doing it at the same time.

Maybe you were sitting peacefully one day, enjoying the beauty of nature, when suddenly you were struck, through and through, with the perfection of it all — and the perfection of you, right where you were and just as you are. Or perhaps you remember a time when it seemed that nothing wrong could possibly come to or through you. These experiences are all signs of being in the flow.

Now imagine that you can be in that flow much more often, perhaps on a monthly, weekly, or even daily basis. What if you could intentionally tap into that flow? You can — by cultivating a whirlpool of present-moment awareness.

Being here, now

Spiritual Wisdom

Don't think about the future. Just be here now. Don't think about the past. Just be here now.
— Ram Dass

Present-moment awareness is like resting in the eye of the storm or the center of a whirlpool. The entire universe swirls around you, but you remain centered in the power of *right now*.

Not only does present-moment awareness help calm your mind and allow you to make clearer decisions, it also brings you into harmony with spirit and opens you to divine guidance. When you're not always looking right or left, up or down, back or forward, past or future, you become more aware of who and where you are right now and can rest in the stillness of your own presence.

Consider

Being completely focused and united with what you're doing is also the secret behind great skills. Rather than thinking about the outcomes or rewards that may come in the future from what your doing, or rehashing factors from the past that are motivating your actions, you keep your focus trained on the Great Spirit that exists beyond all the ephemeral illusions, waves, and fluctuations of the world. From this expanded awareness, great skills flow naturally.

Being totally focused on the present moment also gives you an opportunity to squeeze through the bottleneck of time into the timeless realm I like to call the *eternal now*. This is the highest experience of being "in the moment," because in the eternal now there is only one moment to be in!

The six stanzas of liberation

Sri Shankaracharya was considered to be one of the greatest sages of India. He expounded many scriptures, and began the tradition of ochre-robed swamis or monks. Shankaracharya wrote a popular Sanskrit hymn about the nature of liberation, called *Nirvana Shatakam: The Six Stanzas of Salvation*. Shankaracharya's hymn reveals the enlightened state of his identity with auspicious universal Consciousness (called Shiva) by paring away all the identifications that he is not (and that you are not):

1. I am not the mind, nor the intellect, nor the ego-sense, nor the storehouse of memories. I am not the ear, nor the tongue, nor the nose, nor the eyes. Nor am I the sky (space), or the earth, or fire, or air. I am supreme auspiciousness of the form of Consciousness-bliss. I am Shiva! I am Shiva!

2. I am not what is known as the life-breath, nor am I the five vital airs. I am not the seven constituents of the body. I am not the five sheaths. I am not speech, nor the hands, nor the feet. I am not the genital organ, nor the organ of excretion. I am supreme auspiciousness of the form of Consciousness-bliss. I am Shiva! I am Shiva!

3. I do not have any aversion or attachment, nor do I have greed, delusion, pride, or jealousy. I do not hanker after dharma, wealth, pleasures, or liberation. I am supreme auspiciousness of the form of Consciousness-bliss. I am Shiva! I am Shiva!

4. There is no such thing as merit or sin for me. Nor is there joy or sorrow. I have no need for mantras, or pilgrimage, or Vedas, or sacrifices. I am neither the enjoyed, nor the enjoyer, nor enjoyment. I am supreme auspiciousness of the form of Consciousness-bliss. I am Shiva! I am Shiva!

5. I have no possibility of death, nor distinction of caste. I have no father, nor mother. I have no birth. I have no relations, nor friend, nor guru, nor disciple. I am the supreme auspiciousness of the form of Consciousness-bliss. I am Shiva! I am Shiva!

6. I am all-pervading. I am beyond the organs. I am ever the same. There is neither bondage nor liberation for me. I am the supreme auspiciousness of the form of Consciousness-bliss. I am Shiva! I am Shiva!

These verses demonstrate how the process of spiritual evolution is not so much an adding of more things, but, in fact, a paring away of all the levels of unreal identifications.

Flowing with time

Spiritual Wisdom

The art of life is to live in the present moment, and to make that moment as perfect as we can by the realization that we are the instruments and expression of God Himself.

— Emmet Fox

While living in a monastic-style ashram for ten years, my experience of time went through some interesting fluctuations. At times, I even felt as though I was transcending time by surrendering to time. Some days felt like years, and some years felt like days. Clock time became secondary to all the underlying flows and patterns rippling over the lake of universal time. Sometimes, for example, I would feel as though all the winters were enfolded into the archetype of winter itself, connected more by the qualities of winter than they were divided by the different year numbers or changing seasons of linear time.

You can practice present-moment awareness anytime by keeping your attention focused on whatever you're doing. As you walk, be aware of your feet stepping and how it feels as they touch the ground. Pay attention to the movement of your breath, to the sounds around you, to the thoughts floating through your mind, and to the life-force energy moving through your body. Whatever you're doing, do it fully. Breathe fully! Create fully! Be in the moment fully!

As you begin to flow with time by staying centered in each present moment, the natural flow of the universe begins to move more smoothly and profoundly through and around you.

Looking beyond time

What exists outside of time? What exists before time?

Jesus Christ prayed, "Let me have the glory with Thee that I had with Thee even before the beginning."

This "before" doesn't necessarily mean before in terms of a temporal place in a timeline. Rather, this "before" is co-existing and simultaneous to all creation and all times. It is eternally before everything and everyone — always and forever — and it also remains eternally after everything fades away. This eternal presence doesn't die; it cannot die, for it is the essence of life itself.

Dancing through life

Spiritual Wisdom

When you have the feeling of belonging to God, when your heart is God's heart, you can hear the thunder of his laughter rolling inside you. You feel God's presence in your being, and the pulse of His love moves you forward on His path.

— Gurumayi Chidvilasananda

Life is always moving and changing, like the winds. Your challenge is to move with life's inevitable cycles without being trapped in either the pleasant or the difficult times. Every time has a purpose and potential blessing. For example:

- **Times of poverty** can help you stay humble and keep things in perspective during times of wealth.

- **Times of abundance** can nourish your spirit and remind you that true wealth exists beyond mere outer gain.

- **Lonely times** can help you discover and remember that you truly are never alone.

- **Times of emphatic love** can bring a burst of fresh life force into your heart and soul, along with feelings of divine passion and tenderness.

- **Sad times** can guide you to tap into the peaceful surrender and vulnerability that often come through openhearted grief or tears.

- **Happy times** guide you to enjoy life and trust God, and also remind you to see the world through cheerful eyes.

If you can stay centered in the core of your being, allowing yourself to flow naturally with the winds of change, you may find that in every moment, everything is fine. Even if potential problems seem to be lurking about, you'll be able to move your attention from the spinning world and take refuge in the stillness that exists within every moment, the calm eye that gives rest beneath the storms of life. Even those who have difficult challenges to go through are given the resources to bear what they must, if they can just stay centered in that hub of time's ever-turning wheel.

Don't Forget

By learning to feel and experience each moment, you'll be better able to move with the tides of life, acting when the tides are powerful, and waiting patiently when they're not.

If you ever reach total enlightenment while you're drinking a beer, I bet it makes beer shoot out your nose.

— Jack Handey (Saturday Night Live)

Enjoying the Cosmic Joke

As Charlie Chaplin once said, "In the end, everything is a gag." Life is funny. God is funny. You're funny. The events of this world are funny. Joy is funny, love is funny, and as some have discovered after intense troubles, even suffering can be funny when you have the benefit of hindsight. As comedienne Carol Burnett has said, "Comedy is tragedy plus time."

Spiritual Wisdom

If a person can laugh totally, wholeheartedly, not holding anything back at all, in that very moment something tremendous can happen because laughter, when it is total, is absolutely egoless, and that is the only condition in which to know God, to be ego-less.

— Osho

Beneath this entire universe is the cosmic joke, and tapping into that level of the game is almost like going beyond enlightenment. You're tapping into the very bliss of God, applauding His grand dance, appreciating Her intricate set-ups, and of course, rolling in the aisles at the magnificent punch line.

The punch line of this cosmic joke has many faces:

- You can see the punch line in how big this universe is, in those amazing photos of countless stars, nebulae, and galaxies that exist millions of light years away and are a whole lot bigger than anything you've ever called "big."

- You can see the punch line in how small it all is, in a drop of swamp water seen through the lens of a high-powered microscope that is filled to the brim with invisible legions of life.

- You can see the punch line in how temporary it all is, as those who spend decades ruthlessly pursuing wealth and power end up dying just like everyone else — with their hands empty.

Why do you think they call it realization?

The state of enlightenment is also called self-realization or God-realization. It's called "realization" because the great, enlightened beings have "realized" one fact — a fact that has implications on every element of life as they know it.

They've realized the omnipresence of divinity. They've realized that everything is one, and that knowledge and the knowing of that knowledge are inseparable. They realize that what you see is what you get, what you get is what you see, and what you see is who you are. In other words, it takes one to know one. We are the world, indeed.

Don't Forget

Realization is not just about reading some words and being able to discuss or debate them; but rather to realize the essence behind spiritual insights such as "In the beginning was the word, and the word was God," "Everything is one," "The kingdom of Heaven lies within," or "Thou art That."

Once you realize the essence of spiritual teachings and make them an integral part of your reality, these teachings filter through and transform your entire world. Your sense of limited individuality fades like a mirage that had been blocking the bright sunlight of supreme truth. As this supreme light blasts through you unimpeded by mortal illusions of limitation and separation, you become enlightened. You emanate not only your own personal human light, but also a higher, more universal light.

Consider

Before becoming forever established in the highest realization, you may touch that enlightened space for a while and then return back to limited thinking. Even when you're feeling limited, remembering the higher spaces you've touched helps to keep you moving forward toward your divine birthright of knowing who you are in the highest sense at all times.

And life goes on . . .

Spiritual Wisdom

Enlightenment is the ego's ultimate disappointment.
— Trungpa Rimpoche

One day the master announced that a young monk had reached an advanced state of enlightenment. The news caused some stir. Some of the monks went to see the young monk.

"We heard you are enlightened. Is that true?" they asked.

"It is," he replied.

"And how do you feel?"

"As miserable as ever," said the monk.

Here's the thing: Even after enlightenment, you're still you! For example, if a mopey, sullen person were to somehow become enlightened, he wouldn't necessarily start running around smiling and laughing all the time. In fact, he may not change so much outwardly, although those with eyes to see the light of spirit would see it shining through his eyes, words, and actions.

With enlightenment, you may continue playing your role, but with the awareness that you're the one who's playing your role!

Spiritual Wisdom

The laughter of Hafiz

I'll let the Sufi poet Hafiz have the last word for this part, because he captures so well the cosmic joke behind this book and every other effort to capture reality in words:

> I have a thousand brilliant lies
> For the question:
> How are you?
> I have a thousand brilliant lies
> For the question:
> What is God?
> If you think that the Truth can be known
> From words,
> If you think that the Sun and the Ocean
> Can pass through that tiny opening
> Called the mouth,
> O someone should start laughing!
> Someone should start wildly Laughing —
> Now!

Part Five:

Ten Things

Chapter Eighteen

Ten Small Things You Can Do to Uplift Your Life

Topics in this Chapter:

* Enlivening every day with spiritual awareness
* Bringing goodness to the world
* Appreciating the beauty around you

From a spiritual perspective, small efforts can be as significant as larger ones. Whether you're cleaning up a piece of garbage from the park, selecting a spiritual book to read, or picking up your child from school, your level of spiritual awareness and intention determines the spiritual significance of your actions. Increasing your spiritual focus brings greater significance to all that you do.

This chapter gives you ten simple efforts that can increase your spiritual awareness and intention.

Add Conscious Pauses to Your Day

Practice drawing your attention into a conscious awareness of yourself and the divine nature of this world. Sit quietly and allow your breath and mind to become calm. Bring spiritual thoughts into your mind by remembering or reading them and then allow those thoughts to dissolve into a peaceful awareness of the presence of spirit.

You can add this simple practice to the beginning, middle, or end of your day, or anytime you find a good space to turn down the outer "noise" and absorb your attention into the peaceful vibration of spirit. Even a few minutes of this practice can infuse spiritual awareness into your day.

Centering yourself in the present moment helps to bring your awareness in alignment with your eternal nature, which opens the door for greater blessings to flow into your life. After following this practice for a while, you may be able to settle into a peaceful awareness of spirit even in the midst of a noisy crowd.

One good time to take a conscious pause is when you're about to eat a meal. You have the power to turn regular food into blessed food through your vibration and intention. Before you begin to eat, take a few moments to close your eyes and make the meal sacred:

- Offer your meal to the universal fire of creative consciousness, within whose flames one form of life sacrifices itself to become nourishment for another

- Repeat a prayer or purifying mantra to bless and give thanks for the meal

- Thank all the farmers and other workers whose efforts brought this nourishing sustenance to your plate. Some nonvegetarian Tibetan Buddhist practitioners also thank the animal for giving its body as food, as they pray for it to have a better rebirth.

Along with short, spontaneous pauses, you can also schedule time in your day to sit quietly and alone, without the television set on, without the computer humming, without reading anything — just sitting quietly for however long feels right, with the intention of opening up to spirit. Taking time each day for spiritual remembrance helps to keep your connection with spirit clear and strong.

Read Uplifting Words

Many wonderful ideas and heartfelt spiritual expressions are available to read today. Sure, some spiritual writings come mixed with certain less helpful words and ideas; however, you can train yourself to be a good editor of what goes into your mind (see Chapter 5).

Consider

Reading uplifting words before going to sleep can help give you good dreams and can also color and brighten your day ahead. You don't have to read for a long time. Just open any page of a powerful and positive book and read a few lines or paragraphs. Then close your eyes and allow those uplifting thoughts to come with you into your nighttime adventures.

During the day, you can also take positive thought pauses and fill your mind with uplifting spiritual words and ideas. You can even post favorite quotes around your work or home space to remind you to spiritualize every aspect of your life.

One of the great modern tools for finding uplifting words to read is the Internet. Along with all the gossip, news, politics, and distasteful elements that pervade the worldwide Web are gems from spiritual teachers, scholars, saints, and sages of all traditions — including spiritual scriptures, poetry, questions and answers, articles, videos and audios of lectures and music, photos of exquisite nature and holy shrines, and the writings of all kinds of great and somewhat-great beings.

Just go to a search engine, type spirituality-related words that are of interest to you, and surf through worlds of spiritual information and inspiration. If one Web site doesn't interest you, just click your mouse and go somewhere else. This modern resource of the Internet brings instantaneous entrance to amazing online treasures of interesting and uplifting words and ideas.

Bless Your Day When You Wake Up

Offering a moment of gratitude when you first wake up gives an empowered framework on which to hang all the events of your day. This initial offering of blessings for the day can be as elaborate as long meditations, prayers, and rituals or as simple as bowing your head and thanking God for another beautiful day. What matters more than the outer form of any spiritual practice is the depth and clarity of your feeling.

Every day is like a new birth into your world, and the transition between sleep and wakefulness is a powerful moment for blessing the day that lies ahead. If you have an altar or sacred space, you can stand before it and say a prayer to bless whatever activities will take place for you in this fresh new day.

You may also want to set your alarm for a few minutes before you have to get up and sit or lie quietly in bed for a while before rising. Rest in communion with yourself and with spirit. Feel the divine universal presence surrounding you as you prepare to enter the light of wakefulness and begin your day. This practice also applies to those who work night shifts and would be waking up and blessing your nighttime day.

Play Spiritual Music to Soothe Your Spirit

You can play uplifting music while you work, relax, drive, clean your house, cook, bathe, pay bills, or go to sleep. Harmonious sound vibrations are absolutely magical. Why? Because this entire universe is made up of vibrations. Beautiful music can strum the strings of your soul and the world around you.

Do Your Work with an Attitude of Service

You may want to consider adding an official volunteer or service-oriented practice to your life to help you get into an attitude of service. Maybe you'd like to mentor a child, serve food to the homeless, offer service at your place of worship, or help a friend in need.

Even in the midst of your current work situation, you can find opportunities to serve and benefit others, although you may sometimes have to reflect creatively to find ways to do so. (Not eating your fellow worker's yogurt from the company fridge is a good start!)

Serving others not only brings the joy of kindness to their lives, but also helps to open your heart and soothe your pain. Service takes you out of the dissatisfied lower mind that is always thinking about your own comforts and discomforts, and shifts your focus into the higher intention of being a vehicle of grace and blessings for others.

 **Consider**

One way to transform work into service is to consider every action you perform as an offering to divine spirit.

Surround Yourself with Things that Evoke Positive Feelings

Your subconscious mind is like the Energizer bunny that keeps going and going. Just as your breath continues to flow whether you watch it or not, so your subconscious mind keeps working even when you aren't aware of it.

Even when you think you're doing other things, your subconscious mind is taking in all the information around you like a chef gathering ingredients to use in cooking up your experience of life.

Your choices of what to place in your environment not only represent the contents of your thoughts, but these outer objects also reflect back into your thoughts and back out into your world — like a big feedback loop.

This feedback loop of "positive in, positive out" gives you a way to bring more good energy into your life by choosing to surround yourself with things that inspire and uplift you.

Depending on your personal preferences, you may want to put up photos of breathtaking nature or of one of the many beautiful images that represent spiritual or religious qualities that are meaningful for you (See Chapter 9).

Outer works of spiritual beauty reflect as more spiritual beauty within yourself, which then expresses positively in other areas of your life. Your thoughts create your reality. Therefore, feed your mind with good images and watch your life improve!

Be Friendly to the People around You

Friendliness is a form of divine love. It's an uncomplicated openness of the heart, a feeling of generosity, and an appreciation for whomever God has placed before you.

Along with following general good manners and being courteous to others, you can also go beyond efforts to be polite by also making efforts to connect with their beautiful inner soul. Find joy in greeting others on a soul level with genuine respect and appreciation. See yourself as a vehicle for blessing others (as well as an open heart to receive blessings) and act in harmony with this vision wherever you go.

Don't Forget

When you buy groceries, don't forget that the checkout clerk is a divine flame of God! When you're eating in a restaurant, give your friendliness and gratitude to those who are serving you. Don't forget that divine spirit exists — though sometimes well-disguised — in and as all beings.

Add Symbolic Contemplations to Your Actions

When you understand the symbolic nature of life, you can use your imagination to spiritualize everything you do, including housework:

- As you sweep your floor, contemplate that you're also sweeping your heart clean of old emotional dust and debris, such as anger or fear.

- As you polish your furniture, windows, or mirrors, imagine that you're also polishing your mind so that it will shine more brightly.

- As you tend your lawn or grass, consider that you're also pruning the unending growths of worldly desires.

Applying the power of your imagination and positive symbolic intentions to even mundane efforts can bring surprisingly powerful transformations to your life!

Watch Your Breath

Watching your breath is something you can do anytime and anywhere. Just pay attention to your breathing — to the feeling of the air as it comes in and goes out of your body.

Watching your breath encourages you to take more deep, long breaths. These deeper breaths invigorate your body and bring calmness and nourishment to your thoughts and feelings. Breath is an important part of your connection with life itself, so whenever you can, take a deep, full, conscious breath of life. (Come on, do it now!)

Use Rituals and Affirmations to Invoke Spirit

Rituals and affirmations give you ways to invoke and connect with the supreme spirit that creates and maintains the whole universe.

Invoke spirit by lighting a candle, burning fragrant incense, feeding the birds, creating spiritual artwork, or folding your hands in prayer.

Use positive words that bring you into greater harmony with your own great spirit, and share your positive words with others as well. Positive words can be the strongest medicine for healing whatever ails you — with no long list of scary-sounding side-effects! Choose and create your own personal rituals and affirmations to acknowledge and strengthen the blessings in your life (see Chapters 9 and 15).

Don't Forget

Your intention is the key to turning words into affirmations and actions into spiritually energized rituals.

Chapter 19

Ten Spiritual-Sounding Lines and What They May Really Mean

Topics in this Chapter:

* Taking a moment for humor
* Remembering not to take yourself too seriously

In this chapter, I share ten lines that may sound spiritual on the surface, but could have other not-so-spiritual meanings. Laughing at the foibles of ourselves and others is part of the cosmic joke, and spiritual efforts don't get exempted!

"I Am Detached from All Material Possessions!"

This line may really mean "I'm flat broke and don't have a penny to my name!"

"Make Me One with Everything!"

This statement may really mean "Be sure to put onions, relish, catsup, and mustard on my tofu dog!"

"I Am Not My Body!"

This saying may really mean "So pass another slice of pie!"

"God Bless You!"

This blessing may really mean "May God bless you with the self-control to not sneeze so loudly next time!"

"It Must Be Your Karma!"

This phrase may really mean "Don't ask *me* for help!"

"Buy My New Prosperity Book!"

This statement may really mean "So I can get some prosperity from you!"

"O Lord, My Life Is in Your Hands!"

This surrendering may really mean "What I tried didn't work, and I'm in hot water!"

"I Experience Completeness within Myself!"

This lofty statement may really mean "Nobody likes me!"

"He Who Gives Shall Receive!"

This phrase may really mean "So, fork it over!"

"These Words Were Channeled!"

This line may really mean "I don't want to argue with you about what I just said!"

Don't Forget

Remember, the words in this chapter were channeled!

Chapter 20

Ten Opportunities to See Your Life with Spiritual Eyes

Topics in this Chapter:

* Finding blessings in all situations
* Making your dreams a reality
* Keeping good times good

Life brings a variety of pleasant and challenging experiences: One day everything goes smoothly, but another day is filled with obstacles. One time you are showered with good fortune, but another time you're dragged down by misfortune. You may feel constricted by your past, fearful for the future, or hopeful about a new possibility. You want to find true happiness, but you're not sure how to achieve your dreams. All these different kinds of experiences bring opportunities to see your life with spiritual eyes.

This chapter gives examples of how you can look at real-life challenges and blessings with a spiritual point of view.

When Obstacles Block Your Way

You know those times when you have a goal in mind, but every effort you make seems to meet with resistance from the world around you? Such times can provide an array of lessons for your soul.

For example, when you consider life as a conscious, benevolent experience rather than an unconscious series of events, you're able to look at challenges in a more productive way. You can approach obstacles with a positive spiritual viewpoint instead of getting angry or victimized when things don't seem to be going your way.

One way to approach obstacles with a positive spiritual viewpoint is to think of the universal Consciousness that creates everything in this world as a personally involved friend. Contemplate why God or the universe may have put these obstacles in front of you.

Maybe these obstacles mean that God is saying "No," or perhaps the benevolent universal teacher is using these obstacles to strengthen your resolve to help you achieve your goals. Here are some more explorations of these two possibilities:

When an obstacle is God saying "No":

You may be taking a course of action that would move you away from your highest good, and the compassionate universe has set up roadblocks to alert you about your mistaken course of action. With this kind of obstacle, if you push past one roadblock, another may appear, and another, and another — if you're lucky!

If you think your obstacles may have a message of "No, don't do it," here are some additional ideas to explore:

You can explore the nature of your obstacles by experimenting with surrendering to letting go of the actions they are blocking. Maybe you've decided to write a letter telling someone off, and every time you go to save the document, your computer crashes. Let this obstacle guide you to contemplate whether what you're about to do is the best course of action.

When you experiment with letting go of a particular effort, how do you feel? Is the idea of letting go of this effort upsetting? Is it a relief? Do you feel freer inside when you let go of the desire to pursue this particular goal? Do other priorities naturally arise to take the place of the blocked effort? You can also look for a sign or omen after you do this trial surrender of the action. Sometimes the universe will do something to say, "Yes! You're getting warmer!"

Obstacles are not always a warning from on high, but may also be a reflection of your own inner conflicts about the course of action that is being blocked. Perhaps you've made an offer to purchase a house, but a higher offer beats you out. In this case, you can consider whether somewhere inside you may not have been completely sold on buying this house. Were there elements of the location or deal that may have created a subconscious resistance inside yourself?

Remember that your inner thoughts and doubts express not only through your actions, such as how much you offered for the house, but can also reflect outwardly through the metaphysical connections between your thoughts and the universe. Therefore the obstacles in front of you may be outer reflections of an inner resistance or doubt that you may not even know you have. Once you determine that you do have some resistance to the goals you're pursuing, then the next step is to contemplate whether your inner resistance is right or wrong.

Consider

When obstacles seem to be saying "No" to your efforts, consider that their benevolent purpose may be to get you to change some aspect of your approach to achieving the goal. In the example of wanting to write a letter telling someone off, the constant computer crashes may be the conscious universe's way of suggesting — not that you totally abandon the idea of writing the letter — but that you wait and rewrite it when you're feeling less angry and more diplomatic.

Sometimes obstacles may be guiding you to loosen your extreme attachment to accomplishing a particular goal while you continue to pursue the goal without as much passionate attachment. Letting go of attachments while still putting forth effort is a great way to allow things to unfold more naturally. Efforts that are full of intense desire, neediness, and attachment can actually block what you're hoping to accomplish!

When an obstacle is God's way to strengthen your conviction:

Obstacles aren't always messages that are saying "No," but may be gifts of a benevolent universe to make you strong enough to be able to bear the challenges and responsibilities of the goal you're seeking.

Just think — if your goal is to change from being a minimum wage worker to the CEO of a multi billion-dollar corporation, you'd have to go through a lot of effort and growth to be able to fulfill that role, even if the position were to fall right into your lap.

In the same way, if your goals are beyond your current abilities, the benevolent universe may create obstacles that make you work harder to grow, study, be more courageous, acquire more experience, and spend more time and effort to grow into what you want to be.

Look at your situation and contemplate what you may be learning from certain obstacles: Patience? Loyalty? Dedication? Conviction? Gratitude? Strength? Vulnerability?

Don't Forget

You can find guidance even in obstacles when you consider the universe as your friend.

When You Have a Dream but Don't Know How to Get There

The great thing about wanting something with your heart and soul is that a powerful, enthusiastic vision can help orchestrate whatever universal actions are necessary to achieve your dream.

It's like when you have a clear thought that you want to pick up a coffee mug. You don't have to orchestrate all the muscular and balancing movements of your hand and arm to do it — the mere clarity of intention is enough to set all the subconscious muscular processes into action. In the same way, a clear vision or dream for your life can set all kinds of processes into action — both inside and outside of yourself.

Chapter 15 explains the difference between the first cause (universal spirit) and second cause (material) levels of life. A powerful vision in your mind is able to tap directly into the creative first cause, because the essence of your mind is also the essence of the universal spiritual mind.

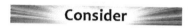 **Consider**

Here are some tips to help you achieve your dreams:

Be clear about what you're really looking for.

Instead of focusing only on specific outer elements, contemplate what you're really, truly looking for in seeking this dream. For example, you may think that your dream is to be happily married to a particular person. You think about her all the time and plan out your strategies for getting her to the altar. The actual essence of your dream is to be happily married, but you've decided that this woman and this woman alone is the one who can fulfill that dream. However, in this case, you're better off getting clear that your real goal is to be happily married to the right person and to focus on that aspiration more than just on "snagging" a specific person to whom you're currently feeling attracted.

It's fine to imagine details of how your hopes and aspirations may look when they take form. Just be sure to also surrender to letting the universe put together the best package deal for whatever essential goals you've ordered through your power of vision and intention.

Clarify your mind through spiritual practices.

A strong and clear mind gives more power to your vision, helps you choose and pursue good decisions, and also allows you to perceive the subtle universal guidance that's guiding your way. You can find spiritual practices to clarify your mind in Chapter 8.

Contemplate to see whether any part of you believes that you don't deserve your dream.

You may think you want something, but deep down, a little parental or childhood bully figure is saying, "You can't do it." Or you may be affected by discouraging words from people who don't have strong faith in your dreams.

Maybe you've heard someone express doubts about your goal, and you've subconsciously woven those doubts into the fabric of your subconscious mind. If you determine that the negative assessments of others have diminished your faith in your ability to achieve your goals, then you can choose to transform those negative ideas into the energy and motivation to be victorious in your endeavors in spite of other people's doubts.

Be clear that this goal is something you really, truly want to do.

Sometimes you think you want something, but really the desire has been sparked by the words of others — including, of course, all those advertising companies who get paid a lot of money to make you want what they're selling. Just ask any child or teenager who would practically give their lives to get that new toy or video game and then ask them again a few years later when they're lusting over an expensive handbag or a fancy new car.

Look at your own goals and question whether they come from your own mind, heart, and soul, or from outer sources such as the marketing efforts of advertising agencies.

Also, ask yourself what outcome you can likely expect if achieve the dream you have in mind. The clearer you are about your goals, the better you're able to work toward them with the empowerment of your own conviction.

Learn what you can about others who have achieved what you want to do.

Allow the successes of good examples to give you inspiration, hope, and strategy ideas. Talk to positive mentors in your field of interest. Read biographies of those who have achieved what you want to achieve. Look through the Internet for examples and lessons from those who have accomplished the kinds of goals you seek.

Remember times in your life when you've come through for yourself and accomplished challenging tasks.

Then move toward your current goal with confidence and remembrance of your strengths.

Be sure that you're envisioning a great dream for yourself and the world. Don't forget that the life you're living is *your* life. Live it! Take chances! It's going to be over one day. How would you feel if you never went for your dreams?

When You're Afraid of Losing Something or Someone

Fear of losing something or someone is an inevitable effect of having people, places, and things in your life that you love. Even while you're enjoying these contacts to the fullest — such as delighting in the company of your family and friends — you may also feel an underlying note of concern that one day you may lose what you're enjoying so much right now.

Don't Forget

If you're experiencing fears over one day losing what you love, this is a good time to remember one of the great universal laws of life: "This, too, will pass." Good times will pass, and bad times will pass. Easy times will pass, and difficult times will pass.

The bad times passing is something you don't mind at all, right? But what about that "good times will pass" part of the equation? How can you enjoy, love, and relish all the great people and things in your life without being fearful of losing them?

The secret of enjoying good times without fear is to:

Stay focused in the present moment.

When you're focused in the present moment, you're enjoying what you have today rather than spending today worrying about what may or may not happen tomorrow.

Live in a higher vision that inspires a sense of detachment.

With a higher vision, you know that all beings and things are made of one supreme spirit that can never die and doesn't really come and go, except in external appearance.

With a higher vision, you free your mind from outer worries and come to experience life through the spiritual heart, which beats with contentment and peace just beneath the waves of your mind, during times of gain and loss.

When You're in Love

Love is life. And if you miss love, you miss life.

—Leo Buscaglia

Being in love is one of the greatest experiences you can have, but it also opens the door for all kinds of tagalongs, such as attachment, jealousy, desire, and anger — and maybe even eventually hatred and the unwrapping of that old prenuptial agreement.

Here's the thing: If you keep your love on the levels of attachment and desire, you'll probably also end up hopping over to their housemates of distress and anger one day. The way around this predicament is to take the love you're feeling and to uplift it into a higher spiritual love that doesn't rest with such unsavory bedfellows.

When your heartfelt love resonates with a higher spiritual love, your love becomes a ray of God's unconditional, divine love. Can you imagine how cool it would be to be totally in love with everything and everyone in life? That's the power of true unconditional love.

Here is a method to help uplift your experience of mundane love into an all-pervasive, universal love. When you're feeling deep love for someone or something:

1. **Pay attention to the loving feelings arising within you.**

2. **Focus on the love, separating it from the image of whatever or whoever is evoking this love in your heart.**

3. **Expand that unattached, free feeling of love so that it begins to pervade everything.**

 **Don't Forget**

Any form of heartfelt love is a good start to opening to higher forms of love.

When You're Under Ongoing Pressures

When you're feeling weighed down by outer pressures, such as health concerns, legal matters, or financial troubles, your attitude can help turn a curse into a blessing. For example, you can use such times to take refuge in God or to train yourself to see beyond outer events and into a deeper awareness of life.

Don't Forget

Times of outer difficulty can give you incentive to look beyond the façade of this world into the precious spiritual realms. When things are difficult on the outside, the inner realms start to look much more enticing!

You can also contemplate why these ongoing pressures may be falling upon your shoulders. For example, if you've been indulging too much in pride or attachment to being in control of everything, the benevolent universe may be creating certain troublesome situations to bring you down a notch or to teach you surrender, compassion, simplicity, honesty, humility, faith, or one of the many other virtuous qualities that come from well-digested troubles.

Think of those daytime TV shows where parents discuss their bad, "out-of-control" teens. I happened to see two of these shows in a row while skimming TV stations a few years ago. The misbehaving teens came into the studio with their blurred middle fingers up, cursing at the booing audience and bragging about how bad they were, while showing no remorse or concern for the pain they'd been causing to their parents and others. Then the prison guards came out and began yelling and screaming into the teens' faces. All the teens were marched offstage and sent to boot camp, where each one was put through a day of physical and emotional challenge where they had no choice but to surrender to the commands of the barking officers.

Somehow, being forced to submit to this traumatic experience broke through the spoiled and shameless exterior shells of these teens. At the end of the show, the teens came back from their ordeal completely transformed! They walked onstage and hugged the prison guards, the host, and their parents, as the audience cheered. It was as though some demonic force had been exorcised from them, leaving behind good, fairly well-behaved teens — at least during the show!

Be Careful

Don't make God send you to boot camp! Be good on your own!

If God or universal Consciousness has given you certain intense challenges to deal with, you can help the process by allowing these ongoing challenges to transform, humble, and uplift you. The key to turning troubles into blessings is to surrender deeply to them through faith and higher spiritual understanding while still making steady efforts to surmount the challenges. Instead of always fighting the waves that are crashing down on you, you can let go and let the same waves carry you to the shore.

When You Don't Like Your Job

If you find yourself unhappy with the job you're doing, this is a good time to contemplate whether certain challenges mean you're in the wrong place, or if you're meant to become stronger by meeting the difficulties head on. In some cases, the challenge may stem from being in not-so-good company at work. After all, like your family, you can't always choose the people you work with — although unlike your family, you can always consider changing jobs!

Don't Forget

Your outer world often reflects your inner feelings. If your job is unpleasant, look inside to see whether you have some hidden conflicts about doing that job: Does doing this job mean that you've given up on a greater dream? Do you feel that you are contributing to the greater good of the world through your position, or is the job focused on taking advantage of others or creating something that is harmful?

Considering whether your job is helpful to the world is a difficult contemplation for some. After all, if everyone who did a job that wasn't truly helpful to the world decided to quit, can you imagine how much of the world would stop?

When I first moved to Hollywood after spending a decade of monastic life in an Indian-based ashram, my goal was to use all the skills I had nurtured there — including video production, editing, and scriptwriting — to serve humanity. However, having had no experience with editing or producing videos in the professional world, I also felt that part of my challenge was to accept whatever work God sent my way.

My first television job in Hollywood was editing *Hard Copy* shows on salacious tabloid topics. Then came some fun work while editing a *Candid Camera* show with Allen Funt, followed by a long stint with Disney's *Prime Nine News,* where I was actually able to produce some positive pieces amidst all the intense news stories.

After these jobs came a fairly violent but innocuous low-budget film produced by Arnold Schwarzenegger's best friend, and on the heels of that came editing and associate producing jobs with the television shows *Mighty Morphin Power Rangers* and *X-MEN.* Sprinkled throughout these jobs were other video-related projects, many of which were charitable in nature and beneficial to the world.

All these projects gave me a chance to hone my skills and work with some very talented folks. However, while working on some of these shows, my desire to serve the world with positive creations had to be shifted to the back of my mind.

One day, I picked up a magazine with an article about childhood violence. The article mentioned both shows I was working on as being detrimental in terms of teaching violence to children. I knew that our writers and producers always tried to include good morals and positive teachings in each episode, but the basic storylines still boiled down to some sort of violent confrontation and fight scene. That's part of what made them the top two children's shows of their time!

Reading this magazine article about the negative social impact of these shows brought together many thoughts and feelings I had buried and not fully dealt with. I knew deep down that I couldn't continue doing that work. This realization was part of a life transition that led to a change in career, through which I would be able to share more helpful offerings with the world in works like this book.

Was it easy to make the transition? No. Did I lose much in terms of material acquirements and wealth? Yes. Was it worth it? Absolutely.

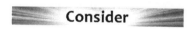 **Consider**

Even if you can't change your job into something you love, you can still do what you love and contribute positively to the world on your own time.

When You've Experienced a Difficult Childhood

Childhood is inherently difficult. After all, growth involves a constant process of destruction and creation: destruction of old worldviews and creation of new ones.

As a young child, you realize at some point that you're not the center of the universe. Then you find out that Mommy and Daddy aren't all-powerful gods. You have to work hard to learn how to print and then write letters and memorize how to spell words. You discover that life isn't always fair, and that you're sometimes on your own. And these challenges all happen in a *good* childhood! Nevertheless, whether you had the best or most horrific childhood, what you can do as an adult is to be the best and happiest of who you are today. Here are some ways that focusing on who you are now can help free you from the harmful effects of a difficult childhood:

- **Focus on who you are now and see how your challenges have come together to create your particular combinations of strength and vulnerability.** For example, in my situation, a lack of parental nurturing during childhood created certain benefits along with the drawbacks, such as a greater sense of inner dependence above outer dependence. Being focused on who you are now helps you to have compassion for your "inner child." You can nourish the vulnerable parts of yourself with maturity and gentle kindness.

- **Being focused on who you are now allows you to be more present and able to help heal others** — and by healing others, you also heal yourself.

- **Being focused on who you are now helps you remember your spiritual nature.** Remember that you are a great and divine soul who took birth on this planet in your specific circumstances because they were the best conditions to help you learn the lessons and have the experiences that will fulfill your soul's destiny.

When You Feel Spiritually Lost

Many people feel lost because they haven't found the right spiritual community or teachings that resonate with their wants and needs. If you're feeling spiritually lost at sea, you can take steps to begin a new road:

- **Clarify inside yourself what you're looking for.** Clarity of intention brings great power to those intentions and can help draw to you exactly the right people, places, and things to keep your spiritual journey vibrant and nourishing.

- **Check out what spiritual paths, communities, teachers, and teachings are available.** Go shopping for spirituality. Visit different places, and read different kinds of spirituality-based books. Check out various houses of worship or spiritual discussions and find out what is available. Notice what you do or don't like about different communities, teachers, and teachings.

  By actively seeking the right path and teachings, you're making a statement to the universe through your efforts that you want to find the right path and community for you. And while you're looking for the perfect path, you'll still be learning and growing from wherever you go. You can find more tips on finding the right path for you in Chapter 5.

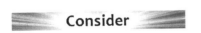 Consider

Reading spiritual books about seekers who have found the right teachers and communities for them can help you to imagine what the right community or teacher could look like for you and can guide you to recognize the right path when it comes along.

When Something Awful Happens

What do you do when you lose a child, or when a big tornado comes along and destroys everything you own? How can you see such times through spiritual eyes? Certainly, the answer isn't to be unfeeling or numb about the loss. That's just a common defense mechanism that your mind may use to cover up your overwhelming grief and pain.

Instead, you must allow your feelings to arise, completely uncensored. Don't act on the angry or vengeful ones, but allow the feelings to arise nevertheless. Even if you feel angry with God, that's okay. At least you're thinking of God! In fact, some people communicate with God only when they're angry about one tragedy or another. Maybe getting these people angry over unfair tragedies is the only way God can get them to relate to Him as real!

Be Careful

Some people use spiritual ideas of personal responsibility to feel guilty about their own tragedies or callous about the traumas of others. Spiritual awareness is not meant to take away your compassion for yourself or others, but rather to add to that compassion a note of faith and higher awareness that gives solace and hope in even the darkest of times.

Terrible disasters can transform your entire relationship to the world around you. These extreme tragedies may rip you out of the roots of materialistic, illusory thinking, forcing you to shed a false sense of security. That sense of security wasn't right; it was too limited. You may fear that after the false sense of security is gone, you'll fall into some horrible state of nothingness, but that's not necessarily the case.

With spiritual eyes, you can see beneath the experience of insecurity to a real security that you may not have known was there. God! Reality! Spirit! Eternality! Nobody dies! Nothing is destroyed! Hallelujah!

Don't Forget

To your deepest soul, even painful experiences are worth undergoing if they lead to a greater unfolding of your small sense of self into the greater divine Self. This is why terrible disasters can actually become great blessings on your soul's journey. An old worldview must crumble before a new one can blossom forth. If it takes a big kick in the butt to get you there, so be it!

When Good Fortune Comes Your Way

Receiving good fortunate is one of the more pleasant lessons your soul gets to go through during its life journey. An unexpected blessing showers down upon your head. Something really great happens. You win the lottery of life. You get the job. You get the girl of your dreams. You meet a great spiritual being. You find the home you've always wanted. Good fortune can enter through many avenues.

One good spiritual response to such times is gratitude. Why? Because gratitude is the perfect companion to good fortune. The two nourish one another and come together to create something even greater than occasional moments of good fortune: the state of grace. When you're in the state of grace, good fortune becomes a natural part of your life.

Another excellent response to times of good fortune is the other "g" word: generosity. Open your heart and ask God to guide you on how to share this great abundance of good fortune. With a smile? With kind words? By sharing what you have or what you've learned? By looking for ways to help the people around you and benefit the world?

Don't Forget

Good fortune gives you a unique chance to practice the gems of gratitude and generosity, so take advantage of the opportunity while you can!

Chapter 21

Ten More Commandments

Topics in this Chapter:

* Following the golden rule
* Keeping good company inside and out
* Being honest, trustworthy, and happy

Even though many folks already have a hard time keeping some of the original Ten Commandments that Moses brought down from his experience of God's presence, I've nevertheless decided to add in ten more that you can also think of as suggestions or helpful advice on ways to honor and follow the laws of this universe.

Do unto Others As You Would Have Them Do unto You

This golden rule is included in the teachings of several traditions, but is generally considered to have originated with Confucius. Another converse version given by Rabbi Hillel in 30 B.C. says, "Whatsoever thou wouldst that men should not do unto thee, do not do unto them."

 **Consider**

Of course, the actual practice of "doing unto others as you would have them do unto you" can bring up sticky questions about whether someone else would want the same things that you do. With people's different styles and preferences, you may end up giving others what *you* would want, but not what *they* would want.

For example, imagine that you're sitting with a friend in front of two slices of pie — a big one and a small one. You love pie and would really like to have the bigger piece, so you follow the golden rule by giving your friend the slice of pie that you would want to be given unto you. But what if your friend doesn't really like pie? What if she is on a diet or is a diabetic? This simple example shows why just following spiritual rules dogmatically isn't enough — you have to grasp the spirit behind the law.

Doing unto others as you would have them do unto you is not about pushing your preferences onto others, but is a stance of generosity that reflects in how charitable and fair you are in all areas of your life.

What is most important about this golden rule is to be in the spiritual frame of mind that allows you to truly do unto others as you would have them do unto you. The only way you can fully enter into this commandment is to have a tangible sense of the oneness and divine nature of everything and everyone in this world. With this awareness, you know that giving to another is inherently giving to yourself.

Think Good Thoughts

Looking at the events of your life with a positive eye enhances the good times and softens difficult times. Your thoughts and feelings also go into everything you cook, build, say, create, and give. Shine good thoughts into your life and into the world!

Look Beyond Matter to Spirit

Within and beyond the realm of matter is spirit. Adjust your focus so that you're seeing not only the external appearance of matter and outer forms, but also the spiritual, inner realms of life.

Too much focus on material things can block your awareness of spirit. Therefore, spiritual scriptures advise seekers to release their attachments to outer sensory experiences so they can more easily perceive the subtle but precious spiritual ones. Just think — if you eat a bowl of hot chilies, your taste buds will get overstimulated and dulled to tasting or enjoying even the most delicious gourmet foods. In the same way, partaking in too many sensory experiences of this physical world can numb your ability to savor the delicious yet subtle spiritual flavors of life.

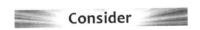 **Consider**

This commandment doesn't mean you should deny yourself the enjoyments of this world. Just enjoy them in moderation and with an awareness of spirit!

Keep Good Company

The company you keep determines to a large extent how you think, feel, and act. Even if you think of yourself as a perfectly individual and independent thinker, the fact remains that human beings are designed to absorb and reflect traits of their associates.

Psychologists have observed that if you put two people in a room together for a couple hours, their movements begin to synchronize with one another. They may start speaking with similar phrases or inflections. Their breathing may become entrained with one another. And these are just two people in a room for a couple hours.

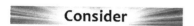
Consider

Just imagine how much people with whom you spend a great deal of time affect you!

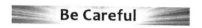
Be Careful

This idea of keeping good company is not meant to create fear or make you run away from people and situations that may not be the best of company. For example, you may be doing volunteer work or performing a job that requires you to be around challenging people who are not always the best of company. In these cases, *you* get to be the good company for *them*!

Turn Within for Guidance

Turn within and make friends with your own wise soul. Let the spiritual grace that expresses in both the inner and outer world guide your steps. Seek a dialogue of continual guidance within yourself through introspection and quiet sitting and relish your own freshly flowing spring of wisdom.

Be Moderate and Balanced

Moderation and balance can be incorporated into all your activities, including your work, lifestyle, diet, relationships, and use of time. When you achieve balance and moderation, you naturally enter into the flow of spirit. In spirit, the stress of opposing qualities gives way to peaceful centeredness.

Remember Death

The death of your body is inevitable. Therefore, the truly intelligent thing to do is to acknowledge and contemplate that which you know is going to happen one day.

Thinking about death isn't a gruesome task, but a realistic one. Remembering that your journey in this world will end one day helps you to see beyond the materialistic level of life. Remembrance of death inspires you to be generous while you're here, makes it easier to let go of ego and false pride, and encourages you to appreciate each moment (see Chapter 4).

 **Consider**

When you become more comfortable with the idea of death, you may also become aware of an essence within yourself that's beyond birth and death. This is a great bonus!

Express Yourself Freely

This entire universe is filled with movements: planets spinning, galaxies twirling, stars being born, atoms smashing, water raining, and flowers growing. This creation goes on and on in every direction — bigger, smaller, higher, and lower — action upon action, work upon work. Do you think God's universal creative power is doing all this work for a big, fat paycheck? No. Everything in nature takes place out of a sense of right action and service, which the Indian scriptures call *dharma*. (See chapter 13 for more on dharma.)

When you act from a sense of dharma rather than from greed-based motivations, then your actions flow smoothly and in harmony with the freely expressing universe. You don't have to limit yourself to accommodate everyone else's judgments or jealousies. You are serving, expressing, and being guided by spirit.

Keep Your Word

Learn to respect yourself and your words so that you find it natural and important to keep your word to yourself and others. If you give your word, you should do your very best to keep your word. When you speak, what you say should be in harmony with your thoughts and intentions. Don't promise things you won't deliver, and don't go around making and breaking commitments all over the place.

When you truly respect your words, all kinds of great new doors open for you. The universe also begins to respect your words. You are able to declare an intention and know that your power of righteousness will bring it to be. You reap the benefits of honesty that I outline in Chapter 10. You trust yourself, and others are also able to trust you. The universe itself is able to trust you!

Have a Good Sense of Humor

As Chapter 17 explains, God is funny. Life is funny. Turns of events are funny. Even suffering can be funny. And more than anything else, truth is funny.

Have you ever noticed that most of the best comedians are usually just saying what they really think? The audience laughs, in part, because the comedian has dared to speak his truth and say what the audience may not have been bold enough to proclaim.

Laughter is the wine of the soul. When you laugh with pure delight, know that God is laughing with you. Like God and spirit, humor is present through the ups and downs of good and bad times. With a good sense of humor, you laugh when you're happy and can even laugh while you cry. Humor is a great friend on your journey!

Never Let Your Creative Spirit Be Limited by Numbers

An appropriate topic for the 11th commandment of this list of ten!

Blessings on Your Path!

With Love and Respect,

Sharon "Kumuda" Janis

51696182R00209

Made in the USA
San Bernardino, CA
29 July 2017